Modern Retellings of Chivalric Texts

Modern Retellings of Chivalric Texts

Edited by

GLORIA ALLAIRE

Routledge
Taylor & Francis Group
LONDON AND NEW YORK

First published 1999 by Ashgate Publishing

Reissued 2018 by Routledge
2 Park Square, Milton Park, Abingdon, Oxon, OX14 4RN
711 Third Avenue, New York, NY 10017, USA

Routledge is an imprint of the Taylor & Francis Group, an informa business

A Library of Congress record exists under LC control number: 98022085

ISBN 13: 978-1-138-32712-2 (hbk)
ISBN 13: 978-1-138-32714-6 (pbk)
ISBN 13: 978-0-429-44944-4 (ebk)

Contents

List of contributors

Gloria Allaire taught Italian at Purdue University, West Lafayette, Indiana while this book was being produced. She has published numerous articles on late medieval Italian chivalric literature, medieval manuscripts, Dante, Boccaccio and Tullia d'Aragona, and *Andrea da Barberino and the Language of Chivalry* (UP of Florida, 1997). She is currently preparing the first edition (with translation) of *Il Tristano panciatichiano*.

Deborah Lesko Baker is Associate Professor and Chair of French at Georgetown University, Washington, DC. She has published *Narcissus and the Lover: Mythic Recovery and Reinvention in Scève's* Délie (Anma Libri, 1986) and *The Subject of Desire: Petrarchan Poetics and the Female Voice in Louise Labé* (Purdue UP, 1996) as well as articles on Labé, Duras, DuBellay and Ronsard.

Barbara De Marco is Managing Editor for *Romance Philology* at the Research Center for Romance Studies, University of California, Berkeley. Her interest in hagiographic literature has led to the study of texts both medieval and modern, including a translation of Giuseppe Bonaviri's *Novelle saracene*.

Christine Herold is Assistant Professor of English at The College of Saint Rose, Albany, NY. Her articles have appeared in *English Language Notes*, *Translation Review* and *Carmina Philosophiae*. Her book-length study on the intersections between Chaucer and Christian tragedy is nearing completion.

Kathleen Coyne Kelly is Associate Professor of English at Northeastern University, Boston, MA. She has published in *Allegorica*, *Arthuriana*, *Assays*, *Parergon* and *Studies in Philology*. She is the author of *A.S. Byatt: A Study*, Twayne English Author Series (G.K. Hall, 1996). With Marina Leslie, she has edited a volume of essays, *Menacing Virgins: Representing Virginity in the Middle Ages and Renaissance* (forthcoming from University of Delaware Press), and is currently completing a book, *Hymenologies: Testing Virginity in the Middle Ages*.

Lee Tobin McClain is Associate Professor of English at Seton Hill College, Greensburg, PA. She has published several articles on medieval romance, and on modern and cinematic retellings of Arthurian legends, most recently in *Extrapolation* and *Studies in Medieval and Renaissance Teaching*.

Stephen D. Powell is Assistant Professor of English at TCU, Fort Worth, Texas. He has articles published or forthcoming in *Anglia*, *English Studies*, *Modern Language Review*, *Names: Journal of the American Name Society* and

Neuphilologische Mitteilungen. He is currently preparing critical editions of *Roberd of Cisyle* and *Sir Isumbras*, and a book on the texts and contexts of Middle English didactic romances.

Myriam Swennen Ruthenberg is Associate Professor of Italian and Comparative Literature at Florida Atlantic University, Boca Raton, FL. She has published articles on Boccaccio, Pasolini and Tomasi di Lampedusa. She has translated *I colpi dei sensi* by Erri De Luca and is currently working on an edition of essays about this new author.

MaryLynn Saul is Assistant Professor of English at Worcester State College, Worcester, MA. This year she will teach a course on Arthuriana. She has published an article on Malory in *Fifteenth Century Studies*. Her doctoral dissertation (Ohio State University) concerned the historical context and ideological function of Malory's Morgan le Fay.

Pauline Scott is Assistant Professor of English at Alabama State University, Montgomery, AL. Her research interests include Ariosto, Boiardo, Woolf and Shakespeare.

Preface

This book owes its existence in part to an informal but intense discussion of modern literary and cinematic refashionings of medieval chivalric texts that took place one evening during the 1994 Modern Language Association Convention in San Diego. The interlocutors were my friends and colleagues Lori Walters, Debora Schwartz and Juliann Vitullo. Our conversation was sparked by a remarkable coincidence: in 1993 I had completed the first critical study of the Florentine chivalric author Andrea da Barberino, and in the same year a modern Italian novelization of Andrea's masterpiece had appeared. Aside from suggesting a literary *Zeitgeist*, the simultaneous emergence of new critical and creative works about a long dead author and one of his texts demonstrated the fascination that modern readers still feel towards chivalric narratives, and opened the way to a consideration of the nature of modern retellings of their medieval and Renaissance models. This impetus indicated a new direction for my own scholarly inquiry.

As part of my subsequent investigation of the appeal that chivalric texts hold for modern readers and writers, I organized three conference sessions: 'Twice-Told Tales: American Literary Transformations of Chivalry' held at the International Conference on Medievalism, Worcester, MA (1995); 'Modern Recastings of Medieval and Renaissance Chivalric Narratives' held at the Modern Languages Association Convention in Chicago, IL (1995); and 'Before/Beyond *Il nome della rosa*: Retelling the Middle Ages' held at the annual conference of the American Association of Italian Studies, Chicago, IL (1998). Shorter versions of essays by Deborah Lesko Baker, Pauline Scott, Stephen Powell, Christine Herold, Barbara De Marco and myself were read in the above sessions. An early version of MaryLynn Saul's study was read at the Worcester conference in a separate session. Finally, Myriam Swennen Ruthenberg originally presented an abbreviated version of her study on Morante at the Purdue University Conference on Romance Languages, Literatures and Film in October 1997. I am grateful to the organizers of these conferences for having created appropriate *fora* for the presentation of our ideas and for allowing the fruits of those early efforts to be published in their present expanded and revised form.

Special thanks are due to my colleagues Anthony Julian Tamburri and Deborah Starewich for technical advice on the production of this volume. I would also like to acknowledge the many interesting submissions which were not selected for this volume; regrettably, I could not include them all. The overwhelming response to my calls for abstracts demonstrates the potential for this area of inquiry: many other modern adaptations of chivalric texts — literary, visual, folkloric, cinematographic, and videographic — await analysis.

Gloria Allaire

Introduction

The stories of chivalry have been told and retold down through the centuries, being reinvented continuously by new authors with new voices for new audiences.[1] This collection addresses the nature of their long-lasting appeal. What is inherent in such texts that they continue to attract the interest of readers centuries after they were originally conceived? What do they contain that speaks to readers at the turn of the second millennium as strongly as they did a thousand years ago? What enables the adventures of Arthur, Tristan, Lancelot, Charlemagne, Roland and others to resist destruction despite dramatic shifts of time, space, genre, medium or cultural context? These stories were the popular entertainments of earlier centuries. Already in the Middle Ages and Renaissance, the chivalric 'matters' served as sources for endless reworkings. Their written versions were the forerunners of the modern novel, a genre that frequently returns to its roots in order to restore, revive and refresh itself.

This book seeks to complement numerous existing studies of medievalism in the Enlightenment and Victorian periods by identifying more recent adaptations of the familiar Arthurian legend and by broadening the enquiry on the nature of the revival to include other medieval or Renaissance chivalric texts and the ways in which they have been adapted. One aim of this collection is to identify as much as possible exact sources to which modern chivalric texts are indebted, and thus to avoid vague, 'once upon a time' versions with fairy tale castles, dragons, and princes on white horses saving damsels in distress. Similarly, we do not consider the numerous popular, late twentieth-century versions that feature muscle-bound adventure heroes who sport weaponry, fight monstrous opponents and engage in combats that their medieval ancestors would scarcely recognize. Although these chapters present new considerations on certain modern adaptations of the Arthurian cycle narratives, another goal of this volume is to broaden the discourse on medievalism to include non-Arthurian texts. Chapters included here signal previously unnoticed or unstudied modern adaptations of well-known medieval and Renaissance antecedents such as *Robert of Sicily*, Andrea da Barberino's *Guerrino Meschino*, Ariosto's *Orlando furioso* and Spenser's *The Faerie Queene*.

This collection includes not only literary adaptations of chivalric material, but also some that have appeared in different media. Lesko Baker discusses a modern cinematic adaptation of a novel that echoes *Tristan*. Two medieval sources, *Robert of Sicily* and *Guerrino Meschino*, have undergone theatrical incarnations (Powell, Allaire). Folkloristic, puppet theatre treatments of Caro-

[1] Throughout this book, the term 'chivalry' should be understood in its broadest sense to denote not only Carolingian battle epics, but Arthurian romances as well.

lingian cycle texts in Sicily have inspired recent literary homages by two Italian novelists (De Marco, Allaire).

Modern authors studied here include representatives of the nineteenth- and twentieth-centuries and of various nationalities, cultures and subcultures: English, Danish, French, Italian, American and Black American. A wide variety of genres is studied as well: poetry, novel, short story, film, oral performance, drama and popular theatre. Five of these chapters explore the ways in which modern authors have absorbed and reshaped the Arthurian legends. These range from the subtle infusion of mythic tropes into contemporary domestic settings to the grafting of romance elements on to post-war adventure tales, from interrogating the role of feminine in the Arthurian world to an ironic exposé of the masculine role in that same world. We have also included a chapter on the modern versions of the legend of Robert of Sicily, a didactic tale that shares certain elements with medieval chivalric texts. Other chapters focus on retellings of Carolingian cycle narratives. Two more examine striking modernist recastings of the well-known Renaissance poems *Orlando furioso* and *The Faerie Queene*, themselves early modern reworkings of still older chivalric material.

The rewriting process is no modern phenomenon, although the authorial intent and actual techniques of rewriting change across the centuries. The medieval scribal redaction process produced, in effect, narratives that were 'retold' either through deliberate compositional choices such as amplification or abbreviation, through translation from one language to another, or through variants introduced consciously or unconsciously into the texts. To the question of what motivates modern authors to return to these centuries-old literary models, no single response emerges, although certain similarities can be identified. The reasons for the modern adaptations depend variously on an individual author's personal perspectives, the world-view of his or her society, and the individual's place within that world. Chapters by Stephen Powell and Gloria Allaire discuss identifiable medieval manuscript sources and their transmission as a backdrop for modern retellings of *Robert of Sicily* and *Guerrino Meschino*. Similarly, chapters by Pauline Scott and Christine Herold focus on a one-to-one correspondence between specific Renaissance texts and their modern literary reinventions. In these cases, plot, characters and narrative motifs have been retained/retold on a large scale. On the other hand, certain retellings employ selected elements from larger myths: Deborah Lesko Baker analyses Marguerite Duras's refigurations of tropes from the pan-European Tristan legend, Kathleen Coyne Kelly discusses four refashionings of the Lady of Shalott character and MaryLynn Saul looks at the deployment of the Holy Grail by various post-war and cold war era authors. In other cases, the medieval sources for the reworkings are less discrete: Lee Tobin McClain studies Thomas Berger's treatment of the complex Arthurian legend and its ethos of chivalric behaviour while Barbara De Marco tackles an even more complex modern interweaving of literary and popular sources, Sicilian and

Arabic folk-tales, and Catholic and anti-monarchist notions fused in a revisionary account of the adventures of Charlemagne's Paladins.

The approaches our contributors bring to bear on their subjects are as varied as modern authors' treatments of their older chivalric material. They address issues such as why a particular model was chosen and how its reshaping depends on the modern author's misreading or rereading of medieval chivalric conventions. Lesko Baker evaluates the relative successes of Duras's novel *Moderato cantabile* and its cinematic adaptation with respect to the way in which each refigures the Tristan myth. She perceptively uncovers various tropes and narrative elements that Duras has incorporated, via Joseph Bèdier's influential compilation of Tristan stories, into her own erotic and transgressive text. Tropes such as the love potion, erotic unattainability, the sea metaphor, the juxtaposition of moderation and excess, and the paradoxical linking of love and death are re-enacted within the constraints of stifling bourgeois conformity. On a deeper level, the notion of re-enactment itself structures Duras's novel. The technique of literary doubling, already present in medieval versions of *Tristan* by Thomas and Gottfried, is employed by Duras herself as she tells and retells a catalytic moment of the narration through her characters' conversations. The intertextual connections between tragic couples abound and rebound from scene to scene, within and between the medieval and modern texts. In the end, re-enactment occurs not only on the literary level, but within the physical and psychological dimensions of Duras's characters as well.

Notions of intertextuality and doubling recur in Kathleen Coyne Kelly's revisionist reading of the Lady of Shalott. She disputes the necessity of looking for sources or of reading texts in a linear, chronological fashion. Instead, Kelly argues that the significance of the character in any one text is dependent upon an intertextual, heteroglossic reading among texts. The idea of the text itself is expanded beyond the boundaries of literature to include a modern painting. Kelly wants to disrupt the sense of linearity and its corresponding notion of literary inheritance by one author from another, choosing to read medieval and modern texts that contain the figure of the Fair Maid, or her analogues, in 'great time'. This Bakhtinian reading enables her exploration of the subject–object split, the tension between male Poet and female Muse, and the difficulty — within phallic discourse — of granting women the subject (writer) position. When read in this theoretical light, the Maid's tower, loom and mirror resonate differently. Her imprisonment is not only the literal one of the tower, but the intellectual muzzling that deprives women of discourse. Although Victorian authors like Tennyson sought to contain the uncontrollable feminine in the object position, modern authors like Pynchon and Zelazny — and even some modern critics — push on the boundaries of this notion, moving the figure of the lady towards empowerment or, even, escape. The technique of doubling, discussed in Lesko Baker's chapter, recurs in one of the modern texts Kelly examines. This time the male and female protagonists double not only the medieval Elayne and Launcelot, but Tristan and Iseult as well.

Whereas Kelly's chapter explores the role of the feminine in Arthurian re-tellings, Lee Tobin McClain interrogates Thomas Berger's deflation of masculine chivalric ideals in his *Arthur Rex*. Berger's is a complex view of his medi-eval sources, detailed even to the extent of including lexicon and minutiae not normally found in modern versions of Arthurian legends. He has inherited certain attitudes toward his material from the legacy of nineteenth- and twentieth-century medievalism. Berger constructs and then dismantles a code of chivalric behaviour in order to critique what for him are antiquated, oversimplified ideals. His reshaping of Malory allows him to show the chivalric code as an inadequate moral system; this is part of his larger agenda to debunk binary thinking and absolute moral systems. Berger's treatment of the chivalric legends is mocking, yet admiring. On one hand, he recognizes modern readers' apparent need for such legends but, on the other, he criticizes legends and magic as suitable only to simple folk or children, thereby scorning his own readers. Yet in the Middle Ages and Renaissance, chivalric texts were read by adults, by kings, queens and the powerful merchant élite. Magic was considered a branch of science to be mastered with serious study, hardly a subject for the amusement of children.

The question of age or sophistication of readers for chivalric tales recurs in several chapters (Saul, Powell, De Marco, Allaire). The fascination with chivalric texts and tropes is continuous and undeniable, but many modern writers and scholars disdain these cultural artefacts by assigning to them a supposedly unlettered and unsophisticated audience. Such ambivalence towards medieval material on the part of modern intellectuals and writers may reflect an anxiety about their own position in the literary tradition: after centuries of reworkings, modern authors may feel inferior to their literary ancestors and react by trying to 'kill the father' — in Freudian family romance fashion — by belittling and deflating their inheritance. However dangerous such reductive readings and rewritings of earlier material may be, they were undeniably a central feature of cultural imperialism begun under the Victorians. Colonizing a text, as Tobin McClain and Powell point out, is a way of containing the threats perceived within it. Such colonization allows the modern writer/reader to explore the unfamiliar terrain without truly becoming part of it, to possess and experience its exotic fascination without allowing oneself to become possessed by it.

Possession of another sort enters into MaryLynn Saul's survey of modern Grail stories. Whereas the originally secular Grail became in its later medieval versions a sacred, Christianized object associated with Christ's passion and visible only to the pure, in modern stories its moral polarity has been reversed from positive to negative. If the Grail quest was a type of religious exemplum in certain early texts, its latter-day counterparts are parables of a technological age bereft of significance, spiritual or otherwise. The new cast of characters in these modern quests are not the knights of the Round Table, but Nazis, journalists, police officers, cult members, fairies, Old West townsfolk and, even, space aliens. Despite the range of settings for these modern versions, the stories share one striking commonality: the Grail is repeatedly recast as a quasi-magical object with powers that corrupt or destroy those who possess it, notions completely extraneous to all medieval models. Saul identifies a range of twentieth-century ideologies and anxieties that inform these varied refashionings: Nietzschean and Sartrean philosophies, the waning of religious faith, the loss of meaning in the face of failing institutions, and cold war era fears of ultimate destruction form the matrix from which these texts emerge.

A similar erasure of religious morality in favour of modern aesthetic ideals occurs in various nineteenth- and twentieth-century transformations of the *Robert of Sicily* story. Stephen Powell indicates ten Middle English exemplars of this widely circulated medieval didactic tale and discusses its reauthoring at the hands of its fifteenth-century scribes. The resulting disunified textual tradition perplexed early modern 'editors' who, lacking rigorous norms for textual editing, resorted to publishing transcriptions of eight of the versions. Various modern rewriters of *Robert of Sicily* seemed motivated by the belief that the story is in need of their 'improvements'. They could also not accept the text's generic slipperiness and sought to confine it to a specific, unified genre recognizable to modern readers. They were also unwilling or unable to accept the polysemous nature of medieval texts or, indeed, of medieval culture itself. Their anxieties about elements that they cannot control leads to a literary colonization of the text in their attempt to dominate and subdue earlier narrative praxes. The faithfulness of the transformation varies from author to author. Leigh Hunt and Rudolf Schmidt both attempt to reduce the didacticism of the tale by casting the story in the mould of determinate history. Schmidt reduces the role of God in the prideful king's affairs, switching the roles of other characters, adding a female love interest and replacing ecclesiastical settings with Romantic landscapes. Henry Wadsworth Longfellow goes so far as to delete the moral that had been explicitly stated at the ending of the medieval versions. Once again, we find modern retellers associating medieval tales with children or simple minds. *Robert of Sicily* undergoes the same treatment in three versions by Frederick J.H. Darton, Ascott R. Hope and Justin Huntly McCarthy.

The next chapters examine surprising modernizations of three well-known Renaissance heroes: Andrea da Barberino's Guerrino, Ludovico Ariosto's Orlando, and Edmund Spenser's Redcrosse Knight. The Italian knights Guerrino and Orlando continue their adventures down through the centuries: their forms and genres may be modified, but the appeal for writers and readers never wanes. Pauline Scott's chapter analyses the connection between the *Orlando*s by Ariosto and Virginia Woolf. Woolf, like Berger, re-examines and rewrites the chivalric code in its broadest sense, this time with the emphasis on the irreconcilable roles of perfect warrior and perfect lover. Whereas Ariosto's Orlando failed at both, Woolf's hero never makes it to the battlefield, given his overwhelming successes in the boudoir. However, this Orlando — descendant of the French warrior Roland, popular hero of medieval Italian narratives and epitomized by Ariosto — becomes the object of a female gaze in Woolf's refashioning. In a startling reversal of gender roles, Orlando, the desiring pursuer of Angelica in the *Furioso*, now becomes the object of desire of Woolf's female characters and, by extension, of her readers. Although his many dalliances would seem to demonstrate his male prowess, in the end he is betrayed and abandoned — Dido-like — by the woman he most desires.

The metaphor of tapestry recurs throughout these chapters: it has been employed to describe the act of writing (Tobin McClain), creation of a world and unbridled discourse, or even imprisoning solipsism (Kelly). Peter DeSa Wiggins used it to unify his important study of Ariosto's poem,[2] the notion of endless threads stretching into the future to be completed — perhaps by another story-teller, perhaps not at all — aptly illustrates the open-ended nature of the romance genre. Woolf was clearly attracted to this feature and she cleverly exploits it in her centuries-long 'biography' of friend and possible lover, Vita Sackville-West. Woolf's novel was not only inspired structurally by the tapestry/romance genre connection, but also reifies the notion with specific references to scenes from *Orlando furioso* that were depicted in a tapestry hung at Knole House, Vita's ancestral home.

Another remarkable recreation of a Renaissance romance hero occurs in Ralph Ellison's revision of Spenser. Although Ellison's debts to other European literary sources have been acknowledged, Christine Herold astutely uncovers clear parallels between Book One of *The Faerie Queene* and *Invisible Man*. Conventional tropes of the knightly hero's humble upbringing, his commissioning for battle, monstrous opponents, female temptresses, even medieval colour symbolism, dream visions, magical elements and the quest motif itself are re-created by Ellison within the context of the Black American civil rights struggle. However, this is no precious academic exercise: the paradoxes inherent within such a project reflect Ellison's integrationist philosophy and produce incredible tensions within the novel, tensions that can only be appreciated when its European model is discerned. Indeed, the very failure of White Americans to recognize their own inherited cultural values comes under scrutiny. When read against the background of romance tradition, Ellison's protagonist acquires the stature not only of an ideal knight on the quest for his own identity, but of a new, inclusive, and culturally diverse Everyman. Ellison's choice of model allows him

---

[2] *Figures in Ariosto's Tapestry: Character and Design in the* Orlando furioso (Baltimore, MD: The Johns Hopkins University Press, 1986).

to expose the narrowness of the canon, to articulate his political philosophy, and to critique the very function of the modern American novel. In the end, his rewriting extends beyond the levels of character and plot to genre itself, a literary agenda that also informs Elsa Morante's *L'isola di Arturo* (Ruthenberg).

The final chapters by De Marco, Allaire and Ruthenberg pertain to modern Italian reworkings of chivalric material by authors who have achieved both popular and critical acclaim. Barbara De Marco's study of Giuseppe Bonaviri's *Novelle saracene* (*Saracen Tales*) includes an admirable introduction to the rich history of chivalric material on Italian soil. She aptly describes the dual channel of transmission — oral and written — that served as a direct conduit between medieval and Renaissance sources and their latter-day folkloristic counterparts. Inexpensive popular editions, serialized publication, street-singers and the marionette theatre kept this material alive, albeit in constantly altered states best suited to the changing tastes and interests of modern audiences. Modern story-tellers were influenced not only by plots and characters, but even by the lexicon and syntax of their models. Bonaviri belongs to a long tradition of *contastorie*: his various novels and poems were deeply influenced by the Carolingian epic cycle. Yet beyond the universal appeal of these stories, Bonaviri's retellings are imbued with a distinctive Sicilian flavour: untameable Nature, fatalism and fervent Catholic piety are commingled with elements of folk-tale and Arabic culture in an exotic and original reinvention of the legends of the Paladins. The compositional process of *rovesciamento*, turning inside out or role reversal, allows Bonaviri to re-create the functions of his characters. Certain wild anachronisms and unorthodox shifts of scene seem plausible when set against a backdrop of the familiar. Conflicting and competing ideologies — as represented by their narrative manifestations — find a harmonious unity in Bonaviri's Sicily, one of the few places where the Carolingian legends flourished well into the twentieth century.

This aspect of Sicilian popular culture also inspired Gesualdo Bufalino's 1993 tribute to a distant medieval source, reinterpreted in his youth by the same puppet masters and popular editions noted in De Marco's chapter. In *Il Guerrin Meschino*, Bufalino frames a brief retelling in prose with poetic glosses that articulate autobiographical themes not found in the original: old age and death, the loss of innocence and the danger and pleasure of illusions. Although parts of his novel are remarkably faithful to the plot, characters and language of Andrea da Barberino's original, elsewhere anachronisms, modern innovations and fantasy abound. Bufalino stands at the end of a long line of admirers and refashioners of *Guerrino*. The Allaire chapter surveys the complex textual history of this important proto-Renaissance epic romance, tracing its various permutations beginning with dialectal changes that appear in incunabula. In the sixteenth century, the book was translated into French twice, into Castilian and versified by Tullia d'Aragona. It continued to be published well into the twentieth century, and appeared in an abridgement for juvenile readers, on the legitimate stage and in folk decorations and puppet theatres of Venice, Naples and Sicily. The stalwart hero and his long quest to recover his birthright captured the imagination of generations of readers in different centuries and countries. The proto-modern Guerrino has been continually adapted and reinvented according to the varying personal, political, religious or artistic needs of later readers and writers.

The volume concludes with Myriam Swennen Ruthenberg's considerations of Elsa Morante's *L'isola di Arturo* (*Arthur's Island*). The title of this 1957 novel shows its clear debt to Arthurian romances; in fact, its subtitle identifies the book's genre as 'romanzo'. Ruthenberg unpacks the semiotic load of the Italian term, a necessary preamble to understanding the true significance of this text. In *L'isola di Arturo*, Morante questions the dichotomy of reality and fiction as related to the genres of novel and romance. This is not simply another case of a modern author imitating a medieval one or of a modern text being copied from a medieval model; instead, it is also an exploration of the way in which the reading experience itself is replicated. The reader's perceptions of a text may lead him or her to confound truth — universal or historical — with fiction and to base future actions on those mistaken impressions. Dante's Paolo and Francesca were guilty not only of the sin of excessive desire, but of reading with 'excessive meaning' (to use Kristeva's phrase). Morante's protagonist Arturo and her readers are similarly implicated. Romances seduce their readers with a spell that is woven out of recognizable and recurrent conventions. Whereas the novel, the presumed representative of true experience, is set within the bounds of real time and real space, the atemporal, aspatial romance world is subject instead to symbolic interpretation. By choosing to write what she explicitly terms a 'romance', Morante is consciously attempting to revise the prescribed neo-realism of the post-war novel in order to present truths that are common to all humans. Through a series of word plays and literary borrowings, Morante engages the reader in a meta-literary game that crosses the boundaries of time, space, text and genre.

There is one more voice we ought to include here: that of the early fifteenth-century compiler, Andrea da Barberino. His texts, especially *I Reali di Francia* and *Guerrino*, served as models for frequent later retellings. Andrea himself was a reinventor of 'ancient' texts and furnishes a rationale for the process in the proem to his best work, *Guerrino*:

> Naturalmente pare che sia di consuetudine che gli uomeni si dilectano d'udire nouelle autori; o sse antiche fossono, non sieno suti palesati alla volgar giente, perchè cose antiche e non palesate paiono n[u]oue alle menti di coloro che no l'àn[n]o più udite. Per questo mi sono dilectato di cierchare molte storie nouelle; et auendo piaciere di molte storie, trovai questa leggienda che molto mi piacque. (Oxford, Bodleian Library, MS canon. ital. 27, f. 1r, punctuation added)

> (Naturally, it seems that men habitually take delight in hearing new authors; or if they [the authors] were old, they have not been revealed to the common herd because old things not revealed [as such] seem new to the minds of those who have no longer heard them. With this in mind, I enjoyed searching for many new stories. And having pleasure from many stories, I found this legend that pleased me very much.)

Regardless of the particular historical or political moment, it is ultimately the pleasure of the narrative itself, the interrelated and interdependent joys of discovering, hearing, reading, writing, telling and retelling these stories that bring authors, readers and critics back to them time and time again.

Chapter 1

Desire and mythic intertext: refigurations of *Tristan* in *Moderato cantabile*

Deborah Lesko Baker

Marguerite Duras attained widespread acclaim and public attention in 1960 as a result of her famous film collaboration with Alain Resnais, *Hiroshima mon amour*. Just prior to this, Duras worked with Peter Brook to adapt her haunting short novel, *Moderato cantabile*, for the cinema. The film, starring Jeanne Moreau and Jean-Paul Belmondo, actually represents a rather loose adaptation of Duras's enigmatic work. As I have previously argued with respect to *Hiroshima*, the treatment of the intersubjective dimensions of forbidden love in Duras's novel represents a fundamental refiguring of the Tristan myth, a myth that informs much of Western love aesthetics from the Middle Ages to the present.[1] Tropes associated with this myth can likewise be uncovered in both the thematic and structural composition strategies of *Moderato cantabile*. The most over-arching of these tropes — unattainability — figures the psychic dissociation of desire and possession, a desire paradoxically intensified by interdiction and separation. Other tropes similarly connected to the Tristan legend include the *philtre* or love potion; the problem of societal restriction and taboo; the binary of moderation and excess; the complex link between obsessive desire and death; and the notion of doubling at the level of the narration itself.

Rooted in ancient Celtic mythology, the Tristan myth as assimilated into modern Western culture absorbed the surviving narrative verse fragments and authorial points of view of several French and German literary versions from the later twelfth and early thirteenth centuries. Foremost among these were the

---

An earlier version of this paper was presented at the 111th Convention of the Modern Language Association in Chicago, Illinois, December 1995.

[1] For a close reading concerning intertextual reminiscences of the Tristan myth both in Duras's dialogic structure and in Resnais's cinematographic imagery, see my 'Memory, Love, and Inaccessibility in *Hiroshima mon amour*', *Journal of Durassian Studies* 4 (1993), pp. 6–16. This essay has been reprinted in *Marguerite Duras Lives On*, ed. Janine Ricouart (Lanham, MD: University Press of America, 1998), pp. 27–37.

versions by Thomas (*c.* 1160), Eilhart (*c.* 1175), Béroul (*c.* 1200), and Gottfried von Strassburg (*c.* 1210) whose extant text is the longest. These versions, along with three shorter twelfth-century poems and a thirteenth-century prose romance (all French) form the basis of Joseph Bédier's now classic, synthetic retelling of the Tristan story in modern French (1900), a redaction that has encouraged the myth's proliferation in twentieth-century cultural and literary consciousness. The objective of this study is in no way meant to offer an exhaustive investigation of precise correspondences between Duras's text and the multiple medieval sources and versions of the Tristan myth. Rather, it will focus on the striking intertextual dimension of Duras's writing and will explore its hermeneutic implications primarily in the novel and, more briefly, in the novel's cinematographic adaptation. My approach here will thus be two-pronged: first, I will discuss how Duras's *Moderato cantabile* incorporates and transforms key elements of the Tristan story, and second, I will address how the film version fails to translate effectively Duras's powerful restaging of human love and suffering inscribed within this pervasive mythic paradigm.

To review briefly the plot of Duras's novel, the action turns around a lonely bourgeois housewife, Anne Desbaresdes, who resides in an unnamed French industrial port and whose object of total devotion is her young son. During a visit to her son's weekly piano lesson, she overhears a chilling scream emanating from the café below the piano teacher's apartment. As she later learns, this scream comes from a woman who has just been murdered by a man that is presumably her lover. Joining the curious bystanders at the entrance of the café, she is transfixed by the haunting look and posture of the murderer who clings desperately to the body of the dead woman, repeating the words, 'Mon amour. Mon amour' ('My love. My love') before turning his delirious gaze to the crowd.[2] Over the course of the following week, Anne returns five times to the same café, where she drinks unaccustomed amounts of wine and is drawn into conversation with a man named Chauvin who, like herself, witnessed the bizarre aftermath of this crime of passion. Through their repeated dialogues, Anne and Chauvin explore their own forbidden attraction for one another by attempting to understand, to reconstruct and, eventually, to re-enact verbally the fatal passion emblematized by the murdered woman and her lover.

The opening scene at the child's piano lesson introduces and helps structure the dynamics of inaccessibility in the novel. As in the Tristan myth, where forbidden passion embodies transgression of the rules of sacred and social law,

---

[2] Marguerite Duras, *Moderato cantabile* (Paris: Minuit, 1958), p. 14; *idem*, *Four Novels by Marguerite Duras*, trans. Richard Seaver (New York: Grove, 1965). Translations are my own except where indicated.

Duras's fictional universe is defined by the stark juxtaposition of two divergent and incompatible worlds: one of societal convention and order and one of immoderate, unacceptable erotic desire. This juxtaposition is metaphorized on the auditory level by the paradoxical rupture between the disciplined production of melody demanded by the authoritarian piano teacher and the sudden, excessive cry arising from the crime of passion in the street. Indeed, the term of musical direction that constitutes the novel's title, *moderato cantabile* (moderately and melodiously), resonates uncannily with an admonitory proverb offered by the medieval narrator during the description of Tristan's charged hereditary background: 'Démesure n'est pas prouesse' ('Excess is not heroism').[3] This proverb appears in Bédier's first chapter where it alludes to both the extremes of passion defining Tristan's parents (Rivalen's coexisting passion for his pregnant wife and for military battle in defence of his lands; Blanchefleur's reciprocal passion for her husband and her inconsolable grief following his death, which results in her own willing death after the physical travail of Tristan's birth) and the moderate prudence of Tristan's guardian, Rohalt (who provisionally yields to enemy forces and passes Tristan off as his own child in order to preserve the orphan's life). The title *Moderato cantabile* may itself be considered a reinterpretation of the medieval proverb concerning the problem of moderation and excess. When read in this light, Duras's musical title becomes not only an explicit injunction of the rigid instructor to the headstrong little boy concerning the performance of his sonatina, but also a symbolic injunction implicitly understood by Anne and Chauvin in their repeated efforts to 'compose' and to 'perform' within acceptable limits the tragic love affair of the original couple.

The physical space of the piano studio establishes an additional, visual metaphor for the broad realms of confinement and liberation at stake in the text. This room in which social grace and acceptability are taught through the ordered execution of musical sound is separated by a vast, open window not only from the chaotic human behaviour on the streets below, but from the boundless sea and horizon beyond the nearby dock. Duras insists on the open window, which from the very beginning figures the inevitable contamination of the two worlds that the female protagonist will be forced to negotiate during her brief, odd relationship with Chauvin. One cannot help but be struck by another parallel between the Tristan myth and Duras's own exploration of illicit passion. In the Tristan myth, the high seas set the scene for the couple's imbibing of the love potion and metaphorize the irrevocable unleashing of their passion. Similarly, in *Moderato cantabile* the visible, yet distant, sea forms a constant reminder of the potential

[3] Joseph Bédier, *Le roman de Tristan et Iseut* (1900; Paris: Union Générale, 1981), p. 19. See also *idem*, *The Romance of Tristan and Iseult*, trans. Hilaire Belloc (New York: Vintage-Random, 1965). The Bédier redaction incorporates in large part Thomas's version.

for a dangerous new freedom that Anne Desbaredes simultaneously desires and fears. Concerning this metaphor, the German poet Gottfried von Strassburg made a significant innovation in the myth's famous love potion episode by having Iseut's servant, Brangien, cast what remains of the drink into the sea, after which the waves grow 'wild and raging'.[4] This version was incorporated by Bédier and thereby made its way into the nineteenth-century French retelling of *Tristan* that has so profoundly influenced modern literary consciousness and culture. In both Bédier and Duras, the stormy movement of the sea mirrors the unleashed desires of the couple, and becomes an important image both of transgression and of ambiguous liberation.

Situating Anne and Chauvin's conversations within the other, seemingly confined space of the café makes their dialogue possible. In *Crack Wars*, a critical work that explores addiction and its relationship to patterns of obsessive, repetitive behaviour in literary texts, Avital Ronell imagines how Duras herself might discuss the café scenes that stimulate the addictive tendencies and psychic crises of her characters:

> I'd saturate my couples, watch them dissolve in cafés. Yes, maybe they would know fusional desire but without all that operatic noise. ... I like to alcoholize my texts, turn down the volume and let them murmur across endless boundaries and miniscule epiphanies.[5]

Like the *philtre* imbibed by the lovers in the multiple versions of the Tristan myth, the wine imbibed by the protagonists — especially by the self-avowedly temperate Anne — catalyses a release of inhibition that allows them to entertain the spectre of their own repressed desire by imagining the story behind the crime and by vicariously seeking to relive that very experience. But, as the above quotation from *Crack Wars* implies, for Anne this is a *philtre* stripped of all romantic clichés and overtones; her engagement in the dialogue is predicated not on a magically transformative potion imbibed in one set of 'fatal' and gratuitous circumstances as in the myth, but rather on a willed intoxication provoked by the kind of repeated, mechanistic drinking that, for Duras, typically links erotic desire with social taboo and with the threat of self-destruction.

Much has been made — both in the various versions of the myth and in the critical response to the medieval and modern French texts — of the structural role

---

[4] Gottfried von Strassburg, *Tristan*, intro. and ed. A.T. Hatto (Harmondsworth: Penguin, 1960), p. 29. By contrast, in Thomas's version Brangien preserves the rest of the potion and presents it to King Mark and to Iseut, but only Mark drinks it: Iseut, already inextricably tied to Tristan, secretly throws away her portion.

[5] Avital Ronell, *Crack Wars: Literature, Addiction, Mania* (Lincoln, NE: University of Nebraska Press, 1992), p. 155.

and moral/ethical implications of the love potion. Denis de Rougemont's famous phrase 'l'alibi de la passion' best expresses the principal issues at hand in considering the *philtre*: those of explanation and of responsibility. In order to 'explain' the inexplicable origin of a passion as intense and transgressive as that shared by Tristan and Iseut and to find the means to render the couple blameless and worthy of sympathy in their unrelenting pursuit of a relationship prohibited by every social and religious law, there needs to be recourse to a magical exterior phenomenon over which there is no possible human control and therefore no moral and ethical human responsibility. Serving as just such a phenomenon, the *philtre* allows for at least a surface romanticization of the chivalric myth, one that is totally swept away in Duras's brutal demystification of the wine trope in *Moderato cantabile*.[6]

The café conversations themselves (with the exception of the final one) manipulate the trope of erotic prohibition and unattainability through two complementary layers of discourse. On one hand, the protagonists seek to know the unknowable story of the murdered woman and her lover through a slowly accreting process of shared speculation and creative reinvention. Their language in this dialogic mode demonstrates a repeated frustration with the impossibility of gaining either certain knowledge or rational understanding of the couple's act and reveals a simultaneous obsession with imagining a narrative to unravel this uncertainty. The following exchange during their first meeting speaks to this desperate hunger for knowledge:

> Anne: Ce cri était si fort que vraiment il est bien naturel que l'on cherche à savoir ...
> Chauvin: Ce que je sais, c'est qu'il lui a tiré une balle dans le coeur ...
> Anne: Et, évidemment on ne peut pas savoir pourquoi? ...
> Chauvin: J'aimerais pouvoir vous le dire, mais je ne sais rien de sûr. (pp. 19–20)[7]
>
> (Anne: The scream was so loud it's really only natural for people to try to find out what happened ...
> Chauvin: All I know is that he shot her through the heart ...
> Anne: And I don't suppose you can tell me why? ...
> Chauvin: I wish I could, but I'm not really sure of anything. [Seaver trans., p. 85])

---

[6] A parallel phenomenon exists in certain modern retellings of the Holy Grail legend. See MaryLynn Saul's chapter later in this volume.

[7] The dialogue in the novel takes place in third-person narration. In citing conversational exchanges, I have added the names of the speakers for clarity.

Similarly, an excerpt from their second meeting reveals the obsessive quest for imaginative reinvention:

> Anne: Dites-moi, je vous en prie, comment elle en est venue à découvrir que c'était justement ça qu'elle voulait de lui, comment elle a su à ce point ce qu'elle désirait de lui?
> Chauvin: J'imagine qu'un jour ... un matin à l'aube, elle a su soudainement ce qu'elle désirait de lui. ... Il n'y a pas d'explication, je crois, à ce genre de découverte-là.
> Anne: Je voudrais que vous me disiez le commencement même, comment ils ont commencé à se parler. C'est dans un café, disiez-vous ...
> Chauvin: Oui, je crois bien que c'est dans un café qu'ils ont commencé à se parler. ... (pp. 31–2)
>
> (Anne: But please tell me, how did she come to realize that that was what she wanted from him, how did she know so clearly what she wanted him to do?
> Chauvin: I imagine that one day, one morning at dawn she suddenly knew what she wanted him to do. ... I don't think there's any explanation for that sort of discovery.
> Anne: I'd like you to tell me about the very beginning, how they began to talk to each other. It was in a café, you said ...
> Chauvin: Yes, I'm almost sure it was in a café that they began to talk to each other. ... [Seaver, pp. 95–6])

Chauvin's imaginative placement of the tragic couple's first conversations in a café obviously links their connection to an incipient re-enactment by Anne and himself. This process of re-enactment bears a strong reminiscence to two variations of 'doubling' that structure portions of the Tristan story, particularly in the versions by Thomas and Gottfried. The technique of literary doubling, i.e. the repetition of situations, themes and images with some degree of variation, pervades the mythic narrative, as does the related phenomenon of psychological doubling, which involves the attempt to re-create oneself in the image of someone with whom one identifies. Recent criticism on Thomas's *Tristan* have explored the notions of doubling in the medieval text. For instance, Susan Dannenbaum has indicated the role of literary doubling to develop the anguish of erotic secrecy as a fundamental tenet of 'courtly love'.[8] Matilda Bruckner has examined how the poet's binary language strategies represent instances of

[8] Susan Dannenbaum, 'Doubling and *Fine Amor* in Thomas's *Tristan*', *Tristania* 5 (1979), pp. 3–14.

psychological doubling.[9] With respect to *Moderato cantabile*, perhaps the most pertinent examples of literary and psychological doubling in the medieval myth entail Tristan and Iseut's implicit reliving of the tragic paradigm of passion, duty, separation and death experienced by the hero's own parents (Rivalen and Blanchefleur) and the courtly couple's attempts to create perfect parity and reciprocity in their acts of devotion towards one another. Indeed, this dual doubling phenomenon begins to illuminate Duras's text from the moment when the frustrating café speculation on the previous history of the doomed lovers becomes intertwined with another slowly developing dialogic process: Chauvin and Anne's gradual revelation and tacit acknowledgement of their own previous history together and the obsessive images and fantasies it has provoked. Chauvin, it turns out, used to work at the foundry managed by Anne's industrialist husband and once attended an employee reception at their home. His memory of that night is haunted by the image of his hostess, of whom he first says: 'Vous aviez une robe noire très décolletée. Vous nous regardiez avec amabilité et indifférence. Il faisait chaud' (p. 34). ('You were wearing a black dress with a very low neck. You were looking at us pleasantly, indifferently. It was hot' [Seaver, p. 98]).

Chauvin returns to this scene several times in his subsequent conversations with Anne, each time tightening the erotic tension of the exchange by the increasingly sensual overtones of his description. Later, he recalls:

> 'Au mois de juin de l'année dernière ... vous vous teniez ... sur le perron, prête à nous accueillir, nous le personnel des Fonderies. Au-dessus de vos seins à moitié nus, il y avait une fleur blanche de magnolia'. (p. 42)
>
> ('Last June ... you were standing ... on the steps, ready to receive us, the workers from the foundries. Above your breasts, which were half bare, there was a white magnolia'. [Seaver, p. 105])

In their penultimate conversation, he even more suggestively muses:

> Vous étiez accoudée à ce grand piano. Entre vos seins nus sous votre robe, il y a cette fleur de magnolia. ... C'est une fleur énorme ... trop grande pour vous'. (p. 59)
>
> ('You were leaning on this grand piano. Your breasts were naked under your dress, and between them there was that magnolia flower. ... It's a huge flower ... too big for you'. [Seaver, pp. 119–20])

---

[9] Matilda Tomaryn Bruckner, 'The Representation of the Lovers' Death: Thomas' *Tristan* as Open Text', *Tristania* 9 (1983–84), pp. 49–61. A senior honours thesis by Zèna-Gabrielle Hailu, Georgetown University, directed by my colleague Carol Dover, provided additional stimulating reading on these issues.

The pervasive magnolia image, functioning with its pungent odour as another metaphor for erotic intoxication and excess — both a rhetorical doubling of the wine motif and a parallel resonance of the medieval *philtre* — reappears as a backdrop in the fantasy-like scenarios developing from Chauvin's obsessional memory. The male protagonist slowly reveals that he has voyeuristically 'scoped out' Anne's house and magnolia-filled garden, and through the pattern of lighted windows has guessed the location of her bedroom and her nocturnal habits. In between their questioning and re-invention of the café crime, both Anne and Chauvin betray their own repressed attraction by rehearsing this nocturnal scenario, exposing once again the conflictive juxtaposition between another suffocating interior space of social respectability (Anne's house) and another intoxicating exterior space of unattained desire (her garden). Speculation on the effect of the magnolia itself dominates the first of these exchanges:

> Anne: Oui, il y en tellement à cette époque-ci de l'année qu'on peut en rêver et en être malade tout le jour qui suit. On ferme sa fenêtre, c'est à n'y pas tenir. ...
> Chauvin: Si vous fermez votre fenêtre à cette époque-ci de l'année ... vous devez avoir chaud et mal dormir. ...
> Anne: L'odeur des magnolias est si forte, si vous saviez.
> Chauvin: Je sais. (pp. 30–31)
>
> (Anne: Yes, there are so many flowers at this time of year that you can dream about them and be ill all the next day. ... You shut your window, it's unbearable. ...
> Chauvin: If you shut your window at this time of year, you must be too hot to sleep.
> Anne: The scent of magnolias is overpowering, you know.
> Chauvin: I know. [Seaver, p. 95])

As their conversations continue, the erotic connotations involving the imagined nocturnal scenario — just as those involving Chauvin's memory of Anne at the workers' reception — become ever more relentless and direct. In this vision, the potential objects of Anne's constrained desire become multiple and indiscriminate:

> Chauvin: Ce grand couloir dont vous parliez reste parfois allumé très tard.
> Anne: Il m'arrive de ne pas arriver à m'endormir. ...
> Chauvin: Quand c'est le jour, au petit matin, vous allez regarder à travers la grand baie vitrée.
> Anne: L'été, les ouvriers de l'arsenal commencent à passer vers six heures. ...

Chauvin: Souvent, vous regardez ces hommes qui vont à l'arsenal ... et la nuit, lorsque vous dormez mal, le souvenir vous en revient.
Anne: Lorsque je me réveille assez tôt ... je les regarde. Et parfois aussi, oui, le souvenir de certains d'entre eux, la nuit, m'est revenu. (pp. 34–6)

(Chauvin: Sometimes there's a light on till late at night in the hallway you mentioned.
Anne: Sometimes I can't fall asleep. ...
Chauvin: The first thing in the morning, you go and look out of the big bay window.
Anne: In summer the workers at the dockyards begin passing about six o'clock. ...
Chauvin: You often watch those men on their way to the dock-yards ... and at night, when you have trouble sleeping, they come back to you.
Anne: When I wake up early enough, I do watch them. And you're right, sometimes at night the memory of some of them does come back to me. [Seaver, pp. 98–9, modified])

The gradual repetition and development of both levels of the protagonists' dialogue — one which focuses on the original couple and the other on themselves — culminate in the powerful juxtaposition of the last two chapters in the novel. The penultimate chapter removes Anne and Chauvin's brief personal history and its attendant fantasies from the realm of café dialogue and places it directly back into the rigidly coded world of bourgeois respectability. Following her fourth — and most unsettling — conversation with Chauvin, Anne makes a late appearance at a formal dinner reception given at her home. Here Duras's narrative descriptions alternate between images of social restraint and those of passionate desire.

During the entire evening, Anne senses instinctively that Chauvin — like the exiled Tristan who first in a fit of fever endlessly hallucinates secret returns to break down King Mark's castle walls, and who later appears nightly in the castle orchard seeking clandestine trysts with his beloved — is wandering back and forth alone between the gates of her garden and the beach beyond. Bédier, following Eilhart, had movingly invoked Tristan's feverish anguish after King Mark, tortured by suspicion, dismisses him from the castle:

Mais, sans relâche, dans l'ardeur de la fièvre, le désir l'entraînait, comme un cheval emporté, vers *les tours bien closes* qui tenaient la reine enfermée; cheval et cavalier *se brisaient contre les murs de pierre*; mais cheval et cavalier se relevaient et reprenaient sans cesse la même chevauchée. (p. 64, emphasis added)

(But in the fire of his fever, desire without redress bore him like a bolting horse towards *the well-girdled towers* which shut in the Queen; horse and rider *broke upon the walls of stone*; but horse and rider picked themselves up and ceaselessly threw themselves into the selfsame ride. [Belloc trans., p. 45, emphasis added])

Bédier then cleverly juxtaposes to this concrete architectural metaphorization of the obstacles confronting the lovers a lyrical description of Tristan's nocturnal visits to a pine tree in the orchard beyond the castle, and the ruse through which he is able to contact and, with Brangien's vigilant help, sometimes see Iseut:

Or, chaque soir, Tristan, par le conseil de Brangien, taillait avec art des morceaux d'écorce et de menus branchages. Il franchissait les pieux aigus, et, venu sous le pin, jetait les copeaux dans la fontaine. Legers comme l'écume, ils surnagaient et coulaient avec elle, et dans les chambres des femmes, Iseut épiait leur venue. Aussitôt, les soirs ... elle s'en venait vers son ami. (p. 65)

(And every evening, by Brangien's counsel, Tristan meticulously cut twigs and bark, leapt over the sharp stakes, and, having come beneath the pine, threw the cuttings into the fountain. Light as foam, they floated down the stream to the women's rooms, and Iseut watched for their arrival. And on those evenings ... she would wander out into the orchard and find her lover. [Belloc, p. 46, modified])

Duras employs a similar juxtaposition of rigid containment and lyrical space. On one hand, Duras's description is filled with details of the elegant cuisine and the tightly controlled, artificial banter of magnificently attired bourgeois matrons cast as show-pieces on the arms of their dispassionate husbands. On the other hand, these descriptions are intercut with those of a desperately desiring man gripping the railings of the gate as he inhales the heady fumes of the magnolias, and the woman inside the house equally obsessed with her own desire, consuming more and more wine and caressing the magnolia she has placed — this time as a subversive emblem — between her breasts. By means of this alternation, the novel's insistent representation of the Tristan-like incompatibility of worlds and its hyperbolization of the tropes of sexual interdiction and inaccessibility reach their climax. Indeed, in the chapter's final scene, when Anne vomits both the food she had forced down at dinner and the wine consumed since her latest afternoon tryst at the café, her act of vomiting figures not only the protagonist's underlying revulsion towards the life mandated by her marriage, but her incapacity to assimilate and embrace as a real-world choice the model of immoderate desire that was played out in the opening crime of passion and explored in her dialogues with Chauvin.

The closing chapter of the novel returns to the café for the protagonists' last meeting. Here the psychic impasse represented by Anne's visceral rejection of the worlds of both enslaving respectability and erotic abandon finds its only possible outlet in a final level of dialogic exchange — and, for the first time, in the consummation of physical contact. Having flirted throughout their conversations with the drive to repeat the excessive, to-the-death passion of the original café couple — itself none other than a reconfiguration of the drive of desire towards death that impels the Tristan myth — they move finally to experience it vicariously in words and gestures. Holding each other's hands and touching each other's lips for the first and only time in deliberate poses that Duras pointedly describes as 'frozen', 'leaden', 'funereal' and 'mortuarial', they try to narrate once again the couple's desire for death until they reach, once again, the impossibility of explaining it. Left as before with this void of uncertainty, they accomplish their own definitive parting by the following stark, verbal enactment of Anne's murder:

> Je voudrais que vous soyez morte, dit Chauvin.
> C'est fait, dit Anne Desbaresdes. (p. 84)
>
> (I wish you were dead, Chauvin said.
> I am, Anne Desbaresdes said. [Seaver, p. 140])

Thus, as Susan Cohen has argued, the text ultimately restages the crime of passion through performative speech acts and concludes with Anne walking away into the red light of sunset that absorbs her in 'the symbolic color of blood'.[10] In so doing, the text also performs a re-enactment of passion's ultimate deathward movement in the Tristan story, demonstrating a crucial impulse on the part of the characters to replace what seems unattainable in reality with a virtual mythification of their experience. This gesture, although compensatory, ritualizes and confers at least provisional closure to their visceral and intellectual quest for psychic knowledge. The important difference, of course, in Duras's reconfiguration of the myth's conclusion (the symbolic re-enactment of the crime of passion by Anne and Chauvin) is the absence of reciprocity created by the 'murder' of one partner by the other. Thus, although *Moderato cantabile* presents the structural doubling between its two protagonists and the couple whose crime brings them

---

[10] Susan D. Cohen, *Women and Discourse in the Fiction of Marguerite Duras* (Amherst, MA: University of Massachusetts Press, 1993), p. 125.

together, the psychological doubling between Anne and Chauvin does not include the balanced unity in death sought and achieved by Tristan and Iseut.[11]

In her provocative study of Duras in *Soleil noir (Black Sun)*, Julia Kristeva compares the literary and cinematic versions of the author's works in a way that suggests a viable approach for evaluating *Moderato cantabile*, the film:

> On comprend désormais qu'il ne faut pas donner les livres de Duras aux lecteurs et lectrices fragiles. Qu'ils aillent voir les films et les pièces, ils retrouveront cette même maladie de la douleur, mais tamisée, enrobée d'un charme rêveur qui l'adoucit et la rend aussi plus factice et inventée: une convention.
>
> (One now understands that Duras's books shouldn't be given to fragile readers. Let these readers rather go to see the films and the plays; they will experience the same sickness of anguish, but filtered, cloaked in a dreamy charm that softens it, and that also tends to artificialize and conventionalize it.)[12]

Kristeva here captures the essence of the problems posed by the cinematic transposition of *Moderato cantabile*. The only two segments of the film that are reasonably faithful to the literary text are the piano lesson scenes and the dinner-party scene. The first of these contrasts well the teacher's regimented discourse and the little boy's unhappily controlled musical performance with the murdered woman's unbridled scream and the ensuing bedlam in the street; later, the dinner-party scene visually reproduces Duras's exquisite narration of suffocating bourgeois ostentation and dramatically juxtaposes it first to Anne's barely suppressed inebriation and then — through a series of anxiety-provoking outdoor tracking shots — to the voyeuristic hunger of Chauvin prowling around the garden.

Elsewhere, however, the moving incompatibility of worlds conveyed in these two segments is numbed and diluted by the film's curious disruption of the central café setting and of almost all the scenes featuring conversations between the two protagonists. Following their initial meeting the day after the murder, Brook's adaptation forces Anne and Chauvin out of the intimate interior space of the café and transplants them into vast, mournful exterior landscapes where they

---

[11] The possible gender-based implications of this imbalance are explored throughout Cohen's study.

[12] Julia Kristeva, *Soleil noir: dépression et mélancolie* (Paris: Folio-Gallimard, 1987), p. 235; *idem*, *Black Sun: Depression and Melancholia*, trans. Leon S. Roudiez (New York: Columbia University Press, 1989), p. 227, modified.

wander aimlessly, alone or together, seemingly preoccupied not so much by a dangerously surfacing, forbidden desire as by a vague, existential ennui that clouds, rather than exacerbates, the painful drama of inaccessibility. Against the backdrop of these grim, empty spaces and away from the site where ritualized wine-drinking catalyses an imaginative exploration and vicarious replaying of an unlivable passion, both layers of Duras's original dialogue between the two characters — speculation on the murder and rehearsal of their personal history — diminish radically. The murder itself is discussed very little and becomes simply a facile pretext for a fall into the clichés of a banal extramarital love affair. The charged references to their long-past previous encounter and the sensual fantasies that it nourishes disappear almost completely from a relationship now dominated by furtive physical embraces and by trite confessions of adulterous desire.

The film's conclusion is a shocking trivialization of the novel's final meeting between the two protagonists. In a state of near hysteria after the dinner-party, Anne escapes into the night and rushes directly to the café that we have barely seen since the beginning of the film, followed in heavy-handed, chase-scene fashion by a husband who had been almost completely effaced in Duras's literary text. Chauvin is inexplicably waiting for Anne in the darkened, empty café. Here, once again, with no verbal 'foreplay' reinvoking the murder that originally brought them together — and with the audience awaiting the inevitable arrival of the punitive husband — Chauvin and Anne utter the final words that in the novel symbolically re-enact the crime of passion. Now gratuitously stripped of their context in this scene, these words cease to have any performative value. By extension, they have lost any sense of ritualized myth-making power. Far from serving as a virtual figure of Tristan's eternalized desire and erotic unattainability, they suggest only Chauvin's brutal rejection of a woman who will clearly be unable to pursue this love affair further, and Anne's sense of abandonment by a callous, would-be lover (played to the hilt by the brooding Belmondo). At the end of the film, it is Chauvin who abruptly leaves the café while Anne dissolves on the floor in sobs before stumbling powerlessly to her husband's waiting car. Duras's carefully nuanced staging of the Tristan myth disintegrates into pure convention: the titillating and sentimentalized torment of thwarted adultery.

In the end, Brook's divergent and frankly forgettable adaptation of the original text of *Moderato cantabile* suggests a discomfort with Duras's stark and intense dialogic exploration of the inaccessibility trope, a discomfort that engages the movie in the process of filtering and conventionalization to which Kristeva alluded. However, the sustained reputation of a film like *Hiroshima mon amour*, which examines related thematic issues, shows that the author's art of this period can achieve an authentic and powerful representation in the cinema. Indeed, the key to *Hiroshima*'s filmic success lies in Alain Resnais's privileging of the Durassian dialogue through which rememoration and re-enactment produce a kind of acceptance and self-knowledge. It is precisely this self-knowledge that, according to Denis de Rougemont's classic study *L'Amour et l'occident* (*Love and the Western World*), represents the positive legacy of Tristan's unattainable passion. De Rougemont views as fundamental the anguishing search and struggle for self-knowledge perpetuated by the experience of unattainable or forbidden passion:

> Passion veut dire souffrance, chose subie, prépondérance du destin sur la personne libre et responsable. Aimer l'amour plus que l'object de l'amour, aimer la passion pour elle-même ... c'est aimer et chercher la souffrance. ... Pourquoi l'homme d'Occident veut-il subir cette passion qui le blesse et que toute sa raison condamne? Pourquoi veut-il cet amour dont l'éclat ne peut être que son suicide? C'est qu'il se connaît et s'éprouve sous le coup de menaces vitales, dans la souffrance et au seuil de la mort.
>
> (Passion means suffering something undergone, the mastery of fate over a free and responsible person. To love Love more than the object of Love, to love passion for its own sake ... has been to love to suffer. ... Why does Western man wish to suffer this passion which lacerates him and which all his common sense rejects? Why does he yearn after this particular kind of love notwithstanding that its effulgence must coincide with his self-destruction? The answer is that he reaches *self-awareness* and *tests himself* only by risking his life — in suffering and on the verge of death.)[13]

In *Moderato cantabile*, too, a type of admittedly vertiginous self-knowledge and acceptance becomes available to the protagonists in the novel, one that never really touches them in the film. While in the film the characters remain on the safe, morally defined terrain of conventionalized adulterous relationships, in Duras's novel Anne Desbaresdes and Chauvin learn to confront their psychic susceptibility to an unbounded, amoral and unfulfillable desire that can never be explained, and to accept mutually that for them it will be pursued and lived only on the level of shared language and imagination.

[13] Denis de Rougemont, *L'Amour et l'occident* (Paris: Plon, 1939), p. 41; *idem*, *Love in the Western World*, trans. Montgomery Belgian (New York: Harper, 1956), pp. 50–51.

Chapter 2

The Lady of Shalott: Malory, Tennyson, Zelazny and Pynchon

Kathleen Coyne Kelly

> Female visionaries are poor mad exploited sibyls and pythonesses. Male ones are prophets and poets. A.S. Byatt[1]

In an essay on Victorian attitudes towards the distant past, J.W. Burrow writes that 'it is tempting to ... draw a line between seriousness and frivolity', between those

> to whom some period or aspect of the past presented itself in full seriousness as a cherished heritage, a spiritual home for the modern world, or an unanswerable condemnation of it, and those who merely used the past as a source for an archaic and hence exotic vocabulary for their trade.[2]

However, those who are determined to respect the 'full seriousness' of the past often end up enclosing it, making it inviolate. In its emphasis on the linear, such a viewpoint leaves little space for what we have come to call intertextuality — for the interplay and interanimation of texts.

Mikhail Bakhtin offers another viewpoint:

> If it is impossible to study literature apart from an epoch's entire culture, it is even more fatal to encapsulate a literary phenomenon in the single epoch of its creation, in its own contemporaneity, so to speak. ... Enclosure within the epoch ... makes it impossible to understand the work's future life in subsequent centuries; this life appears as a kind of paradox. ... Works break through the boundaries of their own time, they

---

I am grateful to Gregory Zuch, who reminded me of the description of Varo's painting in *The Crying of Lot 49*. I thank Susan Wall and Herb Sussman, who read and commented on drafts of this chapter.

1 A.S. Byatt, *The Shadow of the Sun* (1964; London: Vintage, 1991), p. x.

2 J.W. Burrow, 'The Sense of the Past', *The Victorians*, ed. Laurence Lerner (New York: Holmes, 1978), p. 121.

> live in centuries, that is in *great time* and frequently (with great works, always) their lives there are more intense and fuller than are their lives within their own time.[3]

Bakhtin goes on to talk about the 'posthumous life' of a text, and makes a distinction between the factual knowledge of past centuries and the discovery of 'new semantic depths that lie embedded in the cultures of past epochs'.[4] In this view, a text exuberantly resists containment; it actually celebrates what Burrow refers to as an archaic and exotic vocabulary.

Bakhtin's formulation of language as heteroglossic, in which 'every conversation is full of transmissions and interpretations of other people's words', has a special resonance for studies in medievalism.[5] If we apply an intertextual approach to medievalized texts — as opposed to an approach that emphasizes the identification of sources — we might begin to see medievalism as a way of reading, for it is the process, not its results, that makes medievalism so compelling a subject. Medievalism is not only created by what A.S. Byatt calls 'a good and greedy reading, by a great writer',[6] but also by 'a good and greedy reading' by a contemporary reader steeped in both popular and high culture.

In this chapter, I examine what happens when later writers exploit the 'semantic depths' of the Middle Ages. I have chosen to focus on the Lady of Shalott figure as represented in four texts: Elayne in Sir Thomas Malory's 'Fair Maid of Ascolat' (*c.* 1469–70), the Lady in Alfred, Lord Tennyson's 'The Lady of Shalott' (the 1842 revision), Eileen Shallot in Roger Zelazny's fantasy novella 'He Who Shapes' (1964) and Oedipa Maas in Thomas Pynchon's *The Crying of Lot 49* (1966). I should say that Oedipa is not necessarily a direct descendant of the Lady, but a highly allusive analogue to her.[7] In each text, the heroine emerges as a figure through which fate, memory, desire, imagination and the act of story-making itself are constituted. Tennyson's 'The Lady of Shalott' and its critical reception serve as the linchpin for my reading of Malory, Zelazny and Pynchon

---

[3] M.M. Bakhtin, 'Response to a Question from the *Novy Mir* Editorial Staff', 1970; reprinted in Caryl Emerson and Michael Holquist (eds), *Speech Genres and Other Late Essays*, trans. Vern W. McGee (Austin, TX: University of Texas Press, 1986), pp. 3–4.

[4] Bakhtin, 'Response', p. 6.

[5] Bakhtin, 'Discourse in the Novel', in *The Dialogic Imagination*, ed. M. Holquist, trans. Caryl Emerson and Michael Holquist (Austin, TX: University of Texas Press, 1981), p. 338.

[6] Byatt, 'People in Paper Houses: Attitudes to "Realism" and "Experiment" in English Postwar Fiction,', in *Passions of the Mind: Selected Writings* (New York: Random/Turtle Bay, 1992), p. 149.

[7] Sir Thomas Malory, *The Works of Sir Thomas Malory*, ed. Eugène Vinaver, rev. P.J.C. Field, 3rd edn (Oxford: Clarendon, 1990); Alfred, Lord Tennyson, *The Poems of Tennyson*, ed. Christopher Ricks, 2nd edn (Berkeley, CA: University of California Press, 1987); Roger Zelazny, 'He Who Shapes', in *The Last Defender of Camelot* (1964; New York: Avon, 1988); Thomas Pynchon, *The Crying of Lot 49* (New York: Bantam, 1966).

as I violate the chronicity of publication dates and read these texts together in 'great time'.

When we examine Burrow's and Bakhtin's language, we see that they employ similar metaphors and images of containment, but for very different ends. Burrow stresses boundaries; Bakhtin is fascinated by the boundlessness of texts. Although Burrow himself is cognizant of the problem of boundaries, the language that he privileges has erected a formidable tower of criticism around Tennyson's 'The Lady of Shalott'.[8] This criticism, intent on fixing the meaning of 'The Lady of Shalott', shuts out and shuts down the limitless possibilities of creativity, emotionality and play inherent in language — attributes that Hélène Cixous and others describe as feminine in a binary, patriarchal system.

In her questioning of the traditional reading of 'The Lady of Shalott', Flavia Alaya asks: 'If she is a woman, then it is assumed she must give and have love; must it also be assumed that if she is an artist she must not? A chorus of critics answers, yes'.[9] Moreover, numerous critics have been preoccupied with degendering and dehumanizing the Lady in Tennyson's poem, moving her into object position as 'Poet'. Even when, as in some readings, she is made into the Muse or Art itself, she is still subject to the male gaze. We can find such interpretations as early as 1848, when Henry Sutton summed up the poem in this way: 'He who would be a poet, must learn to withdraw himself from trivialities as much as he can'.[10] One cannot help but note the regendering of the Lady here in the pronoun 'he'. This approach has persisted in critical thought, as the following interpretation, found in a popular college anthology, demonstrates:

> The tower, the loom, the Lady herself, have no consistent figurative meaning, but the reader is tempted to consider the Lady in her tower as representing the poet, the loom as art, and the mirror as poetic imagination. ... The poem suggests that the artist must remain in aloof

[8] Criticism on 'The Lady of Shalott' is extensive and varied in approach. See especially Flavia Alaya, 'Tennyson's "The Lady of Shalott": The Triumph of Art', *Victorian Poetry* **8** (1970), pp. 273–89; Lona Mosk Packer, 'Sun and Shadow: The Nature of Experience in Tennyson's "Lady of Shalott"', *The Victorian Newsletter* **25** (1964), pp. 4–8; Edgar F. Shannon, Jr, 'Poetry as Vision: Sight and Insight in "The Lady of Shalott"', *Victorian Poetry* **19** (1981), pp. 207–23. Although these three critics offer new readings of the poem, they concur in interpreting the Lady as a symbol of the artist. Alaya sums up the traditional interpretation of the poem as symbolizing 'the unresolved dialectic assumed to be characteristic of the early Tennyson, artistic detachment vs. social responsibility' (p. 274). For a feminist reading, as well as a guide to other such readings, see Lynne Pearce, *Woman/Image/Text: Readings in Pre-Raphaelite Art and Literature* (Toronto: University of Toronto Press, 1991), pp. 71–85.

[9] Alaya, p. 275.

[10] Henry Sutton, 'The Poet's Mission', *Howitt's Journal* **3** (15 January 1848), p. 39.

> detachment, observing life only in the mirror of the imagination, not mixing in it directly.[11]

In such readings, the Lady's tower on its island is a fixed, stable point, self-contained and safe. Its symbolism as a phallus hardly needs comment. Recall that the Lady herself is often imagined as fixed, sitting in front of her loom, positioned so that the only reality she can see is refracted through a mirror in which the 'shadows of the world appear' (l. 48). I do not mean to imply that all contemporary criticism on 'The Lady of Shalott' is monologic. Indeed, a number of critics (most recently, Isobel Armstrong and Gerhard Joseph) have offered provocative, open-ended readings of the poem.[12] Yet even post-structuralist readings take as their point of departure the troping of Tennyson's Lady as feminine Muse or as male poet. As I hope to show, Malory's Elayne, Zelazny's Eileen and Pynchon's Oedipa both reproduce and resist this trope.

Tennyson said that he wrote 'The Lady of Shalott' before he had read Malory's 'The Fair Maid of Ascolat', naming instead a fourteenth-century Italian novella, 'La Damigella di Scalot' as his 'source'.[13] When I tell this to students in my 'Medieval Literature and Medievalism' class, many of them feel compelled to revise their reading of 'The Lady of Shalott' on the strength of what they understand as an unassailable chronology, from English author to English author. It is in part this sense of linearity that I hope to disrupt here, for my concern is not with sources or context or history, but with the connections that readers make between texts. Real readers do not read texts in some grand chronological order, but jump from period to period, writer to writer, as their interests take them. Real readers read in 'great time', a historical present in which all books are immediately available and thus subject to comparison, deliberate or serendipitous. Recall the famous statements made by T.S. Eliot — 'the past [is] altered by the present as much as the present is directed by the past' — and by Jorges Luis Borges — 'each writer creates his precursors. His work modifies our conception of the past, as

---

[11] Walter E. Houghton and G. Robert Stange, *Victorian Poetry and Poetics*, 2nd edn (Boston, MA: Houghton, 1968), p. 16n.

[12] Isobel Armstrong, 'Tennyson's "The Lady of Shalott": Victorian Mythography and the Politics of Narcissism', in *The Sun is God: Painting, Literature, and Mythology in the Nineteenth Century*, ed. J.B. Bullen (Oxford: Clarendon, 1989), pp. 49–107; Gerhard Joseph, *Tennyson and the Text: The Weaver's Shuttle* (Cambridge: Cambridge University Press, 1992), esp. pp. 102–12.

[13] According to F.J. Furnivall, Tennyson added 'the web, the mirror, island, etc., were my own. Indeed, I doubt whether I should ever have put it in that shape if I had been then aware of the maid of Astolat in *Mort Arthur*' (W.M. Rossetti, comp., *Rossetti Papers 1862–1870* [London: Sands, 1903], p. 341). For a discussion and summary of Tennyson's sources, see Christopher Ricks's headnote to the poem (Tennyson, *Poems*, pp. 387–8).

it will modify the future'.[14] In the space that Eliot and Borges have created, we can imagine a reading in which Malory's tales allude not to the sources that have preceded them, but to the retellings that have followed them. Although Tennyson's poem is not a sequel to or revision of Malory's 'The Fair Maid of Ascolat', Tennyson's Lady and Malory's Elayne share a common genealogy.

The way that I listed my texts earlier, in order of composition (Malory through Pynchon), implies that I am reading them 'vertically', as Michael Riffaterre puts it. However, it is more accurate to say that I am reading 'laterally', inasmuch as each text 'functions as a literary artifact only insofar as it complements another text'.[15] Riffaterre's theory of the 'ungrammaticality' of portions of texts is very useful here, for it explains how a text may take on, as Bakhtin says, a 'more intense and fuller' life in 'great time'. If we accept that all texts refer to other texts instead of to an extratextual reality, then interpretation, argues Riffaterre, lies in the 'recovery of the intertext', which 'demands no special expertise, because the text itself signals its location through ungrammaticalities'.[16] 'Ungrammaticalities' include, for example, such lexical deviations as solecisms and nonsense words, seemingly inappropriate words, phrases and details, as well as sudden shifts in viewpoint, style, or voice. 'The text's ungrammaticality is but a sign of a grammaticality *elsewhere*, its significance a reference to meaning *elsewhere*'.[17] This chapter, then, is a description of one particular search for 'elsewheres' that informs my reading of the Lady of Shalott and her many avatars.

The modern reader who is willing to violate chronological boundaries, to reside in 'great time', might interpret Malory's apparent preoccupation with the literal (as he says, he is bound to the 'letter') in 'The Fair Maid' as an extension of the anxiety that Tennyson's Lady seems to inspire in certain of her readers. At the beginning of the tale, Malory directs our attention to his French source (the story of the *demoiselle d'Escalot* in the Vulgate *Mort Artu*, *c*. 1213–35), as if to suggest that he has no control over the outcome of the story. He writes:

> And, as the booke sayth, she keste such a love unto sir Launcelot that she cowde never withdraw hir loove, wherefore she dyed. And her name was Elayne le Blanke. (pp. 1067–8)

---

[14] T.S. Eliot, 'Tradition and the Individual Talent' (1920); reprinted in *Criticism: The Major Statements*, sel. and ed. Charles Kaplan and William Anderson, 3rd edn (New York: St Martin's, 1991), p. 432; Jorges Luis Borges, 'Kafka and His Precursors', in Emir Rodriguez Monegal and Alastair Reid (eds), *Borges: A Reader* (New York: Dutton, 1981), p. 243.

[15] Michael Riffaterre, 'Syllepsis', *Critical Inquiry* **6** (1980), p. 627.

[16] Riffaterre, *Fictional Truth* (Baltimore, MD: The Johns Hopkins University Press, 1990), p. xviii.

[17] Riffaterre, 'Syllepsis', p. 627, emphasis added.

'As the booke sayth' is a common enough trope in the Middle Ages, and acts as a reminder that the story of Elayne is already enclosed between book-covers; it already has a resolution. Elayne herself is bound in/as a book. She is called Elayne le *Blanke* — as if she owns no words of her own, has no potential for heteroglossia, but is instead a clean white page waiting to be inscribed.

Yet Elayne desires to be more than just written upon. When she is on her deathbed, sick with love for Launcelot (as Malory understands her 'sickness'), her priest tells her that she would be better off if she put Launcelot out of her mind. She replies: 'Why sholde I leve such thoughtes? Am I nat an erthely woman? ... hit ys the sufferaunce of God that I shal dye for so noble a knyght' (p. 1093). Elayne rebels, and rejects the *blanke* label; she tries to break out of her object position by insisting on her femininity: 'Am I nat an erthely woman?' It is this very active femininity that the priest wants to suppress — and the text finally succeeds in suppressing.

Elayne is a writer, too — though writing for her is not a place to begin, but a place to end. She dictates a letter to her brother ('worde by worde lyke as she devised hit') to be placed on the barge that is to take her body to Winchester, where Arthur's court is gathered. Elayne writes:

> Moste noble knyght, my lorde sir Launcelot, now hath dethe made us to at debate for youre love. And I was youre lover, that men called the Fayre Maydyn of Ascolate. Therefore unto all ladyes I make my mone, yet for my soule ye pray and bury me at the leste, and offir ye my masse-peny; thys ys my laste requeste. And a clene maydyn I dyed, I take God to wytnesse. And pray for my soule, sir Launcelot, as thou art pereles. (p. 1096)

Malory/the narrator frames this document, first by saying, 'Thys was the entente of the lettir', and then by saying, 'Thys was all the substaunce in the lettir' (pp. 1096, 1097). By so 'quoting' Elayne, Malory gestures towards an elsewhere, an Other place where authority and tradition are located. Elayne, held fast within this tradition, has no autonomy of her own; like the Muse, she serves the interests of the masculine pen.

When Launcelot is summoned to court in order to have the letter read aloud to him, Malory once again uses the phrase 'worde by worde'. Launcelot's response follows:

> My lorde Arthur, wyte you well I am ryght hevy of the deth of thys fayre lady. And God knowyth I was never causar of her deth be my wyllynge ... I woll nat say nay ... but that she was both fayre and good, and much I was beholdyn unto her, but she loved me out of mesure. (p. 1097)

Thus does Launcelot answer to God and country. Just as Malory binds Elayne in his text, Launcelot, by dismissing the Fair Maid with the verbal shrug 'she loved me out of mesure' — that is, without moderation — attempts to circumscribe, to limit, what he perceives as her uncontrollable and therefore threatening passion. He denies the possibility of intertextuality/intercourse, and tries to take himself out of the web of meaning. Launcelot speaks pointedly to Gwenyver here as well: he also means to say that he gave the Maid no encouragement, and has remained true to the Queen. In other words, Launcelot remains loyal to a monologic order, here represented by Gwenyver.

Arthur's reply, his gloss on the death of Elayne, is that he understands Launcelot's treatment of the Maid, 'for where [a knight] ys bonden he lowsith hymselff' (p. 1097). Imagine reading Tennyson's poem (and its traditional interpretations) as if it came before Malory's story. Revise Arthur's speech in 'The Fair Maid' and substitute the word 'poet' for the word 'knight': 'for when a poet is bound to the world, he loses himself — and loses his art'. This amended statement parallels the judgement of a number of Tennyson's traditional readers of 'The Lady of Shalott'.

Because of the public, performative nature of these recitations and speeches in Malory, any introspection, any sense of interiority, is absent. The central characters in this tale seem to lack any self-awareness; there is little dialogic play as they conform to their assigned roles. However, we can look elsewhere for significance, and this elsewhere lies five centuries in the future. Let us now consider Roger Zelazny's surprising role as a key to, and as a pre-text for, Malory and Tennyson.

Roger Zelazny is best known in science fiction and fantasy circles for his Amber series. His novella, 'He Who Shapes', won the Nebula Award in 1965. (Zelazny then expanded it into *The Dream Master* in 1966.) 'He Who Shapes' is a reinterpretation and conflation of several legends, among which the Arthurian is foremost. In this novella, Zelazny foregrounds heteroglossia; throughout the novella, he plays on and with words. For example, the main character is named Charles Render. He is vain, brooding, solitary, very much the stereotyped figure of the romantic, egocentric artist. His name is open to multiple interpretations that come into play at different times throughout the novel. 'To render' has several meanings: 'to tear to pieces', 'to boil down to an essence', 'to give something up', 'to tell or narrate', 'to give judgement'. Render is a 'neuroparticipation' therapist who manipulates his patients' subconscious through their dreams. We are told that the colloquial name for such a professional is 'shaper' (hence the title of the novella), a word that recalls, among other things, the Anglo-Saxon word for poet, *scop*, a maker or creator, and the word *Scippend*, the Creator.

Render takes a patient named Eileen Shallot — a name whose significance lies elsewhere, in Malory and Tennyson. The meaning of the name is also found in Zelazny's transformation of the word into a reductive, jokey homonym for *Shalott*. Eileen Shallot is blind, and therefore cannot have visual dreams. She wears a silver disc on her forehead in order to help her 'see' well enough to function in her daily life. This is the Lady of Shalott's mirror in miniature. But Eileen Shallot, as we shall see, transforms her therapist Render into a 'mirror' and, like the Lady's mirror, he 'cracks' under the strain.

Render knows that it is extremely dangerous and even unethical to undertake neuroparticipation therapy with a blind patient, but his vanity cannot resist the challenge. If he succeeds in giving Eileen Shallot vicarious 'sight' through therapy, it will be a tremendous boost to his ego and to his reputation. Render is willing to violate the ethical boundaries of his own profession, and risk himself and Eileen in the process.

In Eileen's first assisted dream, she visualizes Render in a suit of armour. Apart from the obvious symbolism of the armour (fixed, rigid, controlling; the costume of the saviour and hero), what is significant here is that Eileen manages to accomplish this without Render's help. As the therapist's consciousness and that of his patient begin to meld — something that is not supposed to happen in therapy of this sort — Eileen begins to assume more and more control, and Render, like Launcelot defeated, is finally left in a permanent dream-state. Dreaming, he is fated to play out endlessly the tragic conclusion of the Tristan and Iseult story. Furthermore, in Render's version of the story, Eileen plays the second Iseult, Iseult of the White Hands, the wife who lies to Tristan on his deathbed. (Why Zelazny chooses to complicate Malory's Launcelot/Elayne story with the continental Tristan/Iseult one is a complicated question. It is as if, in the presence of an excess of referentiality, all signs lose their specificity and collapse together.[18])

Zelazny also recapitulates Tennyson's Merlin and Vivien story (as told by Tennyson in the *Idylls of the King*) in the relationship between Render and Eileen. Eileen/Iseult/Vivien drains Render/Launcelot/the poet and mage of his mystical and creative powers in order to increase her own. Zelazny further exploits heteroglossia by weaving Arthurian material and the 'twilight of the gods' theme together. According to this scheme, Render is Scandinavian, doomed to failure; Eileen is Celtic, idealistic and romantic.[19] On one level, these traditions

[18] Zelazny may have had in mind Canto 5 of Dante's *Inferno*, in which Paolo and Francesca read about Lancelot and his love for Arthur's Queen. Tristan and Paris, other famous lovers, are invoked in this episode. On Dante's adulterous lovers as subtext for another modern retelling, see the chapter by Myriam Swennen Ruthenberg later in this volume.

[19] See Carl Yoke, *A Reader's Guide to Roger Zelazny* (West Lynn, OR: Starmont, 1979), pp. 53–5. Samuel R. Delany, in his assessment of Zelazny's fiction, claims that 'the man who makes fantasies real is an analogue for any artist or scientist' ('Faust and Archimedes' [1968], in *The Jewel-Hinged Jaw: Notes on the Language of Science Fiction* [Elizabethtown, NY: Dragon, 1977], p. 205). He speaks for both Render and Zelazny here: in such a formulation, Render is a

interact with each other, but on another level, they conflict, thus deferring resolution. Given the many significations that attach themselves to the characters of Eileen Shallot and Render, it is easy to see why Joseph Sanders describes Zelazny's intention with respect to his characters as the 'fight to make the world safe for uncertainty'.[20]

Zelazny succeeds in switching Tennyson's Lady/Malory's Fair Maid from object to subject position: it is as if Malory's Elayne breaks out of Tennyson's tower, but does not die. Instead, she takes Render's/Launcelot's place in the world, and it is he who is shut up in the prison-house of his mind. Render is a creator, a renderer of dream-story, who finally sur-renders to Eileen Shallot — the more powerful story-teller. At the beginning of the novella, only Render can see; at the end, only Eileen can speak.

In an early scene in Thomas Pynchon's *The Crying of Lot 49*, we are given a description of Remedios Varo's 1961 painting, 'Bordando el Manto terrestre' ('Embroidering Earth's Mantle').[21] Varo (who, with her long thick hair and strong features, could pass for a Pre-Raphaelite heroine) was an artist of the surrealist school, and the detail and execution of her paintings have something of the texture of medieval illuminated manuscripts, albeit with a dash of kitsch. 'Bordando el Manto terrestre' is a painting grounded in Varo's convent school experience, out of which Varo created a personal, feminized mythology that honours women as the creators — the weavers — of the world. The painting depicts several convent girls, under the stern eye of a masked nun, embroidering a cloak in a high tower. This cloak billows out of the windows and turns into the surrounding landscape's hills, forests and towns. In one small section, one of the young girls has embroidered two lovers entwined and upside-down — a story embedded within the larger story and outside the range of the nun's vision.

Remember that contemporary criticism makes Tennyson's Lady the One, the particular woman, who is assigned the role of Muse or Poet. But Varo portrays

scientist/artist/fantasist in one.

[20] Joseph L. Sanders, *Roger Zelazny: A Primary and Secondary Bibliography* (Boston, MA: Hall, 1980), p. xxi.

[21] For a reproduction, see Janet Kaplan, *Unexpected Journeys: The Art and Life of Remedios Varo* (New York: Abbeville, 1988), pp. 215–16. In Joseph, *Tennyson and the Text*, part of this Pynchon passage appears as epigraph (p. 113) and Varo's painting is reproduced as plate 5. David Cowart says that 'to read *The Crying of Lot 49* with a book of Varo's reproductions at hand is to be struck repeatedly by parallels in imagery and similarities of atmosphere, as if Pynchon has occasionally gone to school to Varo for his images' ('Pynchon's *The Crying of Lot 49* and the Paintings of Remedios Varo', *Critique* **18.3** [1977], p. 20). Dwight Eddins discusses the 'imprisoning solipsism' of the scene in *The Crying*, in which the world is 'a tapestry embroidered by captive maidens who can know only their own embroidery' (*The Gnostic Pynchon* [Bloomington, IN: Indiana University Press, 1990], p. 99).

a whole roomful of women and, in doing so, subverts the iconic power of a solitary woman and forces us to deal with *women* — a grammatical and semantic shift to the plural that suggests a multiplicity of meaning and a multiplicity of readings and readers. I do not mean to suggest that Tennyson's poem was a direct source for Varo; she may or may not have read it in Spanish translation. But in my deracinated reading, Varo's painting is an intertextual link that connects Tennyson's and Pynchon's texts.

When Oedipa Maas, the main character in *The Crying of Lot 49*, hears that her ex-lover Pierce Inverarity is dead, she recalls standing with him in front of Varo's painting. (As in Zelazny, all names have significance in Pynchon's fiction.) As a result of his death, Oedipa, as Pynchon says, will come to 'all manner of revelations. ... There had hung the sense of buffering, of insulation, she had noticed the absence of an intensity, as if watching a movie, just perceptibly out of focus, that the projectionist had refused to fix'.[22] This out-of-focus film recalls the Lady of Shalott's mirror; both are distorted ways of seeing reality. But perhaps 'distorted' is the wrong qualifier. Imagine the projectionist as the good, Bakhtinian reader, refusing to 'fix' the image on the screen. Then imagine the Lady of Shalott/Oedipa Maas as the good, Bakhtinian reader, refusing to accept the monologic image reflected in the smooth surface of her mirror. Here I would like to emphasize Pynchon's verb: 'There had *hung* the sense of buffering, of insulation ...' just like a mirror hangs on a wall. The mirror Tennyson provides for the Lady of Shalott is designed expressly to buffer and insulate her, to refract real emotions, to keep her confined in her tower.

Pynchon describes the young women in Varo's painting as 'prisoners in the top room of a circular tower, embroidering a kind of tapestry which spilled out the slit windows and into a void ... the tapestry was the world' (p. 10). Pynchon's/Varo's tapestry spilling out the window recalls the Lady's own tapestry that 'floated wide': similar images of unbridled, open discourse.

Pynchon goes on to give us Oedipa's memory, her flashback of that day in the art gallery:

> Oedipa, perverse, had stood in front of the painting and cried. ... She had looked down at her feet and known, then, because of a painting, that what she stood on had only been woven together a couple of thousand miles away in her own tower. (p. 10)

He elaborates on the heroine's reveries:

---

[22] Pynchon, pp. 9, 10. Varo herself was strongly attracted to the metaphysical and the spiritual: a friend of Varo's remembers her as 'liv[ing] in perpetual exploration of clues, of revelations' (quoted in Kaplan, p. 7).

> a captive maiden, having plenty of time to think, soon realizes that her tower, its height and architecture, are like her ego only incidental: that what really keeps her where she is is magic, anonymous and malignant, visited on her from outside and for no reason at all. Having no apparatus except gut fear and female cunning to examine this formless magic, to understand how it works, how to measure its field strength, count its lines of force, she may fall back on superstition, or take up a useful hobby like embroidery, or go mad. ... If the tower is everywhere and the knight of deliverance no proof against its magic, *what else*?
> (p. 11, emphasis added)[23]

Imagine reading this passage as Pynchon's response to Tennyson's poem, or at least to Tennyson's poem as it has been traditionally interpreted. Although Tennyson's tower is isolated on an island, Pynchon's tower is as big as the world. In such a world, there is no inside or outside; there are no clear boundaries. There are no safe spaces. Like Eileen Shallot in 'He Who Shapes', Oedipa is 'perverse'; she has 'gut fear and female cunning'. Oedipa refuses the 'rationality' of the phallic, escaping into madness just as Eileen escapes from her blindness and her therapy. To return to Tennyson: some critics, hoping to derive a transcendent meaning from the Lady's end, suggest that her death is an escape, a form of self-empowerment. By doing so, critics reproduce familiar Victorian eroticized idealizations of dying, dead and, often, mad ladies. Death, the ultimate manifestation of monologic discourse, removes the threatening feminine from discourse, takes the feminine out of the loop of time. Pynchon and Zelazny, on the other hand, subvert the idea that madness and death signify feminine empowerment: in Pynchon's works, schizophrenia is inflected positively, and is not tied to gender: *à la* R.D. Laing, Oedipa's delusions are a sane response to an insane world filled with multivalent illusive signs. And in Zelazny's 'He Who Shapes', Eileen does not go mad or die, but comes into her full powers over and through the aggressively male Render.

If we read retrospectively for a moment, Tennyson's many interpreters may be seen as answering Pynchon's question 'What else?' with 'Only art'. But Oedipa Maas, buffeted about by Pierce Inverarity, her husband Mucho, and her current lover Metzger, is hardly satisfied with such an answer. As Oedipa thinks back to Remedios Varo's painting, she begins to see that her own destiny is very much

[23] Another intertextual thread: Giovanni Boccaccio, in his preface to the *Decameron*, writes sympathetically of 'charming ladies' who, 'restricted by the wishes, whims, and commands of their mothers, brothers, and husbands ... remain most of the time limited to the narrow confines of their bedrooms'. Boccaccio goes on to say that he has composed his stories for the 'support and diversion of ladies in love', adding that, 'to those others who are not I leave the needle, spindle, and wool winder' (*Decameron*, trans. Mark Musa and Peter Bondanella [New York: Penguin, 1982], p. 3).

like that of the maidens in the tower, and she realizes that this destiny — her destiny — is never to be the subject of discourse, but always the object. (Oedipa and Tennyson's Lady have interesting analogues in the figures of entowered Rapunzel and Sleeping Beauty.) For Oedipa Maas — and perhaps for Thomas Pynchon — freedom from the subject–object split can come only when one allows for the possibility of multiple realities — even if one is always left pondering a 'useful hobby like embroidery', and remains hovering on the vague border of schizophrenia.

After reading 'He Who Shapes' and *The Crying of Lot 49*, one returns to Tennyson with a new frame of reference. When the Lady says, '"I am half sick of shadows"' (l. 71), it can be read as a sign that she has begun the crucial movement from object to subject. This movement is then hastened along by the appearance in the mirror of Lancelot, singing 'tirra lirra'. Lancelot's song propels the Lady into even more radical action:

> She left the web, she left the loom,
> She made three paces through the room,
> She saw the water-lily bloom,
> She saw the helmet and the plume,
> She looked down to Camelot. (ll. 109–13)

The very triteness of Lancelot's song represents Lancelot as a poet who has displaced the true Muse with the debased muse of the mundane. The Lady's response is a rejection of this song.

Later, in blithe ignorance of the effect his singing had on the Lady, Lancelot stands over her dead body and 'mused a little space', saying, 'She has a lovely face' (ll. 168–9). The verb 'mused' moves us in an unexpected direction, allowing us to imagine Lancelot as the poet who went to the Muse, but returned with the most banal of elegies. This transparently simple statement signifies Lancelot's attempt to put the Lady back in her place. By focusing on her 'lovely' face, he insists on her position as object. Lancelot has much in common with those who feel compelled to protect, as Burrow says, a 'cherished heritage', or what Bakhtin calls a monologic order. The lines 'Out flew the web and floated wide; / The mirror cracked from side to side; / "The curse is come upon me", cried / The Lady of Shalott' (ll. 114–17) describe the shattering of that very monologism. The web (of meaning) flies out of its structuring loom; the shards of mirror become multiple realities, contradictions. The Lady refuses to stay trapped in the phallic. Through the 'curse', the Lady is able to enter into active reality. Along with the Fair Maid of Ascolat, she asserts that she is, in the final analysis, 'an erthely woman'.

At the beginning of this chapter, I invoked Burrow and Bakhtin in order to create a Lady of Shalott whose existence is dependent upon the resonances among a given set of texts. Now I want to add three more voices to the mix, voices that focus our attention not on the Lady as a surrogate for the male poet, but on the Lady as female poet. In a famous statement, Robert Graves proclaimed that 'Woman is ... either a Muse or she is nothing'.[24] Graves also said that:

> Every few centuries a woman of poetic genius appears, who may be distinguished by three clear secondary sins: learning, beauty, and loneliness. Though the burden of poetry is difficult enough for a man to bear ... the case of a woman poet is a thousand times worse: since she is herself the Muse, a Goddess without an external power to guide or comfort her, and if she strays even a finger's breadth from the path of divine instinct, must take violent self-vengeance.[25]

Graves seems to be following the same masculinist script that had inspired so many of the Lady of Shalott's readers in the past. According to Graves, the poet Juana de Asbaje could not bear the 'burden' of her gift which conflicted with her ordained role as Muse. By refusing her role as Muse to man, the female poet is forced to pay a terrible price, here mystified and romanticized as divine fate.

Speaking from an entirely different point of view, Hélène Cixous uncannily echoes Graves when she writes, 'Ou la femme est passive; ou elle n'existe pas' ('Either woman is passive or she doesn't exist').[26] Luce Irigaray also echoes Graves, but where he mystifies, she critiques: 'Woman exists only as an occasion for mediation, transaction, transition, transference, between man and his fellow man, indeed between man and himself'.[27] In each case, position is paramount. Although Graves is comfortably situated within a phallic discourse, Cixous and Irigaray report from the margin.

Cixous gives us an analogue to the Lady of Shalott/female poet in 'The Laugh of the Medusa':

> Every woman has known the torment of getting up to speak. Her heart racing, at times entirely lost for words, ground and language slipping away — that's how daring a feat, how great a transgression it is for a woman to speak — even just open her mouth — in public. A double distress, for even if she transgresses, her words fall almost always upon

---

[24] Robert Graves, *The White Goddess* (New York: Faber, 1948), p. 371.

[25] Graves, 'Juana de Asbaje', in *On Poetry: Collected Talks and Essays* (Garden City, NY: Doubleday, 1969), p. 175.

[26] Hélène Cixous, 'Sorties', in *La Jeune Née* (Paris: Union Generale, 1975), p. 118.

[27] Luce Irigaray, *This Sex Which Is Not One* (1977); trans. Catherine Porter (Ithaca, NY: Cornell University Press, 1985), p. 193.

> the deaf male ear, which hears in language only that which speaks in the masculine.[28]

I would argue that both Zelazny and Pynchon are able to imagine female sexuality/artistry (a 'double distress') from Cixous's margin, in which Eileen Shallot and Oedipa Maas are newly born speakers. In their reworking of Tennyson, the phallic is explicitly engaged with mirroring itself in the feminine; it is obsessed, fix(at)ed on bondage and other-as-object and is, finally, wordless.

---

[28] Cixous, 'The Laugh of the Medusa', trans. Keith Cohen and Paula Cohen, in Elaine Marks and Isabelle de Courtivron (eds), *New French Feminisms: An Anthology* (New York: Schocken, 1981), p. 251.

Chapter 3

Stomping on the shoulders of giants: Thomas Berger's *Arthur Rex*

Lee Tobin McClain

Thomas Berger is one of the most comprehensive and complex Arthurianists of the twentieth century; comprehensive in the breadth of his source material, and complex in his simultaneously ironic and nostalgic attitudes towards that material. Berger's attitude towards his medieval material is usually seen as uniquely modernist. On the one hand, he idealizes the Middle Ages' 'simple' honour and brotherhood as contained in the chivalric ideal; but on the other hand, he scorns medieval chivalry's moral system as something oversimplified and childish. However, this medieval chivalry about which he is so ambivalent is not historical; such unilateral, visionary chivalric values exist neither in historical accounts of medieval knights' behaviour nor in the romance tradition; thus Berger, like many post-medieval Arthurian authors, contributes to a falsely simplified view of the medieval literary tradition. Far from being uniquely modernist, as both Berger and his critics suggest,[1] *Arthur Rex*'s simultaneous admiration and denigration of chivalry closely resembles the attitudes of earlier Arthurian authors, both medieval, such as Chaucer and the Gawain-poet, and post-medieval, such as Tennyson and Arnold. To further complicate matters, much of Berger's denigration of the Middle Ages and of chivalry seem to be unconscious, hidden beneath an outspoken admiration of the period, an admiration most of his critics have taken at face value. Like other tellers of Arthurian tales, Berger is a divided subject, slippery and elusive. His complicated attitude towards chivalry has much to teach us about an institution that has often been portrayed one-sidedly, as either a 'Boy Scout' ideal towards which to strive or a ridiculously antiquated code of upper-class behaviour.

According to the book-jacket of *Arthur Rex*, Berger's encounter with the Arthurian legend began when he encountered a children's version of *Le Morte d'Arthur* at the age of eight; he calls *Arthur Rex* his 'memory of that childish ver-

[1] Thomas Berger, *Arthur Rex: A Legendary Novel* (New York: Delacorte, 1978). Berger enjoys describing his own situation as living in 'the Time of the Cad', and Landon as well as others describe him as emphatically modernist.

sion as edited and expanded according to the outlandish fantasies (and even some of the droll experiences) he has had in the years since'. Despite this self-effacing introduction, the scope of his knowledge is so broad that medieval studies appear to be his life's work; in fact, *Arthur Rex* is the only medieval retelling in his widely varied group of novels. Berger studied at both the University of Cincinnati and Columbia University, and has served as visiting writer and lecturer at a number of academic institutions, so his relation to the medieval tradition goes beyond the level of an enthusiast and approaches that of a professional scholar. Berger names Malory, Chrétien de Troyes, Wolfram von Eschenbach, Tennyson and Wagner as sources he 'ransacked' in the course of researching the novel.[2] However, like his medieval predecessors, he adheres precisely to no single version; instead, as Brooks Landon notes, he follows 'the *example* of Malory, who drew from, mixed together, deleted, expanded on, and sometimes simply copied his own sources'.[3]

When *Arthur Rex* appeared in 1978, it was immediately heralded for its caustic humour;[4] later critics pointed out how closely *Arthur Rex* adheres to its literary and philological roots. For example, Landon describes how, when a reviewer questioned his use of the word 'mammets' for female breasts, Berger broke his usual silence about reviews to trace the term's etymology and prove the merits of his usage.[5] In both scope and use of humour, Berger is exemplary. Starting with the traditional Arthurian *enfances* — Uther Pendragon's passion for Queen Igraine, resulting in the illegitimate conception of Arthur — Berger includes nearly every Arthurian tale, from Tristan and Iseult's tragic love to Sir Gawain and the Green Knight to the less common, 'transformed hag' story popularized by Chaucer's Wife of Bath. Berger is thus more encyclopaedic than that most complete of Arthurian chroniclers, Sir Thomas Malory.

One might think such a large endeavour would result in a diffuse and fragmented retelling, but not so: through his remarkable ironic tone, maintained consistently throughout, Berger creates a unified, coherent treatment of his Arthurian saga. The careful attention to detail throughout Berger's rendition of the Arthur story attests to his admiration for the legend; still, he does not hesitate to laugh in self-mockery at his own modern interpolations. Hence Lancelot and Gawain, the traditional great lovers, discuss venereal disease; Isolde, the high

---

[2] Michael Malone, 'Berger, Burlesque, and the Yearning for Comedy', in *Critical Essays on Thomas Berger*, ed. David W. Madden (New York: Hall, 1995), p. 93.

[3] Brooks Landon, *Thomas Berger*, Twayne's United States Authors Series 550 (Boston, MA: Twayne, 1989), p. 57.

[4] John Romano, 'Camelot and All That', *New York Times Book Review*, 12 November 1978, pp. 3, 62.

[5] Landon, 'Thomas Berger's *Arthur Rex*', in Valerie Lagorio and Mildred Leake Day (eds), *King Arthur Through the Ages* (New York: Garland, 1990), pp. 240–41.

born, 'finds herself' while camping out with Tristram; and Percival armours himself in pots and pans. Indeed, Berger's intimate love of things Arthurian is exemplified by his closing line: 'in these fair laps we must leave King Arthur, who was never historical, but everything he did was true' (p. 449).

The critical tradition surrounding *Arthur Rex* began as scant and largely descriptive, focusing on his themes, his historical and philological accuracy, and his humour; slowly this tradition is growing in both scope and complexity. Most of Berger's critics admire his work, and rightly so; Berger's wit is incisive, his research impeccable. A deeper similarity among his critics is a tendency to see the author as totally in control, aware of and self-conscious about every aspect of his own work. Scholars such as Landon, Michael Malone and David Madden have corresponded extensively with Berger and have thus been able to ask his opinion about many of the issues raised in his books, an opportunity that has contributed to their understanding of his self-awareness as a writer. On such a model, the critic's primary task is to describe and illuminate what the author already knows. Berger himself, however, both in correspondence and in interviews, deflates the idea of his own authorial control by his frequent admission that he can only talk about his conscious intention. In fact, the word 'conscious' is sprinkled through much of his discussion of his own work; he has said, for example, that 'I rarely think consciously of the audience' and 'I have no conscious philosophical intent in my novels'.[6] Berger is perhaps more aware than most authors that the creative mind has its unconscious elements.

Several of Berger's foremost critics have tried to explain away Berger's patronizing attitude towards the Middle Ages, perhaps because Berger expresses so repeatedly his admiration of the period. Although these critics try to reconcile the difference between his ostensible admiration and his actual belittling, they can finally only take him at his word, asserting that he does admire the Middle Ages because he says he does. Raymond Thompson states that Arthur and his knights command our respect in this and other, ironic modern Arthuriana specifically because of their defects:

> We do not admire them *despite* their comic mistakes and misadventures, but rather *because* of them. They have the courage to risk mistakes and to learn from them. And the lesson is *not* to avoid risks, or to seek a compromise that will preserve a selfish pride. Because they have the courage to defy convention and risk looking foolish, regardless of personal cost, they earn the wisdom not only to recognize their own

---

[6] David W. Madden, 'An Interview with Thomas Berger', in his *Critical Essays*, pp. 153, 157.

> limitations, but to keep striving nonetheless, for that alone can create a better world where love and decency can prevail.[7]

Thompson's admiration for modern re-creations of medieval characters is apparent here. However, where he sees only charm in these characters' follies, I detect hostility or ambivalence in authors like Berger who emphasize these characters' mistakes and foolish behaviour. Similarly, Joan F. Dean says that Berger 'demystifies his material while preserving its mythic power to inspire belief and action'.[8] Landon's view of Berger's work seems more subtle; he sees the central tragedy of *Arthur Rex* as the fact that real-world complexity finally overwhelms the black-and-white thinking of chivalry. However, Landon also asserts that 'by pursuing some of the adult and ironic implications of the Arthur legend, Berger's retelling in no way diminishes the glory of Arthur's attempt or the measure of his achievement' and argues that Berger's irony should not be mistaken for absurdity.[9] Landon thus recognizes the mixed attitude Berger takes toward the Arthurian material, but he does not see it as a primary issue. Rather, he takes it as a given part of Berger's ironic mind-set. In the end, Landon, like Thompson and Dean, believes that Berger's prime feeling for the Matter of Britain is admiration.

Michael Malone presents the most nuanced critical reading of *Arthur Rex*: 'in its earthy texture and elegiac wistfulness, in the elaborate weave of its vast interlace structure, Berger's version comes closer to the Gawain-poet and Malory than most of the interpreters in between'.[10] Malone's vision of just how medieval Berger is strikes me as particularly true. However, in trying to ensure Berger a place in the tradition of serious Arthurianists (a place he well deserves), Malone ignores the largely unconscious parodic elements that so resonate for me in Berger's medievalism. Yes, Berger is in many ways 'a twentieth-century weaver at work with medieval threads on a tapestry, not a cartoon', but he is a weaver whose tapestry has a dark underside almost as interesting as the lighter pattern apparent at the front of the work.[11]

---

[7] Raymond H. Thompson, 'Humor and Irony in Modern Arthurian Fantasy: Thomas Berger's *Arthur Rex*', *Kansas Quarterly* **16.3** (1984), p. 48.

[8] Joan F. Dean, 'Thomas Berger's Fiction: Demystification without Demythification', in *Hagiographie et Iconoclastie: Modeles Americains*, ed. Serge Ricard (Aix-en-Provence: Publications, Université de Provence, 1984), p. 56.

[9] Landon, *Thomas Berger*, p. 45.

[10] Malone, 'Berger', p. 93.

[11] Ibid. For tapestry as a metaphor in other modern chivalric retellings, see Kathleen Coyne Kelly's discussion of Pynchon's *The Crying of Lot 49* and Pauline Scott's study of Virginia Woolf's *Orlando* elsewhere in this volume.

Berger has said, 'I adore whichever tradition I am striving to follow, and ... what results is the best I can manage by way of joyful worship — not the worst in sneering derision'.[12] There is no reason to disagree that joyful worship is his conscious intention. However, the heavy mockery that pervades *Arthur Rex* suggests an unconscious ambivalence towards the era. My sense is that there is a depth and richness in Berger's work precisely because he is not always aware of what he is about. It is in his largely unconscious ambivalence about the Matter of Britain and his own relation to it that Berger resonates most profoundly with the post-medieval Arthurian tradition. I wish to elucidate this psychological dimension of Berger's work in an effort to explain his frequent hostility towards the period he claims to so admire.

One of Berger's primary aims is to de-romanticize the Arthurian material, to deflate it and make it humorous rather than awe-inspiring. For example, he uses anachronisms like Freudian psychology to explain such events as Arthur's incestuous relationship with Margawse. He demystifies a hero like Uther, making him end his days living in filth with his dogs and horses. In the realm of style, Berger's 'extraordinary technical and verbal virtuosity' allow him to skilfully mock medieval literature and style.[13] He puts words together in jarring combinations such as 'Certes, the latter' (p. 126); the archaic 'certes' denotes 'certainly' and has seldom been used since the Middle Ages, while 'the latter' is a twentieth-century coinage. He uncannily echoes a historically remote language by sprinkling his narration with archaic forms like 'methinks', 'falleth' and 'seeketh', thereby making his very style humorous and deflationary. With such comic incidents and word choices, Berger attempts to de-idealize the Arthurian material, bringing it down to the level of real life.

Berger specializes in distorted generalizations about the medieval period, some thinly veiled under irony and most rather humorous. For example, Merlin, one of the few characters who is portrayed positively (and who very possibly is Berger's mouthpiece), speaks with a 'unique sense of irony, quite foreign to the mortals of that straightforward time' (p. 18). King Arthur himself, who displays more intelligence than most of the other characters (although, like the other 'mortals of that straightforward time', he has no sense of irony), asserts that 'Treason is unknown in the simple, loyal philosophy of the British folk' (p. 49). In a move that is similar to that of Marion Zimmer Bradley and other medieval refashioners, Berger attributes desire for magic and legend to simple folk, not to sophisticated ones: speaking of Merlin's magic, Arthur says 'I understand the value of such illusions for the people, who require the legendary' (p. 77). It is interesting that

---

[12] Richard Schickel, 'Interviewing Thomas Berger', *New York Times Book Review*, 6 April 1980, p. 21.

[13] Malone, 'Berger', p. 92.

magic and sorcery were seen by Malory, Christopher Marlowe and other medieval and Renaissance writers as a separate and highly sophisticated branch of learning. For Berger, though, admiration of magic seals the fate of the average medieval people: they are simple, naïve and, by extension, inherently ridiculous. Berger's attitude towards his simple medieval creations is complex. He admires them with longing for a constructed nostalgic past. However, Berger portrays Merlin's intelligent irony far more positively than his average medieval character's naïve simplicity.

Another odd twist on Berger's ridiculing of those who 'require the legendary' is the fact that his own reader — and he himself — fit into a similar mould. As a fiction writer, Berger is highly aware of literary legends and their appeal: his extremely popular *Little Big Man* draws much of its life from the legendary American West. Certainly some percentage of the audience for *Arthur Rex* consists of those in our own day who enjoy sword-and-sorcerer fiction, films and video games, as well as the plethora of magic- and legend-filled contemporary Arthurian books.[14] Are we, his readers, as naïve and ignorant as the simple medieval folk who relish Merlin's magic? Is Berger mocking us too? It would not be out of line to ascribe some degree of disdain for his contemporary audience to Berger, who has said that when he thinks of his readers at all, 'it's usually to assume that they will probably not get my point'.[15] However, if Berger's audience is foolish for 'requir[ing] the legendary', what of Berger himself, who confesses to adoring the Arthurian legends? In short, it seems highly likely that Berger's deflation of medieval people is mixed with a healthy dose of social criticism of his own era which has embraced Arthurian stories and self-mockery, for he himself has done the same.

Berger himself would undoubtedly deny any such claim, for he says, 'My interest is in creation, not in commentary. Those who believe my *intent* is to criticize society ... are utterly misguided'.[16] One might then argue that *Arthur Rex*'s condescending portrayal of the Middle Ages belongs not to Berger, but to his narrator or his characters, since Berger as an author conceals his hand. However, elsewhere Berger has explicitly stated his view that medieval texts were simpler than modern ones, not just in his fiction, but in his non-fiction writing. In his 1982 forward to *German Medieval Tales*, Berger explains that 'medieval narratives are not devious in their means or uncertain in their moral focus. ... In the Arthurian tales the reader is seldom in doubt as to the virtues, or lack thereof, of the principal figures'.[17] While there is certainly a grain of truth

---

[14] See the chapter by MaryLynn Saul, 'The unholy grail: recasting the Grail myth for an unbelieving age' that follows in the present volume.

[15] Madden, p. 153.

[16] Michael Malone, 'American Literature's Little Big Man', *Nation* **230** (May 1980), p. 535.

[17] *German Medieval Tales*, ed. Francis G. Gentry (New York: Continuum, 1983), p. viii.

to this assertion, particularly with straightforwardly allegorical characters like Langland's Sloth, one has only to think of Bertilak in *Sir Gawain and the Green Knight*, Malory's Balin, Lancelot in various medieval Arthurian incarnations, or even Langland's Lady Meed, to realize that moral ambiguity is as much a part of medieval as of modern literature. Berger also remarked in a 1977 letter that 'the Arthurian legend is essentially infantile'.[18] His attitude of superiority mixed with nostalgia towards perceived medieval simplicity is characteristic of much nineteenth- and twentieth-century medievalism, such as that of John Ruskin, Kenelm Digby and John Fowles. My point is that this simple, childish medieval world exists nowhere in history or literature.

It is in his depiction of chivalry that Berger's deepest ambivalence resides. Berger sees chivalry as a complicated endeavour, but his descriptions portray a ridiculous ideal — an oversimplified, inherently childish moral system that is ultimately destructive. Accompanying this scornful attitude, however, is a nostalgia for the straightforward honour that chivalry at its best promotes. The novel declares itself, possibly in Berger's own words, as 'Thomas Berger's salute to the age of Chivalry from his own enmired situation in the Time of the Cad'. This succinct book-jacket description implies both scorn and admiration for the chivalric system. The following passage illustrates Berger's ambivalence towards, and oversimplification of, chivalry. Shortly after Arthur has taken the throne, he defines chivalry as follows:

> 'A code for, a mode of, knightly behavior, in which justice is conditioned by generosity, valor shaped by courtesy', said King Arthur. 'The vulgar advantage is declined. Dignity is preserved, even in a foe'.
>
> 'And is that all?' asked Ryons mockingly.
>
> And Arthur saw fit to add, 'Graciousness is sought'. (p. 42)

By using passive voice and 'dictionary style', Berger at once renders the chivalric code impotent. Not only the definition, but Ryons' mockery (he calls it 'shitful rubbish') makes it clear that Berger is far from promoting chivalric values. This device of villainous characters mocking chivalry is used repeatedly. King Mark, for example, thinks Tristram 'womanish' for adhering to chivalric principles (p. 117). Furthermore, when knights go out on quests, chivalry is more often a problem than it is an advantage. At one point, Pellinore courteously dismounts so as not to have an advantage over an opponent, but the opponent jeers at him for so throwing away an advantage. Pellinore explains, 'There is but one manner in which a quest must be pursued, and that is according to the right principles, which do not admit alteration'. The knight responds, 'Then die of excess cour-

[18] Quoted in Landon, *Thomas Berger*, p. 49.

tesy' (p. 103). Obviously, Berger is mocking chivalry by bringing in this sarcastic character who does not believe or participate in it; however, he further twists the scenario by having Pellinore win anyway. In this way, Berger seems to support and admire chivalry even as he mocks it. While he is more than willing to question the chivalric code, he hesitates to completely destroy it. Later, Tristram almost loses a fight due to chivalry:

> Now retaining his own lance Tristram had the advantage, but while he considered whether the principles of courtesy would call for his discarding it, so that the fight could continue with like weapons between equals in chivalry, the other knight chopped his lance in twain. (p. 112)

Once again, however, Tristram narrowly wins the fight. The knights who adhere to chivalric virtue actually do win, but Berger does not explicitly state that such virtue is desirable and helpful in fighting.

All of these events occur early in Arthur's reign. As time passes, Berger complicates his views of chivalry further, showing how morals are relative and no absolute system can really work or do what it is supposed to do all of the time. It is black-and-white thinking of any sort that Berger critiques most strongly, not only in this novel but in all of his work, as Landon has discussed at length (pp. 1–5). If one must adhere to chivalry, fine; but at least mix in some common sense and admit that the chivalric code cannot be applied to every situation without thought. Evil Sir Meliagrant, for example, decides to take up chivalric virtue and in short order he is robbed, shot with an arrow and killed by Lancelot. Shortly before he dies, he confesses privately to Guinevere that honour 'can be a taxing thing' (p. 175). When Gareth works in the kitchens, a chivalric test portrayed positively in Malory and Tennyson, he throws the whole system into an uproar, getting the other varlets in trouble and creating all kinds of chaos; in the end, he has to admit that there is a good dose of vanity in any such attempt to live below one's station. Sometimes chivalric tests appear simply ridiculous, such as in Berger's retelling of the Green Knight story: Gawain is told

> 'Well ... if you are honest you will admit that it is a ridiculous thing. A charlatan dyes his skin and hair and dressed in green clothes bursts into Arthur's court to make a preposterous challenge. Would that be taken seriously anywhere but at Camelot? Now you are likely to die of this buffoonery, and *cui bono*?' (p. 210)

Once chivalry has been reduced through ridicule and once it has been shown to be inadequate as a moral system, Berger's view that it is infantile and simplistic seems justified. Berger's version of Gawain, a great lover and dedicated fighter in his youth, with age turns domestic and thinks reflectively on his life of adventure:

> 'I am happy to have had [adventures] in my proper time, but of a life of adventure it can be said that there is no abiding satisfaction, for when one adventure is done, a knight liveth in expectation of another, and if the next come not soon enough he falleth in love, in the sort of love that is an adventure, for what he seeketh be the adventure and not the lovingness. And methinks this sequence is finally infantile, and beyond a certain age one can no longer be interested in games'. (p. 361)

In the end, Berger wants to deflate and moderate chivalry, showing that 'most [men] were a mixture of virtues and vices whether they wore silk or rags' (p. 419). The implication is that the Middle Ages were the childhood of man, when people believed in absolute systems like chivalry; now that the human race has matured, it sees that life is really complicated, with shades of grey. But what Berger and his critics do not mention is that irony, relativism and shades of grey have been important parts of the Arthurian tradition since it began, and certainly part of medieval literature's broader philosophical backdrop as well. Chaucer is only the best-known example, with his relativistic mixture of tales, his insatiable appetite for irony and his refusal to stick to one firm conclusion. Lancelot articulates the moral of Berger's story: 'Chivalry in general was more complicated than it seemed, for it is not easy always to know what is the noble thing, or what is brave and generous or even simply decent' (p. 461). Most medieval authors, from the Gawain-poet to Chaucer to Malory, would heartily agree.

Berger, like his character Lancelot, seems to ponder 'on the differences amongst men, and how though a company of them might hold the same principles, each member might honestly interpret these in another way' (p. 462). Berger wants to argue for relativism, thus correcting the absolutism he perceives in the Middle Ages — even though he regrets that 'the time of the catiff be upon the world' (p. 495).

But if medieval literature is really quite relative in its own right, then why do Berger and other medieval refashioners persist in attempting to reduce and deflate it? I believe that Berger's attitude towards his medieval material fits into a larger nineteenth- and twentieth-century cultural context. I am not arguing that such deflations, whether individual or cultural, occur intentionally; it has been said that if writers thought consciously about the weight of literary tradition behind them they would never write a word. Rather, I am suggesting that we can understand Berger's otherwise perplexing ambiguity toward his material by fitting it into an overall, primarily unconscious framework. Two explanations for this pervasive trend seem possible, one psychological and one cultural.

Psychologically, Victorian and contemporary authors arrive late in the centuries-old tradition of telling and retelling Arthurian stories, and they have formidable predecessors — Chrétien de Troyes, the Gawain-poet, Malory, Shakespeare, Dryden — whom they may feel they must equal or surpass. As

Harold Bloom has argued eloquently and at length, this situation resembles the Freudian family romance, produces anxiety and may lead to literary efforts to 'kill' the father-poets by belittling them.[19] For the same reason, many contemporary authors resort to powerful irony about medieval romantic ideals: Monty Python's indefatigable Black Knight, for example, keeps fighting as an exasperated King Arthur hacks his limbs off one by one, thus mocking the knightly ideal of fighting to the death. The fact that the Black Knight keeps challenging Arthur verbally, although he is physically incapacitated, enriches the irony — and implicitly ridicules earlier authors who did not 'see through' knightly ideals as did the creators of *Monty Python and the Holy Grail*. Berger's mockery of chivalry, magic and the intelligence of medieval people similarly ridicules both medieval stories and their tellers, suggesting that moderns are superior. However, his frequent references to his own era as 'the Time of the Cad' highlight his negative feelings about his own time. This ambivalence about both his literary predecessors and his own era demonstrates a Bloomian/Freudian anxiety about his position in the literary canon that is typical of much nineteenth- and twentieth-century Arthurian literature.

Belittling earlier eras with an inflated notion of self-heroism may be a move of cultural self-preservation. Medievalism gained the most prominence during two periods of widespread dichotomous thinking — the Victorian era and the present — when a we-good/Other-bad sort of mind-set has prevailed. The Victorian explosion of interest in things medieval, both scholarly (discoveries of lost medieval manuscripts and improved philological and historical research) and creative (exemplified by Tennyson's *Idylls*, Arnold's medievalist poetry and the work of the Pre-Raphaelite brotherhood) corresponds neatly with the age of colonialist expansion. Abdul R. JanMohamed sees the Manichean allegory as a central feature of the colonialist Victorian mind-set, a way of dividing the world into

> diverse yet interchangeable oppositions between white and black, good and evil, superiority and inferiority, civilization and savagery, intelligence and emotion, rationality and sensuality, self and other, subject and object.[20]

---

[19] See Bloom's *The Anxiety of Influence* (New York: Oxford University Press, 1973) and *idem*, *A Map of Misreading* (New York: Oxford University Press, 1975). Although Bloom disregards the medieval 'fathers' as lacking strength, his theories are particularly open to revision and provide a powerful explanation for such Arthurian deflations as Berger's.

[20] Abdul R. JanMohamed, 'The Economy of Manichean Allegory: The Function of Racial Difference in Colonialist Literature', in Henry Louis Gates (ed.), *'Race', Writing, and Difference*, (Chicago, IL: University of Chicago Press, 1986), p. 82.

This mind-set allows a culture to explore threatening topics — evil, savagery, emotionalism, sensuality — without seeming to possess such qualities itself. The generally prevalent oppositional mind-set spills over into medievalism, which deals with a culture far different from nineteenth-century England; Victorian authors like Sir Walter Scott, Arnold and the Pre-Raphaelites variously describe the Middle Ages as inferior, primitive, simple, emotional and sensual.

Similarly, medieval studies as we know them in today's universities developed during the cold war era when, as Anne Middleton explains, 'area studies' had their heyday; the Middle Ages, 'a chronological rather than geographical alien terrain', was considered as 'culturally more homogeneous than diverse, and as irretrievably "other"'.[21] Along with increased academic interest in this supposedly simple Other came increased creative and popular interest, so that books, films and video games all began to partake of things medieval. Middleton goes so far as to claim that even serious, academic study of the period tended to simplify it, creating a sense of present-day superiority. Popularization often simply overexposes certain features of the period, rendering them banal: in my supermarket I recently saw a life-sized cardboard cut-out of a Pittsburgh Steelers quarterback — clad in full medieval armour. The external trappings of an aristocratic, military and literary élite are now reduced to selling groceries. Either approach, the scholarly or the commercial, deflates the earlier era: medievalism can give a whole culture something about which it could feel superior.[22]

There are very good reasons, then, for the reductive exercises performed by nineteenth- and twentieth-century Arthurianists on their setting of choice. But there is also a very real danger. It is much easier to read Berger than Malory, just as it is much easier to watch *Monty Python and the Holy Grail* than to study medieval history. Berger's and other Arthurianists' oversimplification of the Middle Ages may become more familiar than genuine medieval texts, and the popularized renditions of the Middle Ages as a time of absolutes is inaccurate. While some medieval literature is allegorical, it is, on the whole, far less absolute and far more multivalenced than Berger implies — as a glance at *Piers Ploughman* and its recent interpretations will confirm. The Gawain-poet shows the problems in his hero's adherence to the chivalric pentangle, largely via the pragmatic Arthurian court's unchivalric commentary on Gawain's extremism.

---

21 Anne Middleton, 'Medieval Studies', in Stephen Greenblatt and Giles Gunn (eds), *Redrawing the Boundaries: The Transformation of English and American Literary Studies* (New York: Modern Language Association of America, 1992), p. 22.

22 See Clarence Major's discussion of how the presence of an Other has helped American culture shape itself (*Calling the Wind: Twentieth-Century African-American Short Stories* [New York: HarperPerennial, 1993], pp. xvi–xix), and Patrick Brantlinger's similar argument about the Victorians' use of Africa ('Victorians and Africans: The Genealogy of the Myth of the Dark Continent', in Gates (ed.), *'Race'*, pp. 185–222).

Few modern poets are less univocal than Chaucer, whose complexity has kept generations of critics profitably engaged in analysis. Dante and Boccaccio also present complicated world-views from which meaning(s) must be teased.

In sum, Berger reflects the tradition in a different way than either he or his critics have suggested. He deliberately misrepresents an earlier epoch and one of its major codes of social behaviour, chivalry, by simultaneously idealizing and belittling it; in effect, validating and 'making new' his own deeply modernist brand of ironic sarcasm. Yet he cannot avoid falling into pre-existing forms of medievalism. Berger's skilled and pleasing — though inaccurate — presentation of chivalric romance has dangers of which we need to be aware; at the same time, in his complexity, Berger ranks among the most provocative of Arthurian re-fashioners. Some of Berger's early critics have been blinded by his virtuoso performance in *Arthur Rex* into thinking that his view of the medieval period is entirely conscious and under his own control. Berger's creative accomplishment is tremendous and undeniable, but we do it no service if we ignore its depths and its dark side.

Chapter 4

The unholy grail: recasting the Grail myth for an unbelieving age

MaryLynn Saul

> But then the times
> Grew to such evil that the Holy cup
> Was caught away to heaven and disappear'd.
> 'The Sinner King'

So begins a modern version of the Grail legend. Although this quotation elucidates the rationale of one particular short story, it could, by extension, explain the motivation behind many modern rewritings of the Grail myth: the Holy Grail has been recalled to heaven, and in the absence of religious faith we in the modern age must confront evil on an individual basis as best we can. Traditional medieval versions of the story portrayed the Grail as the cup from which Christ drank at the Last Supper, and only the purest knight could see it and no one, no matter how pure, could possess it. In some modern versions, the Grail represents supreme power that can be directed by its possessor for good or evil; in a few versions it has even become unholy and actually motivates the possessor to evil. In spite of the spectrum of morality portrayed in these modern versions, they share one common element: the significance of the Grail has undergone a radical change from the medieval versions of the myth.

In *From Ritual to Romance*, Jessie Weston has traced the development of the Grail story from its probable earliest stage, a version attributed to Bleheris that featured Gawain as the hero of the tale.[1] In its pre-Christian origins, Weston associates the tale to primitive religious beliefs and practices that represented a Vegetation Spirit in a fertility ritual (pp. 52–3). The concept of the Waste Land figures prominently in this tale, and Gawain's task is to heal the Wounded King,

---

A shorter version of this paper 'The Unholy Grail' which was presented at the Tenth International Conference on Medievalism, Worcester, Massachusetts, September 1995, will appear in *The Year's Work in Medievalism 10*.

[1] Jessie L. Weston, *From Ritual to Romance* (New York: Doubleday, 1957), p. 63.

a metaphor for infertile nature, simply by asking questions regarding the significance of the grail and lance brought before the king.[2]

Although there have been many variations of the Grail story over several centuries, with innovations being added by the different writers, most take as a common point of departure the connection of the Grail to the Passion story. Popular modern authors view it, as some medieval predecessors did, as either the cup from which Christ drank at the Last Supper or that which Joseph of Arimathea used to collect the blood from the dying Christ. However, early twelfth-century versions of the Grail story, such as the Welsh Peredur story or Chrétien de Troyes's *Le Conte del Graal* (*c.* 1180), did not identify the vessel as holy nor connect it to Christ; rather the grail belonged to a wounded knight, usually referred to as the Fisher King.[3] Chrétien's *Graal* is typical of this generation of the tale since the grail is not the cup of Christ, and the hero's principle goal is to heal the Fisher King. The hero, Perceval, here 'achieves the grail', i.e. heals the Fisher King, by asking the proper questions at the proper time.

Christianized versions of the story appeared in the late twelfth century. One branch of these featured Galahad as the hero, but by now the Grail has been reinterpreted as a Christian symbol, the Waste Land eliminated, and the Fisher King's role minimized.[4] Robert de Boron's *Roman de l'Estoire dou Graal* (*c.* 1200) is the first to link the Grail to the cup from which Christ drank, thus representing a major change in the development of the tradition.[5] Later, an unknown author wrote the *Queste del Saint Graal* (*c.* 1225), a more elaborate version than Robert's, with the purpose of using a popular story and popular characters in order to teach a spiritual lesson.

The writer of the Vulgate *Queste* very clearly reflects the trend of his times, as can be demonstrated from Jacques Le Goff's research done on the period and its attitudes. Not only did the early Church 'establish a connection between sin and the flesh', but by the early thirteenth century it began to associate the deadly sins to different social groups. To the knightly class, represented in so many chiv-

---

[2] Weston, pp. 12–13.

[3] Chrétien de Troyes, 'Perceval: The Story of the Grail', in *Arthurian Romances*, trans. D.D.R. Owen, Everyman Classics (London: Dent, 1987).

[4] Weston, p. 20.

[5] Even the physical description of the vessel varied throughout the medieval narrative tradition: the Old French term *graal* originally meant a dish or platter (Norris J. Lacy [ed.], *The Arthurian Encyclopedia* [New York: Garland, 1986], p. 257), but later the object was illustrated as a goblet. In modern retellings, the grail's appearance also varies widely — from a simple wooden bowl to an elaborately bejewelled object, but its physical manifestation is less important than its effect on the people who touch or possess it. Its modern function is most frequent as a drinking cup. In my analysis, I will generically refer to it as a 'cup', unless its physical description is relevant to a particular story.

alric romances, church leaders assigned all seven of the sins.[6] In this period, the Church sought to channel aggressive energies of young knights, encouraging them to take up the Crusade instead of harmful tournaments. These themes correspond very closely to the sentiments expressed in the *Queste*, where the greatest knight, Lancelot, is disqualified from seeking the Grail because of his sinful lust for Guenevere. Instead only the purest knights, chief among whom is Galahad, can achieve this quest, which terminates in the 'city of Sarras' — identified by the editor as 'the Heavenly Jerusalem' (*Queste*, p. 280) — where he succeeds an evil man as ruler of the city. Within this plot, the author has envisioned Galahad achieving more than finding the Grail; he has also achieved the successful Crusade.

Early thirteenth-century religious ideas are even reflected in the format of the Vulgate *Queste*, which can be compared to an exemplum. Le Goff has proposed that the use of the popular exemplum in religious teaching increased between the years 1180 and 1240 (p. 181). He also comments on the source of the material for such exempla: they were 'taken for the most part from ancient pagan literature and oral tradition and less often from the Bible' (p. 182). Another contemporary religious practice portrayed in the *Queste* was the importance of penance and confession that superseded other sacraments after the Fourth Lateran Council in 1215 required compulsory confession from every Christian. The Vulgate *Queste* reflects these priorities by having the knights confess to religious hermits while pursuing the Grail.

As we have seen, medieval versions of the Quest legend varied in the religious or societal emphases they gave to the Grail. They did, however, commonly describe it as a sacred object, or at least a positively charged one, with the ability to heal wounds, restore fertility to nature and elevate worthy knights to greater levels of spirituality. Just as medieval authors found the appeal of the Grail story irresistible and took it up time and again, adding new elements, shaping and refashioning the source texts to suit the needs of particular audiences, so have modern authors returned to the old legend reinterpreting it according to the tastes of contemporary readers. The basic plot of a hero on a quest to obtain a powerful, but elusive, object can undergo infinite variations and admit new themes and problematics appropriate to an age of technology as well as to an ancient agricultural era. The most striking commonality among numerous modern reworkings is the negative representation of the grail as unholy. How can this reversal of moral polarities have occurred? One can posit philosophical, spiritual and social reasons for these darker retellings. For example, certain stories are indebted to the philosophies of Nietzsche and of Sartre; some reflect

---

[6] Jacques Le Goff, *The Medieval Imagination*, trans. Arthur Goldhammer (Chicago, IL: Chicago University Press, 1988), pp. 94, 181, 183.

the waning of religious faith so characteristic of the twentieth century; some explore the difficulty of finding meaning when institutions are failing; and others express cold war era fears of the ultimate destructive weapon.

The first factor that may have influenced these modern writers to imagine an unholy grail rather than a holy one is the philosophy of existentialism. The tenets of this philosophy that permeate so much of modern thought have certainly had their effect on these modern retellings since the Grail is no longer interpreted as a pagan fertility symbol nor as the cup of Christ. The Grail has been stripped of all spiritual connotations, these being replaced by totally materialist associations or sometimes even by extraterrestrial ones!

Nietzsche's well-known unequivocal rejection of God ('God is dead and we have killed him') as well as his association of Christianity with weakness inspired Brad Linaweaver's 'Under an Appalling Sky'.[7] The story's epigraph attributes this quote to the philosopher: 'Speak only of that which one has overcome' (p. 91). The questers in this story are Nazis and their plan is described thus:[8]

> 'If only Christ could be made out to be Aryan, and St. Paul (Saul) removed from his position of influence, it would be a mortal blow to the last hold of the Jew over the Christian mind! Getting rid of the Old Testament wouldn't be easy, but it might work if the New Church could satisfy the age-old dream of finding the Holy Grail. He Who Held the Grail could change the rules to ... anything. Lutherans and Catholics would lose their influence in Germany and the new Christianity would be exactly what Hitler wanted.' (p. 93)

Despite the flaws of logic in this plan, the Nazis' motives are well established: they perceive the Grail as a powerful tool that could allow absolute rule and lead to the extinction or dilution of three major religious groups. The

---

[7] 'Christianity has sided with all that is weak and base, with all failures; it has made an ideal of whatever *contradicts* the instinct of the strong life to preserve itself; it has corrupted the reason even of those strongest in spirit by teaching men to consider the supreme values of the spirit as something sinful, and something that leads into error — as temptations' (Friedrich Nietzsche, 'The Death of God and the Antichrist', in Richard Ellmann and Charles Feidelson Jr (eds), *The Modern Tradition: Backgrounds of Modern Literature* [New York: Oxford University Press, 1965], pp. 906, 909); Brad Linaweaver, 'Under an Appalling Sky', in Richard Gilliam, Martin H. Greenbert and Edward E. Kramer (eds), *Grails: Visitations of the Night* (New York: Penguin USA, 1994), pp. 91–106.

[8] The recurrence of Nazis in these stories as the ultimate representatives of earthly evil belongs to a thematic that is also present in Stephen Spielberg's cinematic retellings *Raiders of the Lost Ark* and *Indiana Jones and the Last Crusade*. Both these films imagine powerful weapons created from once holy ancient and medieval objects, and narrate the heroic quests to retrieve them.

expedition sets out seeking a grail of conventional medieval characteristics; however, this is not the kind of grail the group ultimately discovers. In a cave in the Himalayan mountains, the group encounters the keepers of the grail, strange creatures between nine and ten feet tall. 'The features of the face were one of the few parts of its anatomy not covered in hair, as were the hands. And it was the most beautiful face Karl had ever seen, a face to match the pure light that seemed to stream forth from the eyes' (pp. 104–5). Despite the positively charged adjectives in this passage ('beautiful', 'pure'), the story is more deeply pessimistic as shown by the adjectives in its title and in its final sentence: 'appalling' and 'abominable'. The grail found at the end of the story has nothing to do with either its pre-Christian or medieval models. The origin of these previously unknown creatures is never explained, but an alien connection suggests itself. The extraterrestrial grail has an intriguing effect on the group:

> '"If you are of the true blood", said the voice, "your spirit eye will be awakened. If not, then your flesh will serve others who are awakened. Even the remains of the body will live, transformed into the humble creatures [as large as his arm, all black and shiny with dozens of squirming legs] you have already seen in this, our home"'. (p. 105)

Although the group's chances of being initiated into a higher level of consciousness are deemed remote, they each drink in turn from the grail, an action explicitly referred to as 'communion', and the narrator comments that this forced transformation to another life form 'was abominable' (p. 106).

Although Sartre may not have been as vituperative as Nietzsche in his rejection of religion, he theorized that 'everything is indeed permitted if God does not exist'. This lack of divine rules means that a person is entirely free and, consequently, 'from the moment [man] is thrown into this world he is responsible for everything he does'.[9] Therefore, while Sartre believed man is free to act in whatever way he pleases, he also believed man is burdened with responsibility for his actions, with no excuses permitted. Since Sartre does not accept any *a priori* morals or rules, each person must invent his or her own morality.

This Sartrean lack of divine guidance resulting in a clash of individual moralities is played out in Brad Strickland's 'The Gift of Gilthaliad'.[10] Here, the Grail is the cause of violence and destruction even though it has no inherent power. As in so many of these stories, no Arthurian knightly characters appear,

[9] Jean-Paul Sartre, 'Existence Precedes Essence', in Ellman and Feidelson Jr (eds), *Modern Tradition*, p. 837.

[10] Brad Strickland, 'The Gift of Gilthaliad', in Gilliam, Greenbert and Kramer (eds), *Grails: Quests of the Dawn* (New York: Penguin USA, 1994), pp. 60–73.

but fairies and elves do. Gilthaliad, of the Fair Folk, constructs a material wedding gift with his own hands for his human friend Davel rather than giving a gift more characteristic of the Fair Folk, such as long life. The Fair Folk consider the cup Gilthaliad made to be 'a toy, a piece of childish vanity not becoming one of Gilthaliad's lineage, station, and age' (p. 61) Humans, on the other hand, see it as having 'a surpassing, eerie loveliness' that 'enraptured the eye, gladdened the heart, and made all mundane cares recede to unimportance' (pp. 60, 61). One notes here the invention of an interesting new myth of origin for the Grail: it is created by fairies. As such, this retelling conflates the myths of fairies and of the Grail.

Even at the gift's presentation, danger is foreshadowed when all the court looked at it with 'admiration — and envy' (p. 61). The gift does not bring happiness; instead, it ironically destroys the marriage for which it was a gift since the wife envies the time the husband spends admiring the cup rather than with her. Therefore, she convinces her lover to steal it, and as a result the husband kills her through torture trying to find out where the cup was taken. Finally, the friendship between the Fair Folk and humans deteriorates and leads to a war. As the story continues, every human who comes into contact with the cup is obsessed with its beauty and suffers in some way because of it.

In the end, after many years have passed, children find the cup in a box. Gilthaliad declares, 'It was but a toy. ... No enchantment went into it, and it had no importance' (p. 73). Strickland's story, then, has a bitter irony not present in the other reworkings. One would not expect a gift of love and friendship to produce such destructive effects. What is seen by the Fair Folk as a simple valueless cup becomes a site upon which humans write the stories of their own greed, jealousy and ambition. Its material nature is a metaphor for the materialism of the unspiritual modern world. The friendship and support of supernatural beings now counts for less than a trivial object.

Another story which may be inspired by Sartre's idea that humanity is responsible for its own behaviours and not guided by any divine plan is 'Siege Perilous' by Jerry and Sharon Ahern.[11] The disparate interpretations for the Grail in this story reflect our modern age's nihilistic confusion and inability to create meaning for itself. The story alludes to the traditional origin of the Grail as the cup of Christ's Passion. Despite this firm grounding in medieval tradition, however, the grail that these characters seek is a kind of 'decoder cup' which could allow its possessor to 'decipher the knowledge of the ancients, the transmutation of lead into gold least among them. He who has the cup and the tablets holds the key to

[11] Jerry and Sharon Ahern, 'Seige Perilous', in Gilliam, Greenbert and Kramer (eds), *Grails: Visitations*, pp. 191–212.

molding all of nature to his will, the ultimate temporal power over mankind' (p. 198). The priest who spent his life trying to find the grail laments, 'And if this cup was [Christ's] cup, then why was it His? He was the Son of God. Why did He drink from the cup of arcane knowledge when He always was and always will be the Sum of All Time and Wisdom because He and the Father are One?' (p. 199). But these questions are never answered; instead, the story only adds more speculations as it fast-forwards from biblical antiquity to the space age: certain tablets that the cup will help translate 'might be the writings of an extraterrestrial race which came to Earth and interacted with early man. Or even the last remnants of a culture which pre-dated man on Earth' (p. 207). One might even say the confusion over the meaning of this grail and the authors' refusal to clarify its significance reflect the uncertainty of a world where God has been declared dead, but where no clear substitute — except perhaps a space alien Other — has been found. The existentialists, of course, offered no substitutes, but rather urged action in the face of Nothing. Yet this story suggests that modern humans need some meaningful order in the world and illustrates our inability to accept Nothing.

The tension in the Aherns' story is derived from the desperate attempt of two priests to prevent the grail from falling into the Nazis' possession. In the climax of the story, the dilemma of what to do with the grail is contemplated. Should it be destroyed to prevent the enemy from acquiring its power? One character asks, '"What's the greater peril, Father? ... That we destroy the cup forever or let it fall into the hands of the Nazis"' (p. 207). In the end, Father Hastings, the priest who sought the grail, is admonished by another priest who intimates that perhaps he had searched for the grail to confirm his faith in God, but may instead have found another cup because his faith was not firm without proof. In the end, the cup is destroyed, and Father Santini murmurs, '"Amen"' (p. 212). While this story raises the issue of a traditional Catholic faith in conflict with a disbelieving age, we note once again the connection of doubt to a material proof. Just as the doubting disciple Thomas needed to touch Christ's side to believe, this priest must find an object to convince himself that his faith is valid. This notion recurs explicitly in Robert Weinberg's 'Seven Drops of Blood'.[12]

In Weinberg's story the villains acquire the grail, yet despite their evil intentions the cup has a purifying effect on them. The protagonist, called a 'New Age detective', is hired to find the Holy Grail and locates it in the possession of a mob leader. As in other stories, the power of the grail can only be activated by blood from a specific donor, in this case 'a righteous soul' (p. 386). The connection of the cup to blood echoes the medieval notion that the Grail was used

---

[12] Robert Weinberg, 'Seven Drops of Blood', Gilliam, Greenbert and Kramer (eds), *Grails: Visitations*, pp. 373–90.

to catch the blood of the dying Christ. Once Weinberg's cup has been activated with the blood, the mobster, King Wedo, picks up the goblet, and by this action alone he is purified: he now detests evil, which in this case includes himself and his own past deeds. Once the repentant criminal is 'overwhelmed by his monstrous crimes, [he] resorted to suicide' (p. 390).

At the end of the story Weinberg offers this spin on the origin of the Grail, which he calls a cup of treachery: 'The Chalice was a gift to Christ from one of his disciples ... who doubted and thought to use the Grail as a final test. And thus began a tale of treachery — and eternal damnation' (p. 390). The writer has not drained the tale of all its religious meaning, but he has changed the essence of the Grail. It is no longer associated with Christ and holiness; it is instead associated more with punishment and distrust than with love and enlightenment.

A modern retelling that portrays a more complete modern loss of faith set within the various medieval conventions of the Grail legend is 'The Sinner King' by Richard T. Chizmar.[13] The grail in this story is worshipped by a renegade religious cult called the New Order. Their grail is likened to that belonging to the so-called 'Sinner King' of the supposedly traditional story:

> But one of [the keepers of the Grail] failed and thus began a terrible myth, that of the Sinner King. This man was supposed to have looked at a partially disrobed female and, according to legend, the sacred spear then fell upon him, inflicting a fatal wound, thus, crowning this man as *Le Roi Pescheur* or The Sinner King. (p. 221)

Here the revision of the Grail legend depends on a clever wordplay based on the similarity of French nouns: *pécheur* ('sinner') and *pêcheur* ('fisher'). The idea of calling the king a sinner glosses the punishment: the wound is usually described as being in the thigh, a euphemism for impotence. Chizmar was not the first to speculate about the nature of this unusual title. In discussing its significance, Weston saw the name 'Fisher King' as 'the very essence' of a primitive ritual of seasonal renewal (p. 136). The fish was an ancient life symbol found in Syrian, Buddhist, Jewish and Christian religions. Chrétien's *Perceval* offers the more pragmatic explanation that the king goes fishing to keep himself occupied while his wound is healing (p. 420). By changing the traditional character's name, Chizmar has changed the very nature of the story.

Chizmar's use of the character may have an unsuspected, northern European source. It resembles more closely *Sone de Nansai* which recounts the history of 'Joseph d'Abarimathie' (referred to as the Fisher King) who is 'ensnared by the

[13] Richard T. Chizmar, 'The Sinner King', in Gilliam, Greenbert and Kramer (eds), *Grails: Visitations*, pp. 213–28.

beauty of the Pagan King of Norway, whom he has slain; he baptizes her, though she still an unbeliever at heart, and makes her his wife, thus drawing the wrath of Heaven upon himself.[14] God punishes him by causing a pain in his loins; the punishment seems to fit the crime. The medieval story is not only connected to the fertility-rite versions of the Grail (fish are part of nature; fish can be used as fertilizer), but also by the fact that his wound recalls the land's barrenness. In Chizmar's story, the Sinner King committed a similar sin (thus his appropriate name), but his punishment — banishment — and its significance differ since the land is unaffected by the King's potency. Playing off the sin of lust, Chizmar has created a 'cult of the New Order' whose task is to punish sinners (usually men) who succumb to lust by banishing them after the first offence, but by burning them to death for a recurrence.

This story contains both parallels to, and surprising variations on, medieval Grail conventions. In medieval texts, an old hermit is often an affirming figure who provides material assistance and spiritual advice to those knights or others who are pursuing journeys of spiritual purification. In Chizmar's story, many of the external trappings of the medieval hermit are retained in the person of Lew Perkins, a man banished from the cult who teaches the younger, first-person narrator, Bill, about his 'religion'. Like a medieval hermit, he has retreated from society, living in a remote log cabin with no telephone and avoiding contact with the civilized world (pp. 216, 219). He also serves the function of physically helping heal Bill after his escape from the New Order's camp. Lew finds him with 'a broken leg, broken wrist, bruised ribs ... and probably one whopper of a concussion' (p. 217). In a sense, Lew also serves as Bill's confessor when he listens to Bill's story of how he came to be wounded and lost in the forest. However, Lew was actually a former cult member himself who had been banished from the very cult Bill was investigating because of practising the aforementioned sin. This helper figure, Lew, is himself a criminal and a sinner according to the norms of his society, hardly the religious recluse or holy man of the medieval legends.

More extraordinary is the way that Chizmar refashions the Grail knights and their function of serving a holy object into a sinister and dangerous cult on the fringe of society. In his retelling, the cup seems ominous first because it is explicitly described as not the cup of Christ; second, because it becomes the object of worship itself, like an idol; and finally, because the religious group worshipping it commits murder. Instead of the noble knights of Arthur's Round Table who pursue the holiness and purity which the Grail represents, the seemingly insane cult members of 'The Sinner King' appear to have lost touch with reality to the point of committing violent crimes against their fellow men. This

[14] Weston, p. 22.

story critiques the effect of cult membership on individuals and suggests how easily one can be seduced into joining a cult. By the end of the story, the main character, a clear-thinking journalist whose original mission was to expose the questionable practices of the New Order, is himself referring to the cup as 'the Holy Grail'.

Several of the modern stories present the frightening idea that any individual — not just the righteous — could possess and use the power of the Grail. In the French *Quest del Saint Graal* only the most worthy knights, namely Galahad, Perceval and Bors, were even able to see the Holy Grail, let alone possess it. They could not use the Grail to satisfy their earthly desires, but instead through its intervention were permitted a glimpse of the glory of God. In contrast to this untouchable, divine Grail, several modern stories degrade the grail into a thing that can be grasped and exploited, even by those people most unworthy of it. Modern popular retellings allow incarnations of evil such as Nazis and mobsters to find, handle and exploit the grail to their own ends. The theme of unimaginable destructive power in so many modern novels and movies may have at its inception the existence of nuclear weapons and the psychological effect their existence has had through the cold war era and beyond.

One such story that includes a grail that can provide power over others for evil purposes is 'The Unholy' by Doug Murray.[15] Although the story retains many of the familiar characters from the Arthurian legend such as Merlin, Lancelot, Mordred and Morgana, the action centres on an interesting new character, Giles, Arthur's son by Guenevere's cousin, conceived in an attempt to produce an heir because Guenevere herself was barren. Whereas the Holy Grail is described as the cup from which Christ drank at the Last Supper, Murray's unholy grail is said to be the cup from which Judas drank. Morgana plans to use this anti-grail to destroy Arthur and seize power for herself and Mordred. Murray uses the traditional antipathy between Morgana and Arthur as the motivation for the use of the grail. The notion of a powerful enemy possessing an invincible weapon with which s/he intends to overthrow the existing political order plays on the modern reader's fears of nuclear war or terrorism.

The remarkable physical description of the grail in Murray's story merits discussion. It is formed from a human skull 'covered with silver ... the metal inset with ruby eyes and emerald teeth' (p. 31). The symbolism of this object with respect to medieval or Renaissance beliefs sheds light on the process of narrative refashioning. The use of a human skull imbues the object with connotations of death and mortality. Skulls were an important visual element in medi-

---

[15] Doug Murray, 'The Unholy', in Gilliam, Greenbert and Kramer (eds), *Grails: Visitations*, pp. 30–51.

eval art, cautioning the viewer to ponder his corruptible human nature. While Murray may or may not have researched actual cultural beliefs of earlier centuries, the aggregation of precious stones and metals in his Grail suggests a potent amulet or even a reliquary. Silver, emeralds and red stones like the ruby were traditionally believed to have the power to ward off demons.[16] Here, Morgana is not concerned with protecting herself from demons, rather with using diabolic power: the triple combination of such materials resonates with older beliefs in creating an object which is the seat of awesome power. We have seen the need for blood to activate other modern grails. In order to generate this one's evil magic, Morgana needs the 'seed, blood, and skin' (p. 35) of Arthur's son in order to aid her take-over of the country.

The presence of Morgana recalls parallels to Sir Thomas Malory's *Le Morte d'Arthur* (*c.* 1485).[17] As in Malory, Murray's Morgana is invincible and violates all the expected rules, ultimately provoking Lancelot to wound her with his sword. Merlin comments, '"Aye, that wound looks mortal enough, but to a mage of her power ..."' (p. 49). This confrontation and wounding calls into play the 'rules' of the chivalric code by which knights were not to fight the helpless such as women, unarmed opponents or old men. As a true knight, Lancelot ponders the code of behaviour that prevents him from killing her. Yet Morgana is no ordinary helpless woman. This is quite different from Malory's version in which Morgain can turn herself to stone to escape injury or death. The modern author preserves the threat of an invincible feminine power, but nevertheless allows Morgana to suffer physically for her treachery. In Malory, she suffers, too, but her grief is emotional rather than physical, due to the loss of her lover Accolon who was killed in the confrontation with Arthur. The scene of her grieving for her lost lover humanizes Morgain and presents a more vulnerable side of the sorceress; in Malory's text she is not, therefore, the embodiment of pure evil that she is in many modern versions. This focus on malevolence may reflect the ideology of nuclear conflict today where both the nuclear weapon and the enemy who wields it are demonized.

Even though Morgana has been prevented from using the power of the grail destructively, it can exert its own destructive power over whomever holds it. Murray makes another interesting innovation to the story: after Morgana is wounded, Giles gains control of the grail and gives it to Lancelot, 'the perfect protector — the bravest, noblest man in Christendom' (p. 50). Yet while displaying the evil object at court, Lancelot suddenly realizes how beautiful

---

[16] Hans Biedermann, *Dictionary of Symbolism*, trans. James Hulbert (New York: Penguin USA, 1992), pp. 117, 308–9.

[17] Sir Thomas Malory, *Malory: Works*, ed. Eugène Vinaver (New York: Oxford University Press, 1971).

Guenevere is, and thus begins their adulterous affair. Murray thus makes the grail the instrument of sin, a kind of Edenic 'apple', that causes Lancelot to betray his lord, and Guenevere her marriage vows, and that brings about the downfall of Arthur's court. Quite in contrast to medieval versions where Lancelot is chastised by holy hermits for his sins (loving Guenevere) which prevent him from achieving the Holy Grail, in this modern version it is the grail itself that causes Lancelot to take the path of sin.

A story that puts a similarly destructive spin on the Grail is Connie Hirsch's 'Judas'.[18] We recall Murray's inclusion of the betrayer Judas as a rationale for inventing his 'Unholy Grail', and Hirsch gives her evil cup the same origin, with a similar corrupting effect. Just as Lancelot was the champion of women, but then became transformed into a sinner who could destroy the Round Table, the main character of Hirsch's story, Paulita, is transformed from a police officer who protects battered wives trying to escape their abusive husbands into an abuser of those very women. As the story begins, Paulita's new room-mate, Maggie, brings with her an unusual cup: 'It was more like a ceramic cup or goblet, done in a white crackle glaze with an illegible design on the side. It had a wide base, good to hang onto, comfortable in the hand' (p. 277).

As in other modern versions of the Grail story in which a bodily fluid is required to activate the evil power, here Paulita pricks her finger on the rim furnishing the requisite blood. In inspecting the damage to her finger, Paulita observes that the drop of blood on her finger looks 'like a ruby' (p. 277), recalling the rubies on Murray's skull-cup. That the cup would need blood to activate its power shows similarity to Christ's cup. Since Christ's blood represents his ultimate redemptive sacrifice, blood represents great power. Here, however, that power is reversed from saving to damning. Maggie's ex-husband Joe repeatedly appears demanding the return of an object which is very important to him, presumably the cup. He never specifies what it is he wants, and the two women cannot guess. In these confrontations, Paulita steadfastly protects Maggie. She has not yet succumbed to the corrupting influence of the cup.

Nevertheless, over time, the power of the cup begins to exert its influence over Paulita. Like the Tree of the Knowledge of Good and Evil in the Garden of Eden, the cup functions as the apple. When she drinks out of it, Paulita thinks, 'I had been waiting all my life for knowledge, for power like this' (p. 288). In a perversion of the hagiographic tradition of holy objects speaking to saints, the cup begins to talk to her 'whispering, saying things [she] wanted to hear' (p. 288). The former saviour and champion of women now turns abusive. When she finds

---

[18] Connie Hirsch, 'Judas', in Gilliam, Greenbert and Kramer (eds), *Grails: Visitations*, pp. 275–99.

Maggie in her room where she has hidden the cup, Paulita comments, 'I hadn't really had to hit her, just shake her up a bit, and the tongue-lashing, of course. Joe's physical battering had been nothing compared to my power' (p. 291). In other modern retellings, we have seen the notions that the cup produced jealousy, envy and aggression (Strickland) or personality change among humans who possessed it (Weinberg). As Paulita investigates the history of the cup, a previous possessor informs her that '"More than once ... many times in fact, the records show a striking personality change in the owner"' (p. 295). She even murders her informant, a previous owner, with poison that he drinks from the cup. The story concludes with Paulita envisioning other murders, saying, 'Better I should manipulate Joe into confronting me or the police so he could be shot down like a dog; Maggie's death could wait. Perhaps an overdose of sleeping pills ... ' (p. 299). In addition to these homicidal thoughts, she anticipates the great power that can be hers because of the cup. How many people she will affect remains unanswered.

The cup seems to have the same destructive effect on men and women. Previous owners of the cup, such as the abusive husband Joe, were men, and the fact that a woman possesses the cup now appears to be coincidental rather than symbolic. Male or female, all possessors of the cup are seduced by its power, and their lives are inevitably destroyed. More significant than her gender is Paulita's occupation as a police officer, a person sworn to uphold the law and protect the innocent. That she has been a responsible and caring person up until the time she drinks from the cup we do not doubt since she has chosen to room with battered women in order to offer them personal protection. In just the way that Paulita, sworn to do good, is seduced by great power to harm others, individuals holding the power of nuclear weapons may find their good intentions corrupted by the ultimate weapon.

A symbolic Grail that can also be a nuclear bomb substitute appears in 'Ashes to Ashes' by Jack C. Haldeman II.[19] As the title implies, the holy and powerful object sought by the greedy is really no more than ashes and bones of an unnamed saint. The grail embodied as the traditional cup does appear, but is not considered important by the enemies of good because

> the power of the grail cannot be used for personal gain, nor can it be used for any evil purpose. It may only be used to better the fate of all humanity. Of course the bones can do that too, if the holder is stupid enough to have a weakness for benevolent actions. But the bones do not carry the same restrictions as the grail. (p. 260)

---

[19] Jack C. Haldeman II, 'Ashes to Ashes', in Gilliam, Greenbert and Kramer (eds), *Grails: Visitations*, pp. 238–62.

Although the story preserves the traditional power of the grail for good motives, in the medieval story the grail could not be used at all. Therefore, the action centres around the evil characters attempting to acquire the bones and ashes. This power of the saints' bones is quite in keeping with medieval ideas of the miracles performed by such relics. However, in medieval legends the relics of saints always had positive functions.

In much the same way as in the story 'Judas', the potentially unlimited power of these bones is corrupting. However, even more than in the last story there is tension about what the people pursuing the bones will do with the power they acquire. Since they specifically reject the bowl — the traditional grail — because it can only be used for benevolent purposes, we know that their intentions are evil. While Paulita in 'Judas' seemed to only be able to affect one person at a time, there is the possibility in 'Ashes to Ashes' that a person in possession of the bones could affect all of humanity at once, much like someone in charge of detonating a nuclear bomb. In contrast to the fear of nuclear weapons this may represent, the bones and ashes are almost all destroyed, while the bowl itself, the grail, is rescued. This is a reassuring scenario in that not only have the dangerous people been prevented from acquiring the bones, but most of the objects have been destroyed and so will never be able to be used against humanity. However, all is not perfect since in the end Haldeman's narrator tells us he saved 'a tiny sliver of a bone' (p. 262). Since as readers we have come to trust this apparently good-hearted narrator, this does not cause us a great deal of concern; yet the haunting possibility exists that the sliver could still fall into untrustworthy hands. Moreover, the corrupting effects of the grail in stories by Murray and Hirsch may cause us to wonder if even this tiny sliver would someday corrupt this narrator as well.

The similarities of these unholy grails to a nuclear bomb include the possibility of unscrupulous people using the power of the object to increase their own power to the detriment of others. If these authors are in some sense using the idea of an unholy grail to express a fear of nuclear weapons, they have also made the threat more manageable, less threatening. While the bones and ashes might have been used in destructive ways, with world-wide consequences, the threat of one group of people holding a single weapon is less threatening than the thought of governments around the globe holding thousands of nuclear weapons. Also, unlike the bomb, these unholy grails cannot be reproduced; once they are destroyed, the power is irrevocably gone with no knowledge of how to re-create it. Therefore, these authors may have created threats to humanity that can be more easily defused than the real situation — a fantasy of destroying the threat that is not available in reality.

A more optimistic fantasy is the homespun treatment of the Grail legend 'What You See ... ' by Alan Dean Foster.[20] This story transports the Grail to the mythical Old West. It begins with a snake-oil salesman pitching his 'Elixir of the Pharaohs' to gullible townspeople (p. 133). 'Doctor' Mohet Ramses is clearly a trickster: despite his exotic Egyptian name, the only Cairo he has ever visited was Cairo, Illinois!

The 'doctor' reveals a heartless cruelty when he tries to sell the elixir to an old woman who is worried about her elderly husband who has been kicked by a cow and is in danger of dying. The doctor's lack of moral concern is apparent: not only does he try to sell bogus medicine to a seriously injured man, but he stands firm on the price of his elixir — one dollar, a sum that the poor woman can scarely afford. Happily, before the transaction can be completed, a large man happens by and tosses the phoney cure away; instead, in a Christ-like gesture, he offers the man a drink of water from a simple wooden cup and the injured man instantly improves. Foster describes this stranger as a 'mountain man' wearing 'thick buckskins' and having 'salty black hair that hung to his shoulder' (pp. 139, 140), resembling in many ways the hermit-helpers of medieval stories.

Seeing the real power of the stranger's cup, the 'doctor' becomes determined to steal the magical vessel and awaits the opportunity to rifle through the stranger's saddle-bags. When he takes out what appears to be the same cup, something creeps out of the bowl and clutches him, pulling him inside:

> As he didn't fit inside the bowl of the vessel nearly as efficiently [as the creature], there ensued a great many cracking and rending noises as he was pulled in, until only his spasmodically kicking legs were visible protruding beyond the smooth rim. Finally they too vanished, and lastly his fine handmade shoes, and then he was all gone. (p. 147)

When the unnamed stranger returns to his saddle-bags, he surmises what has occurred and wryly comments, "'Course, it didn't help him that he got ahold o' the wrong grail'" (p. 148). Unlike the other stories, the co-presence of a 'wrong grail' comes as a surprise to the reader and calls to mind the trickery of a huckster's shell game. Although this 'wrong grail' seems to share the characteristics of the other unholy grails that brought danger to whoever touched them, the twist in this story — that the thief got what he deserved — embues the retelling with a more affirmative moral outlook. In other modern grail stories, good people were influenced to behave in negative ways and as a result destroyed themselves or others, but in this instance a corrupt man received a swift and sure punishment for his nefarious deed. Perhaps due to its Old West setting, the Foster story

---

[20] Alan Dean Foster, 'What You See ... ', in Gilliam, Greenbert and Kramer (eds), *Grails: Quests*, pp. 133–48.

resurrects the old-fashioned notion that goodness will triumph over evil: nameless heroes appear when we need help, and potent objects are in the hands of the good. Surely this is the ultimate reassuring fantasy for an age of disbelief.

Chapter 5

Transforming the proud king transformed: *Robert of Sicily*

Stephen D. Powell

'How came Shakespeare to let such a subject escape him?' wonders Leigh Hunt about the Middle English story of King Robert of Sicily. 'Or Beaumont and Fletcher? or Decker (*sic*)? or any of the great and loving spirits that abounded in that romantic age?'[1] The exemplary tale of this proud king humbled by God was immensely popular in the late Middle Ages, if we may judge by the number of surviving manuscripts: nine complete versions and a fragment.[2] But the story, which Hunt called 'an especial delight of our soul' (p. 13), was passed over by most early modern writers before it achieved a resurgence of popularity in the nineteenth century.[3] In that century, and in the early part of the twentieth, this didactic tale, often classified as romance because of its chivalric elements, was transformed by a series of authors — Hunt, Henry Wadsworth Longfellow, Rudolf Schmidt, Frederick J.H. Darton and others — as part of the era's larger project of resurrecting interest in the Middle Ages. More recently, however, the story of this fictitious Sicilian monarch, who is relegated to the position of court fool until he mends his prideful ways and is restored to the throne, has once again

---

An earlier version of this paper was presented at the Tenth International Conference on Medievalism in Worcester, Massachusetts, September 1995. I am grateful to Alan Shepard for his helpful comments on this revision.

[1] *A Jar of Honey from Mount Hybla* (1848); London: Smith, 1883), p. 13.

[2] Oxford, Bodl. Engl. Poet. a.1. (Vernon); Oxford, Trinity College 57; London, British Library, Add. 22283 (Simeon) and 34801 (fragment); BL Harley 525 and 1701; Cambridge, University Library Ff.2.38 and Ii.4.9; Cambridge, Gonville and Caius College 174/95; and Dublin, Trinity College 432.

[3] Donna B. Hamilton suggests, not implausibly, that Shakespeare did know the story, but her argument that he had it in mind during the composition of *King Lear* is unconvincing ('Some Romance Sources for *King Lear*: Robert of Sicily and Robert the Devil', *Studies in Philology* 71 (1974), pp. 173–91). To my knowledge, no other early modern literary remnant of the tale survives, although there are records of dramatic productions from that period (see Stephen D. Powell, 'Textual and Generic Instability in the Middle English *Roberd of Cisyle*: A Study with Critical Edition', dissertation, University of Toronto, 1995, pp. 185–6).

been shelved by some literary critics.[4]

The reasons for the tale's transitory fame and 'canonization' and 'decanonization', especially in the early modern period, are numerous and at least partially unknowable. Despite the number of surviving medieval exemplars, we cannot be sure that these manuscripts enjoyed wide circulation in the Renaissance, although the diversity of their dialects does confirm that the poem travelled far and wide within England in the century or so they represent (*c.* 1375–*c.* 1500). Even if the poem did appeal to early modern tastes, the lack of incunabula and early printed versions confounds our ability to prove the continuity of readership in the period and, in fact, suggests a decline in popularity. This chapter focuses on the much more extensive evidence of later centuries. In the nineteenth and early twentieth centuries, the didactic story of Robert of Sicily, which had existed on the generic boundary between the secular romance and the pious tale, was recast as a more generically unified and less overtly didactic text than it had been for its medieval readers. The poem was thus made to conform both with modern aesthetic regulations and with modern notions of medieval artistry. As it was changed, it became one of a number of texts important to the era's understanding of the medieval underpinnings of European culture.

We have abundant evidence for the poem's reception in the period following the appearance of Thomas Warton's *History of English Literature* (1774). Warton printed extracts of the medieval poem, and his example was followed by George Ellis (1805).[5] The first modern edition of the complete poem was E.V. Utterson's in 1839, and that was quickly followed by editions by James Orchard Halliwell-Phillipps (1844), W. Carew Hazlitt (1864) and Carl Horstmann (1878 and 1879).[6] What is most interesting about these early 'editions' — actually just

---

[4] The story was removed from the most recent revision of the *Pelican Guide to English Literature* (now titled the *New Pelican Guide to English Literature*, 1982). More encouraging is the new student edition by Edward E. Foster, *Amis and Amiloun, Robert of Cisyle*, and *Sir Amadace*, TEAMS Middle English Texts series (Kalamazoo, MI: Medieval Institute Publications, 1997), pp. 89-110.

[5] Thomas Warton, *The History of English Poetry from the Close of the Eleventh to the Commencement of the Eighteenth Century*, 3 vols (London: Dodsley, 1774–81), vol. 1, pp. 184–90; 'Robert of Cysille', in *Specimens of Early English Metrical Romances, Chiefly Written during the Early Part of the Fourteenth Century*, ed. George Ellis, 3 vols (London: Longman, 1805), vol. 3, pp. 143–52.

[6] *Kyng Roberd of Cysyle* [ed. E.V. Utterson], (London: Whittingham, 1839); 'Robert of Sicily', in *Nugæ Poeticæ: Select Pieces of Old English Popular Poetry, Illustrating the Manners and Arts of the Fifteenth Century*, ed. James Orchard Halliwell [Phillipps] (London: Smith, 1844), pp. 49–63; 'Kynge Roberd of Cysille', in *Remains of the Early Popular Poetry of England*, ed. W. Carew Hazlitt, 4 vols (London: Smith, 1864), vol. 1, pp. 264–88; 'Roberd of Cisyle', in *Sammlung altenglischer Legenden*, ed. C. Horstmann (Heilbronn: Henninger, 1878), pp. 209–19; 'Roberd of Sicily. Nachträge zu den Legenden', [ed. C. Horstmann], *Archiv für der neueren*

transcriptions — and those that followed is the inability of the various editors to reach a consensus about which of the manuscripts to use as a base text for their work. Of the poem's complete manuscripts, eight were transcribed and published by different editors between 1839 and 1940. The reason for the lack of scholarly certainty about the 'best' manuscript stems from the poem's radical variations from manuscript to manuscript. Over the course of the fifteenth century, for example, *Robert of Sicily* did more than just circulate widely through medieval England: it also grew in length from 444 lines to 516 lines. These extra lines are an important piece of evidence we have of scribal reauthoring of the poem; apparently the lack of a named author as originator of the text made reauthoring especially permissible.[7] With few exceptions, modern editors have been unwilling to imagine these reauthored versions as authoritative. Yet at the same time, paradoxically, modern editors have in effect validated the variant readings by their own profligate printing of numerous different versions.

In addition to its many modern transcribers and editors, *Robert of Sicily* also attracted the attention of Hunt and a number of other nineteenth- and early twentieth-century writers, each of whom recast the story in a new light. In other words, just as the medieval scribes felt authorized to reinterpret and rewrite their material rather than to recopy it 'mechanically', writers in the modern period have authorized themselves to rework the medieval story. Although the poem's medieval reauthorings have complicated but not stopped the work of editors, they have been completely ignored by the poem's transformers — the revisers, rewriters, and translators who have in their turn reshaped *Robert of Sicily*. The refusal to acknowledge the polysemous textual tradition that is part of the heritage that was being appropriated corresponds with the belief, implicitly or explicitly expressed by all the transformers, that the story of *Robert of Sicily* was in need of various kinds of 'improvement'. Their admiration for the story, then, was tempered by the certainty that they could and should make it better.

Although Hunt and the others praised *Robert of Sicily* in glowing terms, they did more in their transformations than simply 'translate' the Middle English verse into more modern diction. In the introduction to his collection of stories *A Jar of Honey from Mount Hybla* (1848), which includes 'The Legend of King Robert', Hunt laments that he has not yet accomplished his goal of transforming the tale into the masterpiece he believes it to be: 'O Fate! give us a dozen years more life, and a lift in our faculties, immense; and let us try still if even our own verses

---

Sprachen und Literaturen **62** (1879), pp. 397–431.

[7] For a full explanation of the different generic valences of the scribal versions, see my article 'Multiplying Textuality: Generic Migration in the Manuscripts of *Roberd of Cisyle*', *Anglia* **116** (1998), pp. 171–97.

cannot do something with it' (p. 13). But were a dozen more years really necessary to transform this tale? It already contained, as Hunt writes, 'the most striking dramatic points; extremes of passion were in the characters; pride and its punishment were in it; humility and its reward; a court, a chapel, an angel; pomp, music, satire, buffoonery, sublimity,tears' (p. 13). Were Hunt a less forthright critic, we might wonder if he were exaggerating his praises, but bearing in mind Clarence Thorpe's observation that Hunt's taste generally favoured literature 'that delights and entertains through sensuous appeal or charm of wit, humor, or narrative'.[8] we can be certain that Hunt was much taken with *Robert of Sicily*. The poem as it had come down to him simply did not satisfy his own aesthetic needs.

Hunt's writing about the reasons for his revision of the Robert story is only one clue we have about the perceptions held by the poem's nineteenth- and early twentieth-century transformers. When we examine the various rationales for, and products of, these transformations, we find that the transformers attempted to foreclose the further production of meaning made possible by a consideration of the complete manuscript tradition. They did this because they failed to recognize the multiplicity of meaning that the poem's various manuscript versions allow; or were discomfited by the challenge to literary authority that scribal reauthoring suggests; or were unable or unwilling to acknowledge the sophistication of medieval writers. Whatever the reasons, which varied from transformer to transformer, the result is that all of them colonized the textual centre of the story, added their own generic spins, and marginalized the generic polysemy of the original versions. The product of these transformations, though admittedly charming, violate the spirit of the medieval originals.

The original versions of *Robert of Sicily* shed a brighter light on the straightforwardness of medieval popular piety than does the much flashier Chaucerian canon. Even though some modern readers may find its overt didacticism and continuous moralizing, relieved by few exciting chivalric deeds, boring, the story is affecting in its simplicity. Thus, although George Kane has called *Robert of Sicily* 'a crude, sprawling and morally unimpressive story which, by the correct use of emphasis and heightening, could have been made into something both artistically better and successfully didactic', Kane's judgement that the poem is 'a tasteless and ill-conducted exemplum' has met with few seconders.[9]

Hunt's praise, however, shares with Kane's scorn the common feeling that the medieval poem, as it stands, is in some way insufficient. Indeed, Hunt's trans-

---

[8] Quoted in Paul M. Clogan, 'Chaucer and Leigh Hunt', *Medievalia et Humanistica*, n.s. 9 (1979), p. 165.

[9] George Kane, *Middle English Literature: A Critical Study of the Romances, the Religious Lyrics, Piers Plowman* (1951; New York: Barnes, 1970), p. 19.

formation of the story seems to anticipate Kane's call for correction. Both critics ignore the poem's medieval popularity and the fact that the emphases of the different versions are demonstrably different. Surely all of the versions cannot be as bad as Kane claims. In fact, the version most often reproduced, that found in the famous Vernon Manuscript (Bodl. MS. Eng. Poet. a.1, ff. 300r–301r), seems to have been laid out with a strong sense of plot balance: exactly one-quarter of the story (111 lines) is devoted to each of its main events — Robert's pride, the usurpation of his throne by God's angel, his recognition of his own sinfulness and his restoration as ruler of Sicily. Other versions alter the narrative weighting of the tale, but they do so for reasons which seem to accord with designs imparted to the poem by its manuscript context.[10] The much later version in Cambridge University Library, MS Ff.2.38, ff. 254v–57v, for example, provides additional information about the deposed king's sufferings and quest for redemption and restoration. These emphases are in concert with the emphases of the other romance poems that appear in the manuscript anthology. Medieval scribes saw the possibility of reworking the text, but they did so for reasons other than what they perceived to be weaknesses or lacunae in the text; instead, according to their various spiritual, political or artistic agendas, they felt free to reshape the familiar story by mixing together bit and pieces of romance, exemplum, saint's life, and history in new and different combinations. On the other hand, Kane and Hunt both imply, perhaps because of its generic heterogeneity and perhaps because of its moralization, that the text itself is inherently faulty.

The first move in Hunt's transformation was to cast the story more closely in terms of actual history than the medieval versions do. Although there are several illuminating parallels between the medieval versions and the history of the Norman rulers of Sicily, it is not possible to establish exactly who 'Robert' might have been intended to represent. The poem's pope, Urban, shares his name with a number of popes who were much involved in Sicilian politics, while the Emperor Valamound, said to be Robert's brother, bears little resemblance to any known historical figure. There is, then, an air of historicity about the medieval versions, but there is no effort to make the poem cohere with specific historical facts or dates. This lack, however, which Hunt acknowledges by admitting his inability to determine the identity of King Robert, does not stop him from leaving open the possibility that 'antiquaries' may be able to 'determine' the identity of Robert (p. 109). In other words, whether or not he is being disingenuous about the plausibility of such an identification, Hunt implies that his tale should be read

---

[10] My 'Manuscript Context and the Generic Instability of *Roberd of Cisyle*' (*Neuphilologische Mitteilungen*, forthcoming) discusses the relationship of the poem's textual variants to different reception environments provided by conjoined texts, and manuscript size and decoration.

as having a determinate — if not determinable — place in history. The effect of this is to recast *Robert of Sicily* along the lines of a historical legend, rather than as an artificial — that is, a historically timeless, 'literary' — parable.

In one sense, Hunt is merely continuing the grand tradition of pseudo-historical chronology, so common in the late Middle Ages, just as his appeal to written authority ('Writers ... inform us' [p. 109]) echoes the romance tradition of invoking anonymous textual witnesses. But since Hunt's age is one of 'scientific' not 'chronicle' history, his attempts — sincere or not — to make Robert speak like a historical figure are in vain. The immediate effect of remaking the exemplary tale in the mould of a historical legend, suggested by Hunt's title 'The Legend of King Robert', is less profound than the nearly complete break Hunt thereby makes with the moral-didactic tradition that gave birth to the story in the first place. Although it is interesting to speculate whether the scribes had any idea of which Pope Urban they were writing about, the pseudo-anonymity of the main characters is a principal element of the medieval poem's diffusion of the historic in order to maintain the focus on its important didactic lesson.

Although the moral of the poem remains intact in Hunt's transformation, supporting details have been altered to make the history more lively. According to all the medieval versions, Robert, who has fallen asleep in the church and is locked in when the usurping angel leads his followers out, commands the sexton to open the door. Despite worrying that Robert is a thief, 'Þe sexteyn þouhte a non wiþ þan / Þat he was sum wood man, / And wolde þe chirche dilyueret were / Of hym, for he hedde fere, / And openede þe chirche dore in haste' ('The sexton thought that [Robert] was a crazy man and, for fear, wanted the church to be delivered of him. And he opened the church door in haste' [V ll. 85–9]).[11] In contrast, Hunt's Robert violently breaks out of the church on his own, having been kept prisoner by a taunting sexton:

> Now, whether King Robert was of the blood of that Norman chief who felled his enemy's horse with a blow of his fist, we know not; but certain it is, that the only answer he made the sexton was by dashing his enormous foot against the door, and bursting it open in his teeth. (p. 112)

Beyond increasing the amount of dramatic conflict in the tale, Hunt's alteration here also blurs the medieval focus on the king's conflict with his own short-

[11] All quotations from the medieval tale are taken from my own edition and are cited by manuscript and line number. I have quoted from two of the manuscripts, the late fourteenth-century Vernon (V) and the late fifteenth-century CUL Ff.2.38 (F), which reveal the surprising degree of textual variation that occurred as scribes reauthored the poem.

comings and his paralysing inability to recognize his own madness, so apparent to both the sexton and the audience/reader.

More evidence that Hunt's 'Legend of King Robert' gives a historic rather than didactic interpretation to the story is found in the conclusion. Whereas the medieval poem's king had disclosed his faults to his brothers in an ostensibly private letter, Hunt's king records his faults for posterity: 'after a blessed reign, he died, disclosing this *history* to his weeping nobles, and requesting that it might be *recorded* in the Sicilian Annals' (p. 122, emphasis added). In both cases, the king is anxious to disclose his faults, but the effect of the disclosure in the medieval version is to provide material for the pope to use in preaching against the dangers of pride. Hunt's disclosure effaces the didactic purpose. Rather than being left with a sense of the danger of pride, the reader is left with a mouldering Sicilian history book. That book, of course, is also an official archival record and as such a tool of power that upholds the rights of the ruling class. Hunt has thus turned a gesture of spiritual humility into a justification for earthly hierarchy.

More fundamentally, as he appropriates the story of King Robert for his political and aesthetic purposes, Hunt seems unwilling or unable to grasp that the scribes who copied the medieval poem were untroubled by scruples about generic unity and straightforwardness. The textual evidence of the medieval poem *Robert of Sicily* suggests that scribes were quite comfortable with, and perhaps even actively sought out, a poem that defies pure generic categorization and that resists narrative impulses that foreclose generic possibilities. In short, the scribes resisted the limiting authority of unitary authorship. Indeed, as the poem was reauthored, its generic fissures enlarged as the emphasis of the tale was repeatedly redirected. Hunt's version, however, as a product of a literary culture that gave primacy to authorship and valorized the originality of the isolated creative genius, works to impose on the tale the supposedly unified and unifying generic direction of the epic romance, with its quasi-history, martial deeds and adventure. At the same time, paradoxically, given his century's greater distrust of divine authority, he tries to downplay didacticism, which, while nearly omnipresent in Middle English romance, is largely absent from modern understandings of the genre.

Longfellow's version of the Robert of Sicily story is found in *Tales of a Wayside Inn*, which was first published in 1863.[12] Like Hunt's 'Legend of King Robert', 'The Sicilian's Tale' is one of a series of tales. These tales are all ostensibly part of a pseudo-Chaucerian story-telling session at the famous hostelry in Massachusetts. That fact suggests that Longfellow's poem is to be judged as a

---

[12] Henry Wadsworth Longfellow, *Tales of a Wayside Inn* (1863; *The Poetical Works of Henry Wadsworth Longfellow*, vol. 4 [Boston, MA: Houghton, 1886]).

part of a whole evening of tale-telling rather than exclusively on its own merits. Thus, although there are striking similarities between the medieval poem and Longfellow's, the narrative potential of the story rather than its didactic moral is ultimately the *raison d'être* of 'The Sicilian's Tale'.

In many other ways, however, Longfellow's retelling remains quite faithful to the original Middle English versions. His use of understated humour captures well the occasional wry comedy found in all the versions of the medieval poem. When Robert is told the meaning of the Latin verse from the 'Magnificat', 'Deposuit potentes de sede / Et exaltavit humiles' ('He has put down the mighty from their thrones, / and exalted those of low degree' [Luke 1.52]),[13] Longfellow's hero mutters:

> "Tis well that such seditious words are sung
> Only by priests and in the Latin tongue;
> For unto priests and people be it known,
> There is no power can push me from my throne!'
> And leaning back, he yawned and fell asleep,
> Lulled by the chant monotonous and deep. (p. 46)

Longfellow's rhyme of 'asleep' and 'deep' emphasizes the humour of the situation: the mighty king is acting like a fidgety boy anxious to get out of church and scornful of the church's teachings, just as he is in the medieval versions: 'Hym þouhte he dwelled þer ful long' ('It seemed to him that he had been there a very long time' [V 32]). But Longfellow's poetry follows the later medieval versions in their more elaborately humorous descriptions of Robert as the fool, rather than the more economical earlier ones. Longfellow's fool rides 'Upon a piebald steed, with shambling gait, / His cloak of fox-tails flapping in the wind, / The solemn ape demurely perched behind' (p. 51) just as in the late medieval redactions in which the king rides 'Clad in a full sympull garment, / Wyth foxe tayles to renne a bowte: Men myght hym knowe in all þe rowte!' ('Clad in a very simple garment, with foxtails running around: People could recognize him in the crowd!' [F ll. 278–80]). Whether or not he was conscious of all the manuscript variations, Longfellow's transformation imposes on the poem a unified humorous tone, present in only some of the medieval versions.

The didactic theme that pervades all of the medieval versions of the Robert of Sicily story, however, is mostly absent from Longfellow's version, a transformation that must have been deliberate. In particular, the beginning and the ending of 'The Sicilian's Tale' place the medieval poem in a new light. Notably,

---

[13] *Oxford Annotated Bible, Revised Standard Version*, Herbert G. May and Bruce M. Metzger (eds), (New York: Oxford University Press, 1962).

in Longfellow's version, before the king distrusts the priest's words about being removed from power, Robert is never called proud. Consequently, instead of being an exemplar of the deadliest of sins, Robert is reduced to being a rather flippant doubter of divine authority. While a medieval audience might readily equate such doubt and defiance with the sin of pride, a modern audience would be less likely to leap to a theological conclusion. In any case, by weakening the linkage between Robert's private sins and his public actions, Longfellow dilutes the story's didactic impact.

Moreover, at the end of the story, Longfellow removes the original medieval ending and thus radically alters the narrative's thematic content. 'The Sicilian's Tale' ends immediately after Robert has been restored to the throne. No attempt is made to prove a moral either for those who are listening at the inn or for the reader, nor does Longfellow's version attempt to convince the audience of divine power. Unlike the medieval version, in which Robert undergoes almost ritualistic self-cleansing to rid himself of his sin and prepare for a holy death, Longfellow's king is left to live happily ever after.

I do not mean to suggest that Longfellow (or Hunt) was morally bound to provide the same didactic spin to his version of the story, only that such an omission is telling. Most obviously, it may reveal the start of a paradigm shift in the relative importance of religious instruction in a literary work with artistic aspirations. But that shift, more subtly, would also include the need to efface such instruction from previous texts of cultural foundation; in other words, it would be not only undesirable to write religious didactic literature, but also impractical for Longfellow to imagine that his literary forebears saw such didacticism as central to their literary missions.

The Danish play *Den forvandlede konge* (The Transformed King) by Rudolf Schmidt provides a very different version of the Robert of Sicily story.[14] Performed in Copenhagen in 1876 and translated into German in 1889, the play is more interesting for what it reveals about modern transformation of the medieval than for any intrinsic literary merit. Whether the play was ever performed in Germany or elsewhere after 1876 is unclear. Schmidt's verse play is a far looser adaptation of the story than Longfellow's or Hunt's, incorporating some elements of the Robert the Devil stories and *Jovinianus*, an analogue of *Robert of Sicily* found in the *Gesta Romanorum*. Along with switching the roles of some of the characters, Schmidt also adds new characters, including a female love

---

[14] Rudolf Schmidt, *Den forvandlede konge* (Copenhagen: Den Gyldendalske Boghandel, 1876). See also *Der verwandelte König*, German trans. Hermann Varnhagen (Erlangen: Deichert, 1889).

interest, Dione, for the king. The effect of these extra characters is to dilute somewhat the medieval poem's relentless focus on the main character as exemplar and to portray him instead in a more naturalistic way unknown to most medieval poetry, as one component in a larger sphere of social structures. As the play progresses, the king's actions are shaped not just by his interactions with the angel, as they are in the medieval poem, but also by his redemptive contact with Dione and his advisers. As a consequence, God's involvement in the king's affairs becomes less important than it is in the medieval poem.

Another significant change is that the main character is renamed Rodger in an attempt to make the action more congruent with actual Sicilian history for there was, as Hunt hints, no historical king Robert of Sicily. The Norman conqueror of Sicily, Robert Guiscard (the Astute, *c.* 1015–85), was never king; his nephew, Roger II (b. 1095), was the first king of Sicily, reigning from 1130 to 1154.[15] Schmidt seeks to provide his story with historical validity as Hunt does, but Schmidt's change is clearly more profound because it rejects any lingering remnant of medieval chronicle 'history' and replaces it with something that is, for Schmidt, far more satisfying: actual historical fact. Again, the movement away from the medieval poem's didacticism is clear; Schmidt maintains a positivistic, 'scientific' presentation through his appeal to verifiable history.

More startling than these changes are those which Schmidt makes to the medieval story's setting and theme. Schmidt keeps Sicily as his play's background, but it is clearly a differently conceived Sicily from that proposed by the medieval English poets. As he claims in his foreword, 'this island, which is notable for its natural wealth and bounty as well as for the fact that it has been home for vastly different races and nationalities, provided a good playing ground for the fantastic action'.[16] The nineteenth-century Romantic conceptions of nature and society, hinted at in this quotation, permeate the play's setting and action. Instead of the vague, interior scenes at court and church of the medieval poem, Schmidt's is a meticulously rendered *al fresco* Sicily. The stage directions, for example, reveal that the action in the first act takes place on 'an open, rocky field on the Ereta mountain near Panormus', i.e. Palermo, with a path crossing the bare mountain in the background.[17] Furthermore, in that rocky landscape, there is a chapel with the engraved inscription 'Deposuit de sede potentes et exaltavit humiles' (p. 1).

---

[15] John Julius Norwich, *The Normans in Sicily* (1967–70; Harmondsworth: Penguin, 1992), pp. 332–4, 754–5.

[16] 'Denne Ø, der er mærkelig ved sin Naturs Rigdom og Mangfoldighed saavelsom derved, at den har været Hjem for vidt forskellige Folkestammer og Nationaliteter, afgav en god Skueplads for den eventyrlige Handling' (Schmidt [p. v]). All quotations of Schmidt's play are from the original Danish. Translations in the body are my own.

[17] 'En aaben Klippeflade paa Bjerget Ereta i Nærheden af Panormus' (p. 1).

In short, the play commences in the outdoors, and the key Latin verse first appears in that outdoor setting rather than inside a church.

The verse becomes the focus of attention in Act 1, Scene 4, after Rodger's sin has become apparent. On the mountain path, a monk and children appear, singing the 'Deposuit' as they head home. While the characters are listening to the singing, a shrouded figure appears from inside the chapel and, standing on the church doorstep, declares, 'Listen to the song, Rodger; it sounds for you'.[18] Pointing to the chapel's inscription, the figure warns, 'The words of the song speak again from the stone!' and disappears.[19] Although the verse is sung by mortals, as it is in the medieval tale, the implication is clear that the monk and children are acting as mortal intermediaries for God's will. As a stunned character declares, 'Oh, King, Heaven's voice has spoken to you!'[20] That voice, again, has spoken to Rodger, not inside a church, but in the outdoors. In other words, while maintaining a 'Gothic' sensibility, Schmidt has here abandoned the medieval tale's emphasis on the centrality of the church's teaching. Perhaps to bolster Protestant notions of God's direct intervention in human affairs, Schmidt marginalizes the role of the monk, who appears in the background, and emphasizes that God himself has spoken directly to Rodger.[21] Even more, Schmidt seems interested in quasi-Romantic claims that ultimate truths are revealed in nature rather than through human institutions such as the Church.

That emphasis on the pre-eminent role of the earthly is continued in the resolution of Rodger's crisis. When Rodger eventually realizes his fault, he has learned it not by example of a biblical figure such as Nebuchadnezzar, the model for the medieval Robert, who sees the parallel unaided, but rather by talking to the rustic's daughter, Dione, who loves him. Having proclaimed 'My love is rich',[22] Dione is answered by Rodger, suddenly struck by the accuracy of the deposing angel's words: 'It was really true! In the speech of your lips I understand it.'[23] Here the link between the earthly (Dione's love) and the sacred is made fully explicit. In the rest of the play, Rodger shares his new-found humility — and the reasons for it — with all those he encounters. He even orders that the cap and cloak he has worn as a fool be carried before him at celebrations (p. 88), and the play closes with his declaration that 'the fool's bell-cap and his cloak shall, on this

---

18 'Til Sangen, Rodger, lyt; for dig den lød' (p. 17).

19 'Fra Stenen taler Sangens Ord paany!' (p. 18).

20 'O, Konge, Himlens Røst har til dig talt!' (p. 19).

21 This is not a strictly pro-Protestant move, however, since a picture of the Virgin Mary is visible through the chapel's open door (p. 17).

22 'Min Kærlighed er rig ... ' (p. 79).

23 'Det var dog Sandhed! / I dine Læbers Tale jeg forstaar den' (p. 80).

day, and onward till my death, constantly be found hung up on my throne!'[24] The king's fault, then, is transformed directly, through visual imagery, into a hortatory public reminder of the danger of pride. Although the emphasis is not historical, as it is in Hunt's version, the didacticism here is separated from the overtly religious environment that sponsors it in the medieval versions and replaced with Romantic (or even Wagnerian) conceptions of salvation. *Den forvandlede konge* is, in short, a moralistic play, but one which resists the medieval association of moral instruction with the Church and which portrays morality as an essentially public matter.

Darton's prose translation of *Robert of Sicily*, published as part of his 1907 collection entitled *A Wonder Book of Old Romance*, brings us closer again to the original medieval plot.[25] In abridging the tale, however, Darton shifts its emphasis again. The extent of Robert's penitence, for example, is greatly diminished, as the medieval refrain 'Lord, on þi fool þow haue pite!' ('Lord, have pity on your fool!' [V l. 348]), which reappears, in slightly different wordings five more times, is reduced by Darton to a single 'Have pity on Thy fool, O Lord' (p. 63). The ending, too, has a less religious tone. Darton's 'this is the tale that has been handed down concerning him' (p. 64) substitutes for the medieval prayers, admittedly conventionalized, that appear in different forms to close each of the medieval scribal versions. Moreover, while Hunt, Longfellow and Schmidt all treat the story of the proud king humbled as worthy of careful, adult attention, as did the medieval scribes,[26] this modern transformation of the poem is clearly aimed at children. This is obvious from the simplicity of the prose Darton uses and from the illustrations that accompany the text. Admittedly, the story of King Robert requires no special adult knowledge, but Darton's agenda for the tale seems patronizing, especially in light of his later claim in *Children's Books in England* (1932), that 'whatever their parentage and contents and literary form, [Middle English romances] all had this in common ... they were what they ever since remained, wonder-tales for simple minds'.[27] In other words, Darton felt not only justified but actually obliged by his view of literary history to make his version of *Robert of Sicily* seem like a children's story. A similar conception of medieval

---

[24] '... skal Narrens Bjældehue med hans Kappe / paa denne Dag, some til min Død fremdeles, / bestandig findes ophængt paa min Trone' (p. 90).

[25] Frederick J.H. Darton, *A Wonder Book of Old Romance* (London: Wells, 1907); reprinted as *Stories of Romance from the Age of Chivalry* (New York: Arlington, 1984).

[26] Of the surviving manuscripts, none shows any evidence that it contained texts directed at children or, indeed, anybody other than the reasonably well educated.

[27] Darton, *Children's Books in England: Five Centuries of Social Life* (Cambridge: Cambridge University Press, 1932), p. 34.

literature seems to have motivated two other transformers, Ascott R. Hope, who retells the tale in *Stories of Old Renown*, and Justin Huntly McCarthy, who weaves the tale (much elaborated) through his novel *The Proud Prince*.[28] Both of these also seem aimed at juvenile audiences. In each case, the shift of audience attacks the very foundations of the medieval poem's morality, which has no regard for age. In suggesting that medieval romance is a mode fit only for children, these transformations seem also to imply that only the young need worry about moral uprightness.

For aesthetic and ideological reasons, consciously perceived or not, Darton and the other transformers participated in a rewriting of the medieval aesthetic. This rewriting involved a recasting of sensibilities and narrative praxes to align them more strictly with modern conceptions of the interplay of art, religion and entertainment. The rewriting also depended upon a redrawing of the boundaries of medieval creativity and intellect. The tool of this rewriting — and also its effect — may be thought of as a sort of colonization of the medieval tale of Robert of Sicily.

Any twice-told tale may inevitably involve colonization of the original story, and that colonization may or may not be justified by the end result. In the case of the nineteenth- and twentieth-century versions of Robert of Sicily, the colonization did bring to light tales worth repeating in aesthetic environments suitable to a modern audience. The appropriation of the Robert story, however, was also undertaken as part of the nineteenth- and early twentieth-century quest to control what was to that culture the fascinating but dangerously polysemous Middle Ages. By limiting the text's production of meaning, whether by dismissing its original audience as naïve or by extracting the narrative's textual centre and discarding its original generic directions, these literary imperialists attempted to assert their dominance over the older historical period.

Hunt — in his day no mean expert on things medieval — and the other transformers were influenced by their culture's primary reaction to a historical and cultural 'other' in which, ironically, the roots of modern European culture were to be found. As Hans Aarsleff describes it,

> the Middle Ages [was] the most important object of literary and historical studies because much more than learned and academic matters was at stake. The sense of national identity, even of legitimacy and

[28] Ascott R. Hope, *Stories of Old Renown* (London: Blackie, 1883); Justin Huntly McCarthy, *The Proud Prince* (New York: Russell, 1903).

> autonomy, demanded possession of a past that was one's own, the older the better.[29]

It was therefore vital that the past be fully comprehensible, but inherent in Aarsleff's observation is the corollary that the past must also be relegated to a position of subjection, as both the origin of the current culture and its distinctly inferior predecessor.

When Hunt writes that he wants to 'make' something of *Robert of Sicily*, his implication is twofold. He does see the poem as valuable, worthy of preservation and a window on to the past. Yet at the same time he proclaims that past to have been less capable than Shakespeare and other Renaissance playwrights or, even, than he himself of fulfilling the story's promise. Caught up by his praise and distress, however, he ignores the untidy, uncontrollable multiplicity of meaning suggested by the radical scribal reauthoring in the poem's manuscripts, a multiplicity of meaning that proves that *Robert of Sicily*, far from being easily categorized by its medieval audience, was worthy of repeated generic reinterpretation. Medieval scribes had, in fact, 'made' something of the poem, but what they made of it would later confound the Romantic notion of a limited medieval capability and so would be conveniently brushed aside.

To say that the re-creators of *Robert of Sicily* wantonly misunderstood the text and violated the philosophy and aesthetics responsible for its medieval creation and preservation is not to say that the products of their labours are themselves without value. While enjoying these new artistic creations on their own merits, we would, however, also be wise to see these texts as heretofore overlooked signals in our own consideration of both nineteenth-century and current interpretations of the Middle Ages.[30]

Multiple and multifarious cultural, social and textual signification has, of course, frequently been ignored by revisers of the Middle Ages. As Alice Chandler points out in a discussion of Sir Walter Scott's medieval novels, 'While admitting the brutality of the middle ages, most ... historians [of Scott's era] thought that the period was redeemed by the chivalric insistence on the sanctity

---

[29] Hans Aarsleff, 'Scholarship and Ideology: Joseph Bédier's Critique of Romantic Medievalism', in Jerome J. McGann (ed.), *Historical Studies and Literary Criticism* (Madison, WI: University of Wisconsin Press, 1985), p. 104.

[30] As a caution, we would do well to recall Peter Faulkner's assessment of Furnivall's failure to engage with the complexities of 'historical development or civic institutions. ... If this strikes us today as naïve, we may find it useful to interrogate the politics of our own sophistication' ('"The Paths of Virtue and Early English": F.J. Furnivall and Victorian Medievalism', in John Simons (ed.), *From Medieval to Medievalism* ([New York: St Martin's, 1992], pp. 156–7).

of women and the inviolable right of the innocent and the weak'.[31] Chandler's observation, one of many comparable remarks that could be cited, reminds us that such an unproblematized view of medieval social interaction makes nonsense of medieval historical developments. A similarly unproblematized view of textual practice led the transformers of *Robert of Sicily* to be distressed at what recent scholars see rather as the happily disunified chorus of medieval voices, giving the lie to views of a supposedly unified, monolithic medieval world.

At the same time, these transformers were also deeply troubled by what probably still bothers most readers of the medieval poem today: its unrelenting and only occasionally optimistic didacticism. Of the four transformations discussed above, only one approaches the didacticism of the medieval versions, and even in that case the moralization is displaced from an origin in religious instruction. If we seek reasons for the recent literary decanonization of *Robert of Sicily*, we need not look much further than the medieval poem's strict morality, so much less genial, so much less forgiving than that of Chaucer or the Gawain-poet. Such a conclusion raises the uncomfortable possibility that, although we at the turn of the millennium may be more careful to acknowledge the complexity of the Middle Ages, we are only slightly more willing to embrace all its aspects than were the modern transformers of *Robert of Sicily*. Although they rewrote, recast and effaced the poem's religious basis, our scruples do not permit us to take such liberties with medieval literary history. They do, however, allow us to transform the legend of the proud king transformed in another way: if we ignore it, we seem to hope, it might just go away. In short, our interest in effacing the tale completely (through decanonization) coexists uneasily with our struggle to keep it on the scholarly agenda. This tension goes a long way towards elucidating and confirming the mixed motives of the modern transformers of the story of Robert of Sicily.

[31] Alice Chandler, 'Chivalry and Romance: Scott's Medieval Novels', *Studies in Romanticism* **14** (1975), p. 187.

Chapter 6

The modernist Orlando: Virginia Woolf's refashioning of Ariosto's *Orlando furioso*

Pauline Scott

In his seminal work *The Rise of Romance*, Eugène Vinaver referred to the romance genre as a 'carefully planned design ... charged with echoes of the past and premonitions of the future'.[1] This description indicates the degree to which romance as a form is characteristically open-ended: the complexity of its interwoven structure is never closed down or tied off, but stretches instead into a future when another story-teller picks up the threads and weaves on. This open-endedness is very likely the feature that most attracted Virginia Woolf to the genre as she prepared to write her novel *Orlando: A Biography*.[2] *Orlando* is a rather unique work in Woolf's *oeuvre*: bordering on the fantastic, it begins with a young nobleman in sixteenth-century England who lives about 300 years, inexplicably becomes a woman midway through his life,[3] marries, gives birth and is only 36 years of age when the story ends in 1928, the very moment at which Woolf was writing it. As the subtitle indicates, the novel was conceived as an imaginative biography of Woolf's friend (and possibly lover) Vita Sackville-West.[4] In her novel, Woolf both adopts and pokes fun at the conventions of biography while also intermingling elements of the chivalric romance. Woolf's

---

An earlier version of this paper was presented at the 111th Convention of the Modern Language Association in Chicago, Illinois, December 1995. I would like to express my gratitude to readers Jane Tylus, Robert Rodini and Dorinda Williams for their insightful comments and suggestions on the revision of this essay.

1 Eugène Vinaver, *The Rise of Romance* (1971; Totowa, NJ: Barnes, 1984), p. 92.

2 Virginia Woolf, *Orlando: A Biography* (New York: Harvest/Harcourt, 1928).

3 This plot twist either purposefully or coincidentally echoes Renaissance fears of gender instability. In sixteenth-century medical discourse, 'there were documented cases of women turning into men ... raising the unwelcome possibility ... that men could turn into women' (Valeria Finucci and Regina Schwartz [eds], *Desire in the Renaissance: Psychoanalysis and Literature* (Princeton, NJ: Princeton University Press, 1994), p. 6.

4 The exact nature of their relationship is the subject of much speculation. See, for example, Louise A. DeSalvo, 'Lighting the Cave: The Relationship between Vita Sackville-West and Virginia Woolf', *Signs* **8** (1982), pp. 195–214; Sherron E. Knopp, '"If I Saw You Would You Kiss Me?": Sapphism and the Subversiveness of Virginia Woolf's *Orlando*', *Publications of the Modern Language Association of America* **103** (1988), pp. 24–34.

incorporation of various literary forms demonstrates what Bakhtin has noted as the peculiar strength of the novel form: its ability to embrace other genres while maintaining its own integrity. In Bakhtin's words:

> The novel parodies other genres (precisely in their role as genres); it exposes the conventionality of their forms and their languages; it squeezes out some genres and incorporates others into its own peculiar structure reformulating and re-accentuating them.[5]

In adopting, parodying and reformulating other genres, the novel also revitalizes them and pays homage to its predecessors even as it concomitantly moves beyond them.

For Woolf, the peculiar tension between subversion and encomium was a hallmark of the position in which the woman writer inevitably finds herself. Woolf situates the first half of *Orlando* in the sixteenth century in order to establish the long tradition of Sackville-West's ancestry, but also in order to emphasize the overwhelming weight of the patriarchal literary tradition that confronts the modern woman writer. This tradition is symbolically represented in the novel by the poem that the protagonist works on through the centuries, a poem that significantly utilizes sections from Sackville-West's own prize-winning poem, *The Land*.

The first part of *Orlando* includes a fictionalization of Vita's actual affair with a married woman, Violet Treyfusis. The scandalous affair, which included a brief elopement to Paris, is represented in the novel in the story of Orlando's love for an exotic Russian woman named Sasha. Because of the potentially explosive nature of the subject of lesbianism in her day, Woolf was sensitive to the need to handle her representation of the episode with care.[6] Working as she was with themes of love and betrayal, and mindful of the need to couch the scandalous material in a more innocuous form, Woolf turned to the chivalric romance epic, in part because she considered the romance form to be an excellent means of 'disguise' for matters too personal (and perhaps too controversial) to write of directly. Her own comments on Sidney's *Arcadia* address this point:

> When Sidney hinted that his friends would like the book for its writer's sake, he meant perhaps that they would find there something that he

[5] M.M. Bakhtin, *The Dialogic Imagination* (Austin, TX: University of Texas Press, 1981), p. 5.

[6] An extensive account of the affair and Vita's love for Violet may be found in Nigel Nicolson, *Portrait of a Marriage* (London: Weidenfeld and Nicolson, 1973). See also Joanne Trautmann, *The* Jessamy Brides*: The Friendship of Virginia Woolf and Vita Sackville-West*, Penn State University Studies 36 (University Park, PA: Penn State University, 1973), p. 42.

> could say in no other form. .... There may be under the disguise of the Arcadia a real man trying to speak privately about something that is close to his heart.[7]

Like Sidney, Woolf was dealing with themes close to her heart in *Orlando*, and perhaps her own need for disguise led her to the romance as a viable vehicle for her own private communications.

In *Orlando* Vita is imagined as the sum of her ancestral parts, and events from her personal life are incorporated into an imaginatively reconstructed history of her ancestors. One of the primary inspirations for the historical trajectory of Woolf's novel was *Knole and the Sackvilles*, a book in which Vita chronicled the history of her ancestral home and its occupants.[8] Woolf was reading this book while she was writing *Orlando*, as we know from a letter she wrote to Sackville-West on 9 October 1927.[9] The other major subtext for Woolf's novel was Ariosto's chivalric epic *Orlando furioso*. In part, the *Furioso* as subtext may have been suggested to Woolf by Knole House itself. Louise De Salvo has pointed out that the opening passages of Woolf's novel refer specifically to a feature of one of the rooms at Knole: a tapestry depicting scenes from the *Orlando furioso*.[10] The presence of the tapestry in the first pages of the novel is not mere coincidence; the same arras is mentioned no less than five times throughout the course of the novel — at least once in each century described — and in every extended reference to Orlando's estate. The tapestry holds *Orlando* together and, as in its Ariostan predecessor, is both figured in the text and used as a figure for the text.[11] In *Orlando* the tapestry is an omnipresent background, fluttering in the slight breeze, always in motion, almost animate: 'The green arras with the hunters on it moved perpetually' (p. 14). The tapestry forges a direct link between the *Orlando furioso* and Woolf's novel. The opening passages of the novel evoke the world of the chivalric epic in their depiction of heroic battles fought by Orlando's ancestors against a 'pagan' foe, represented by a shrunken Moor's head:

---

7 Woolf, *The Second Common Reader* (New York: Harcourt, 1932), pp. 133–4.

8 Sackville-West, *Knole and the Sackvilles* (London: Heinemann, 1922).

9 On the influence of Vita's work on *Orlando*, see James Naremore, *The World Without a Self: Virginia Woolf and the Novel* (New Haven, CT: Yale University Press, 1973), pp. 202–8. For direct citations of Vita's book in *Orlando*, see Frank Baldanza, '*Orlando* and the Sackvilles', *Publications of the Modern Language Association of America* 70 (1955), pp. 274–9.

10 DeSalvo, 'A Note on the Tapestries at Knole House', *Virginia Woolf Miscellany* 12 (1979), pp. 3–4.

11 Peter DeSa Wiggins, *Figures in Ariosto's Tapestry: Character and Design in the* Orlando furioso (Baltimore, MD: The Johns Hopkins University Press, 1986).

> [Orlando] was in the act of slicing at the head of a Moor which hung from the rafters. It was the colour of an old football, and more or less the shape of one. ... Orlando's father, or perhaps his grandfather, had struck it from the shoulders of a vast Pagan who had started up under the moon in the barbarian fields of Africa; and now it swung, gently, perpetually, in the breeze which never ceased blowing through the attic rooms of the gigantic house of the lord who had slain him. (p. 13)

But Woolf's Orlando is woefully behind the times, the Moor's head is a shrunken remnant of a time long past, and the legendary battles of Christendom are now reduced to a child's game in a relic-filled attic. Given his noble lineage, Orlando both belongs to that past and yet is historically displaced from it. There is an indication that the men of the family are still occupied in missions of foreign conquest, and this accounts for the absence of male figures other than Orlando and the old gardener Stubbs. Precisely because of their absence, Orlando is able to deify them and to fantasize about one day escaping from the domestic, maternal sphere into the world of men and history:

> Orlando's fathers had ridden in fields of asphodel, and stony fields, and fields watered by strange rivers and they had struck many heads of many colours off many shoulders and brought them back to hang from the rafters. So too would Orlando, he vowed. But since he was sixteen only, and too young to ride with them in Africa or France, he would steal away from his mother and ... go to his attic room and there lunge and plunge and slice the air with his blade. Sometimes he cut the cord so that the skull bumped on the floor and he had to string it up again, fastening it with some chivalry almost out of reach so that his enemy grinned at him through shrunk, black lips. (pp. 13–14)

From the start, the relation of Woolf's novel to the chivalric epic tradition in general and to the *Orlando furioso* in particular is characterized by her protagonist's imitation of his chivalric epic predecessors. Patricia Feito has noted that 'with this exemplary modernist/deconstructivist "beginning" Woolf destabilizes at once the privileged position of historical discourse by making her initial scenario that of the most popular of sixteenth-century romances, the *Orlando furioso*'.[12] In fact, the entire first part of Woolf's novel, the story of Orlando's first love for the Russian princess Sasha, parallels the story of Orlando, the greatest of Charlemagne's Paladins, and Angelica, the Eastern princess who betrays his

[12] Patricia M. Feito, 'Gender, Sexuality, and Authority in the Modern British Novel: Virginia Woolf's *Orlando*, E.M. Forster's *Maurice*, and Joseph Conrad's *Chance*', dissertation, University of California-Irvine, 1990, p. 18.

love by marrying a lesser man.[13] Woolf's striking structural and thematic echoes of Ariosto's poem heighten the element of parody already found in the *Furioso*'s own relation to its lyric and chivalric predecessors. Ariosto had both reproduced and ironically challenged the Petrarchan representation of the ideal lady as a sum of perfect parts (golden hair, alabaster forehead, rose-red lips, etc.) by granting Angelica a mind and a libido of her own. Woolf turns this 'poetics of fragmentation' on its head once more by presenting a consummately romantic description of the beauty of Orlando as the sum of his parts, thereby subjecting the male to a voyeuristic, and ostensibly female, gaze.[14] Woolf's narrator introduces Orlando piece by piece:

> The red of the cheeks was covered with peach down ... the lips themselves were short and slightly drawn back over teeth of an exquisite and almond whiteness. Nothing disturbed the arrowy nose in its short, tense flight; the hair was dark, the ears small, and fitted closely to the head ... he had eyes like drenched violets, so large that the water seemed to have brimmed in them and widened them; and a brow like the swelling of a marble dome pressed between the two blank medallions which were his temples. (p. 15)

From the outset, Woolf's Orlando is objectified by the female gaze. After only one early encounter with Queen Elizabeth, the old woman is so struck by the young man's grace and physical beauty that she summons him back to her court when he comes of age. He quickly gains a coveted place by virtue of 'the finest legs that a young nobleman has ever stood upright upon; and violet eyes; and a heart of gold; and loyalty and manly charm ... ' (p. 23). The interest that Queen Elizabeth takes in her young cousin is clearly erotic; in a reversal of traditional gender roles, he is the object of her desire. The sexual aspects of their relationship are closely connected with her power as sovereign: 'At the height of her triumph when the guns were booming at the Tower ... she pulled him down among the cushions. ... "This" she breathed, "is my victory!" — even as a rocket roared up and dyed her cheeks scarlet' (p. 25).[15]

---

[13] It was with characteristic irony that Woolf selected her niece Angelica Bell to pose for the photograph in Orlando representing Sasha as a child. The identification of Bell as model was made by Trautmann (p. 42).

[14] The term 'poetics of fragmentation' is borrowed from Giuseppe Mazzotta, "The *Canzoniere* and the Language of the Self," *Studies in Philology* 75 (1978), p. 274.

[15] Woolf's representation of the rather comic lusting of the old Queen after the young Orlando may well be an irreverent parody of the relationship between Elizabeth I and the Earl of Essex; a relationship chronicled by Woolf's friend Lytton Strachey in his *Elizabeth and Essex: A Tragic History* (New York: Harcourt, 1928).

As Orlando moves closer to the centre of political power via the Queen's desire, he ironically moves further away from his dream of becoming a knight and winning fame in battle. Because of the depth of her attraction to the young man, the Queen can neither part with him nor allow him to risk any injury in service to his country. 'He was about to sail for the Polish wars when she recalled him. For how could she bear to think of that tender flesh torn and that curled head rolled in the dust? She kept him with her' (p. 25).

Like his counterpart in the *Furioso* who abandoned Charlemagne to pursue Angelica, Orlando is torn between the irreconcilable roles of warrior and lover; however, his subjection to the authority — and the desiring gaze — of the Queen keep him from having the opportunity to ever prove himself on the battlefield. In contrast to the romantically challenged Orlando of Ariosto's poem, the modern Orlando's conquests are exclusively of an amorous nature: 'He was young; he was boyish; he did but as nature bade him' (p. 28). In this way, Orlando is the inverse of his epic predecessor; somewhat effeminate in his looks, as much pursued as pursuer, sheltered and pampered rather than battle-worn and weary, Orlando's sense of adventure is satisfied only vicariously as he slips from the sheltered confines of the court to the beer gardens and docks to hear sailor's tales of far-off places and to pursue his pleasure with women of questionable virtue. As a man, Orlando can be forgiven his dalliances (even with the serving maids) as well as his excursions among the commoners, as long as he does not flout the responsibilities of his class. But when loyalty to his liege and position conflict with the pursuit of his desires, the result is disgrace and exile.

The love of Orlando's life, and his downfall, come during the extraordinary period of The Great Frost, a section of the novel fantastic in its hyperbolic extravagance:

> The severity of the frost was so extraordinary that a kind of petrifaction sometimes ensued; and it was commonly supposed that the great increase of rocks in some parts of Derbyshire was due ... to the solidification of unfortunate wayfarers who had been literally turned to stone where they stood. (p. 34)[16]

As a result of the frost the Thames freezes solid, immobilizing ships from around the world and forcing everything to a standstill. It is in this magical, static time that Orlando, by now betrothed to a rather dull but worthy noblewoman, encounters Sasha, a mysterious Russian:

---

[16] This sort of hyperbole, directly reminiscent of the type of wildly improbable events that Ariosto's poem attributes to the Archbishop Turpin, is particularly strong in this section of Woolf's narrative.

> He beheld, coming from the pavilion of the Muscovite Embassy, a figure, which, whether boy's or woman's, for the loose tunic and trousers of the Russian fashion served to disguise the sex, filled him with the highest curiosity ... extraordinary seductiveness ... issued from the whole person. (p. 37)

Although on first view he is unable to determine this person's sex, Orlando is none the less attracted as never before. Woolf again inverts gender roles, as the initial description of Sasha focuses on her strength and speed rather than her looks, thus causing Orlando to mistake her for a boy.

> When the boy, for alas, a boy it must be — no woman could skate with such speed and vigor — swept almost on tiptoe past him, Orlando was ready to tear his hair with vexation that the person was of his own sex. (p. 38)

For the first time in his life, Orlando is at a loss as to how to approach the object of his desire. The inevitable seduction is the result of Orlando's facility with languages: unable to speak English, Sasha communicates with the court in French, but only Orlando is able to respond. Like his poetic ancestor, Orlando is a polyglot whose linguistic ability is a double-edged sword. Whereas Ariosto's Orlando was able to decipher Medoro's poem and discover Angelica's marriage because of his ability to read Arabic, Woolf's Orlando is able to gain access to Sasha because of his fluency in French. As a result of his linguistic ability, Orlando succeeds in consummating his desire; yet because of that very success, he suffers the worst defeat of his life: abandonment and betrayal by the woman he loves.

Orlando's affair with Sasha effectively parodies the chivalric theme of divided loyalty to duty. His constant attention to this dubious foreigner and slighting of his wealthy and noble fiancée becomes the scandal of the court; by extension, it constitutes a betrayal of his class and his duty to his liege, by this time James I. At the same time, Woolf ironically describes the complete transformation of the inappropriately infatuated Orlando into the epitome of the perfect lover:

> the change in Orlando himself was extraordinary. ... In one night he had thrown off his boyish clumsiness; he was changed from a sulky stripling, who could not enter a lady's room without sweeping half the ornaments from the table, to a nobleman, full of grace and manly courtesy. (pp. 41–2)

Despite his new perfection as a lover, the inappropriateness of the object of his desire — apparent in the repeated disdainful references to Sasha as 'the Muscovite' and in Orlando's suspicion that she is of relatively low birth — presages the inevitably tragic outcome.

In the *Furioso*, Orlando's greatest fear had been that someone else would come along and pluck the flower of Angelica's virginity before he got the chance:

> e il fior ch'in ciel potea pormi fra i dei,
> il fior ch'intatto io mi venìa serbando
> per non turbarti, ohimè! l'animo casto
> ohimè! per forza avranno colto e guasto. (11. 8.77.5–8)[17]
>
> (And your flower, which could have set me among the heavenly gods, the flower which I preserved for you intact, so as not to sadden your chaste heart, will they, alas, have plucked and despoiled it? [Waldman trans., p. 79])

His impulse was to contain and control her sexuality through his insistence on her chastity and his absolute possession of her. Woolf's Orlando is similarly tormented by doubts and subject to fits of obsessive jealousy. Although he initially enjoyed Sasha's passion, he gradually comes to fear the very nature of her enticing sensuality. Even at the peak of his passion, marvelling that the ice beneath them does not melt from their sexual heat, his lingering doubts about her crop up from time to time to disturb his happiness: 'however open she seemed and voluptuous, there was something hidden; in all she did, however daring, there was something concealed' (p. 47). The dark forebodings he experiences are an eruption of his repressed fears about her assertive sexuality, the passionate jealousy he feels causes him to flare out in uncontrollable rages.

> What, then, did she hide from him? The doubt underlying the tremendous force of his feelings was like quicksand beneath a monument which shifts suddenly and makes the whole pile shake ... then he would blaze out in such a wrath that she did not know how to quiet him. (p. 49)

The force of Orlando's wrath is uncontainable, and it rises out of his perception that Sasha's sexuality is similarly uncontainable and ultimately impossible to possess. He thinks only of 'making her irrevocably and indissolubly his own' (p. 50).

In the climactic scene of the *Orlando furioso*, Canto 23, the hero came face to face with proof of Angelica's active sexuality in the form of a poem written by her new husband that graphically detailed their love-making. The poem is carved into the wall of a cave located in an idyllic bower where the weary Orlando had

[17] Lodovico Ariosto, *Orlando furioso*, ed. Marcello Turchi, 2 vols (1974; Milan: Garzanti, 1982); *idem*, *Orlando furioso*, trans. Guido Waldman (Oxford: Oxford University Press, 1974).

stopped to rest. Upon entering the bower, Orlando had first seen the names of Medoro and Angelica inscribed into rocks and trees, and recognized the handwriting as that of Angelica. Faced with evidence of Angelica's attachment to another man, Orlando initially attempted to revise the meaning of the inscriptions, reasoning that perhaps 'Medoro' was a code-name for himself. However, with the discovery of Medoro's poem and later confirmation by a shepherd that Angelica had indeed married, Orlando inevitably goes insane. Just as Ariosto's Orlando continued to repress his doubts and fears about Angelica's virginity for as long as he could, Woolf's Orlando repeatedly suppresses his own suspicions of Sasha's too open sexuality. His fervent desire to idealize Sasha, however, suffers the final blow in an incident that takes place on the Muscovite ship, an incident significant for its many parallels to the bower scene in the Ariostan model.

In Canto 23 of the *Furioso*, Orlando was forced to finally confront the truth that Angelica had rejected his love and replaced him with a man he deemed undeserving because of his lower class and lack of heroism. Medoro, the man with whom Angelica falls madly in love, is a mere Arabian foot-soldier who has never distinguished himself in battle; in fact, he is captured and wounded while in the process of killing enemy soldiers as they lay sleeping. Medoro stands as the opposite of Orlando in nearly every way, not the least in his delicate, almost feminine appearance. In describing the effect that Medoro's beauty has on the smitten Angelica, Ariosto subverts the courtly tradition by reversing gender roles, casting the formerly cold, disdainful maiden in the role of Love's thrall:

> Assai più larga piaga e più profonda
> nel cor sentì da non veduto strale,
> che da' begli occhi e da la testa bionda
> di Medoro aventò l'Arcier c'ha l'ale. (ll. 19.28.1–4)
>
> (In her own heart she felt a far wider, deeper wound made by an unseen arrow shot by the Winged Archer from the dazzling eyes and golden curls of Medor [p. 219]).

Medoro's feminized beauty finally succeeds where other suitors' masculine prowess had failed. Whereas Orlando had always assumed that Angelica belonged to him by dint of his fame, she slips from the position of passive object of his — and every other man's — desire into the role of desiring subject. Her pursuit of Medoro is aggressive, and her desire for him insatiable:

> Se di disio non vuol morir, bisogna
> che senza indugio ella se stessa aiti:
> e ben le par che di quel ch'essa agogna,
> non sia tempo aspettar ch'altri la 'nviti.

Dunque, rotto ogni freno di vergogna,
la lingua ebbe non men che gli occhi arditi;
e di quel colpo domandò mercede,
che, forse non sapendo, esso le diede. (ll. 19.30.1–8)

[...]

Più lunge non vedea del giovinetto
la donna, né di lui potea saziarsi;
né, per mai sempre pendergli dal collo,
il suo disir sentia di lui satollo. (ll. 19.34.5–8)

(If she was not to die of longing, she would have to help herself without delay: it was clear to her that there was no time to wait until she was invited to take what she craved. So, snapping the reins of modesty, she spoke out as boldly with her tongue as with her eyes and asked for mercy there and then — which he, perhaps unknowingly, conceded to her. ... The damsel could look no further than the youth. She could never have enough of him: though she clung constantly round his neck, her appetite for him never cloyed. [p. 220])

Medoro's seeming *naïveté* and Angelica's usurpation of the role of sexual aggressor neatly reverse their roles: Angelica is transformed from pursued to pursuer. This change is so radical that, upon discovering that she has married Medoro, Orlando is completely unable to comprehend how such a thing could have happened.[18] The tripartite configuration of Orlando as pursuer, Angelica as pursued turned pursuer, and Medoro as pursued, creates a frightening sense of instability as traditional gender roles are interchanged. Ariosto's triangulation blurs the bipolar opposition of male and female, with Medoro functioning as a middle point:[19] although he does not embody the overtly masculine qualities of Orlando (strength, bravery, etc.), he nevertheless succeeds in winning the most sought after woman for his wife. For the triumphant Medoro, his beauty is his greatest asset.

---

[18] Deanna Shemek discusses Angelica's assumption of the position of desiring subject as a disruptive force in Ariosto's poem, even suggesting that 'Orlando's case suggests that belief in ... pure otherness is perhaps the most destructive force within the narrative of the poem' ('That Elusive Object of Desire: Angelica in the *Orlando furioso*', *Annali d'Italianistica* 7 [1989], p. 117).

[19] The foundational study of the triangular dynamic of desire and its relation to the novel is René Girard's *Deceit, Desire, and the Novel: Self and Other in Literary Structure*, trans. Yvonne Freccero (Baltimore, MD: The Johns Hopkins University Press, 1965). Both Ariosto's and Woolf's depictions of triangulated relationships, however, represent variations on the Girardian paradigm.

If we take into account the presence of Medoro in the Orlando–Angelica story, and read that story as a subtext for the Orlando–Sasha relationship in the modern novel, we may read Woolf's Orlando as a complex amalgam of qualities. Like his namesake, Woolf's Orlando possesses the attributes of nobility and a brilliant reputation (though his fame is for feats of love rather than of arms). But like Medoro, Woolf's Orlando also possesses grace and beauty and, as a result, is the object of female desire from women throughout the kingdom, even from no less a personage than the Queen herself. As such, this modern Orlando unites the seemingly disparate qualities of masculinity and femininity in a way that prefigures his ultimate transformation from man to woman.

Woolf gradually dismantles the bipolar, male/female opposition by means of her emphasis on androgynous appearance in the initial descriptions of both Orlando and Sasha. The first words of the novel allude to some degree of androgyny in Orlando's appearance, an effect attributed to 'the fashion of the time' (p. 13). Similarly, the description of Orlando's first impression of Sasha also attributes her gender indeterminacy to her clothing:

> he beheld, coming from the pavilion of the Muscovite Embassy, a figure, which, whether boy's or woman's, for the loose tunic and trousers of the Russian fashion served to disguise the sex, filled him with the highest curiosity. (p. 37)

The narrator's comments on their respective attire imply that English dress is the more effeminate and helps to obscure Orlando's masculinity, while Sasha's looser Russian clothing hides the womanly curves of her body. In each case, it is not merely the apparel, but also the physical attributes of the individual — Orlando's delicate features and Sasha's athleticism — that contribute to effacing gender. This implies that the clothes only complement an underlying indeterminacy that is intrinsic to the individual.[20] The androgyny attached to each of these two characters is one way that Woolf's novel dismantles the bipolar opposition of gender. It is a strategy similar to that described by Marjorie Garber in her analysis of the function of contemporary cross-dressing as 'an undertheorized recognition of the necessary critique of binary thinking, whether particularized as male and female, black and white ... or in any other way'.[21] Even though Orlando and Sasha are not really cross-dressed, but ambiguously and therefore androgynously clothed, Woolf's presentation of the essential androgyny of each lover functions

---

[20] For another view of androgyny and dress in *Orlando*, see Sandra M. Gilbert, "Costumes of the Mind: Transvestism as Metaphor in Modern Literature," in Elizabeth Abel (ed.), *Writings and Sexual Difference* (Chicago, IL: University of Chicago Press, 1982), pp. 206–8.

[21] Marjorie Garber, *Vested Interests: Cross-Dressing and Cultural Anxiety* (New York: Routledge, 1992), pp. 10–11.

as a critique of the social roles ascribed to each by means of their gender. Woolf further confounds gender categorization by linking the characters' androgyny to cultural practices. The effeminacy of Elizabethan dress implies a certain effeminacy in a culture where the warrior has been replaced by the courtier and, by the same token, Sasha's dress is customary to the practical considerations of her culture. Her clothing is as mysterious and unreadable to Orlando as her sex; its indecipherability stimulates and provokes his intense curiosity.

Unlike Ariosto's presentation of the Medoro–Angelica relationship, however, Woolf's Orlando–Sasha coupling does more than merely reverse gender roles; it confounds them in increasingly complex ways. Utilizing a dynamic similar to the one found in the *Furioso*, Woolf presents a complex triangulation of desire in her account of the Orlando–Sasha relationship in a scene that closely parallels the account of the onset of Orlando's madness in the *Furioso*, Canto 23. Orlando's discovery of Medoro's poem detailing the events of his marriage to Angelica and his attempts to wilfully misinterpret it constituted a kind of primal scene through which Orlando was symbolically emasculated by the image — presented in the poem — of a nude Angelica in Medoro's arms. Unable to reconcile himself to this image and to his replacement by an inferior rival, Orlando lapsed into madness. In Woolf's recasting of this scene, Orlando waits dreamily for Sasha on the deck of the Russian ship, while his beloved, accompanied by a crew member, goes below. Realizing that she has been gone for some time, Orlando's suspicions return:

> Seized instantly with those dark forebodings which shadowed even his most confident thoughts of her, he plunged the way he had seen them go. ... For one second, he had a vision of them; saw Sasha seated on the sailor's knee; saw her bend towards him; saw them embrace before the light was blotted out in a red cloud by his rage. He blazed into such a howl of anguish that the whole ship echoed. ... Then a deadly sickness came over Orlando, and they had to lay him on the floor and give him brandy to drink before he revived. (p. 51)

Whereas Ariosto's Orlando arrived belatedly at the scene of Angelica and Medoro's nuptials and experienced Angelica's betrayal of his love second-hand through reading Medoro's poem, Woolf's Orlando actually witnesses his betrayal by Sasha. Unable to face his beloved's infidelity, Orlando falls senseless to the floor. Regaining consciousness, Orlando immediately begins to doubt what he has seen. As Sasha hovers over him 'now cajoling, now denouncing', Orlando begins to 'unremember', to engage in the same kind of self-deception and wilful misinterpretation of the evidence as did his predecessor in the *Furioso*. 'Looking at them together ... Orlando was outraged by the foulness of his imagination that could have painted so frail a creature in the paws of that hairy sea brute' (p. 52).

To a large extent, Orlando's inability to believe what he has seen results from his deeply ingrained sense of class distinction that causes him to recoil from even imagining a sexual union between a noblewoman and a 'common seaman'. The immense physical presence of this man, his inferior social position and the darker colour of his skin all contrast sharply with the refined nobility of Orlando. The sailor 'stood six feet four in his stockings; wore common wire rings in his ears; and looked like a dray horse' (p. 52). Comparing the man to a 'dray horse', a 'sea brute', and a 'tawny wide-cheeked monster', Orlando objectifies his humanity and equates difference with bestiality; the man's tawny skin and wide cheeks mark him as monstrous in the protagonist's eyes and further enable him to reject even the idea that Sasha could have any involvement with such a man. Orlando is here caught up in the beginnings of the subtle paradox that will ultimately undo him, denouncing the sailor for his difference while trying simultaneously to deny his own cultural, social and sexual differences from Sasha. The major aspects of Woolf's scenario — the assumption of entitlement on the part of the noble lover, the assertive sexuality of the woman, the encounter of the male lover with evidence of sexual betrayal — all duplicate the basic elements of her Ariostan subtext. Woolf further replicates the multiple permutations of difference represented in the Orlando–Angelica story: class, sex and race. Orlando's horror at the seaman's dark skin and exotic looks leads him to consider the sailor as a 'tawny wide-cheeked monster' who is not only culturally, but even racially different from himself. What Orlando fails to acknowledge, and finally is forced to confront, is the common bond of nationality shared by Sasha and this 'monster'. Just as in the *Furioso* where the Eastern princess Angelica ultimately bonds with a man of a non-European race, the reality that the bond between Sasha and the sailor is one in which Orlando can never share is evidenced in his feeling of exclusion as the two converse in their native tongue: 'Sasha paused with her hand on the ladder and called back to this tawny wide-cheeked monster a volley of Russian greetings, jests, or endearments, not a word of which Orlando could understand' (p. 52).

Woolf's description of Orlando's response to the sailor's 'brute' physicality is psychologically rich. As he witnesses the reality of Sasha's infidelity, it is initially the spectacle of her sexuality, directed toward another man, that strikes him as monstrous. But as she turns her attention back to him 'now cajoling, now denouncing', he begins instead to project the 'monstrosity' of his vision solely on to the sailor. In the process he restores Sasha in his mind to the purer, utterly unrealistic image he has struggled all along to maintain of her, even going so far as to beg her pardon. However, just as Ariosto's Orlando was unable to purge the vision of Angelica coupling with Medoro from his tormented mind, the vision of Sasha on the sailor's knee, once seen, can never been entirely eradicated from the modern Orlando's consciousness. Yet we must recall that the sexual indiscriminacy demonstrated by Sasha that so offends Orlando is the very behaviour of which he himself had been guilty in his many dalliances with women of the lower classes. Underlying this episode is Woolf's implicit critique of the hypocrisy that was part of not only of her protagonist, but of his entire culture.

Consumed by doubt about what did or did not happen on the Russian ship, Orlando's ire is momentarily placated by Sasha's tender flattery. This momentary calm is broken, however, as Orlando and Sasha view a court production of Shakespeare's *Othello*. The subsequent violence of Orlando's feeling towards Sasha is related to his inability to deal with her sexuality: he now imagines killing her with his bare hands. His wish to control and to dominate her extends to murderous thoughts and causes him to feel a strange identification with the protagonist of the tragedy: 'The frenzy of the Moor seemed to him his own frenzy, and when the Moor suffocated the woman in her bed, it was Sasha he killed with his own hands' (p. 57). The violence that Orlando wants to wreak on Sasha's body is proportionate to the violence that his love for her has done to his naïve conception of love as eternal and transcendent — of the soul and heart, rather than of the body — and echoes the violence wrought by Ariosto's Orlando on the trees and rocks of the bower containing Medoro's poem.

When confronted with the irreconcilable contradiction of his love and hate for Sasha, and frightened by the intensity of his reaction to the dramatic enactment of the murder of Desdemona, Orlando's response is the desire to act on his prearranged plan to run away with her, and to symbolically flee his fears and doubts in the process. Orlando invests everything in Sasha's going away with him; if she goes, she will have chosen him, she will have renounced her people, her position and, most importantly, any other men, to be with Orlando.[22] Like the protagonist of the *Furioso*, Orlando wants to see himself reflected in his lover's eyes; by being everything to Sasha, Orlando himself can finally be something. She will invest his life with new meaning to replace the emptiness he has always felt among his own countrymen.

The appointed hour approaches while he waits for her at their prearranged meeting place at an inn near Blackfriars. As the clock rings out the strokes of midnight with Sasha nowhere in sight, Orlando begins to realize that he has been betrayed:

> The passionate and feeling heart of Orlando knew the truth. Other clocks struck, jangling one after another. The whole world seemed to ring with the news of her deceit and his derision. The old suspicions subterraneously at work in him rushed forth from concealment openly. He was bitten by a swarm of snakes, each more poisonous than the last. He stood in the doorway in the tremendous rain without moving. (p. 61)

[22] Interestingly, Orlando does not seem to consider the equally bleak reciprocal consequences for himself.

Orlando's humiliation is complete; the 'whole world' seemed to know that Sasha had made a fool of him. Meanwhile, The Great Frost comes to an end. Orlando stands as if frozen while the ice melts around him, as stone-like as was the other Orlando when faced with Medoro's poem.[23] Nature expresses the fury and chaos that Orlando feels: 'The downpour rushed on. In the thick of it, great guns seemed to boom. Huge noises as of the tearing and rending of trees could be heard. There were also wild cries and terrible inhuman groanings. But Orlando stood there immovable ... ' (p. 61). Sasha's betrayal echoes that of Angelica, and the tearing and rending of the oaks, the wild cries and inhuman groans echo the earlier Orlando's 'furor': in Woolf's version, nature itself is rendered 'furioso' by Sasha's departure. When the dumbfounded Orlando finally regains his mobility, he rides to the river in search of the Russian ship. The flag, far out at sea, announces definitively that Sasha is gone. Again, Woolf stands literary convention on its head: gender roles are reversed as Sasha sails off while Orlando is left behind, alone on the coast like the archetypal abandoned woman, a Dido, an Ariadne, an Olimpia.

In both Ariosto and Woolf, the inversion of the courtly ideal of the perfect lover is accomplished by means of a reversal of gender roles: in each relationship, the woman rides or sails off to new adventures, leaving the lover behind and bereft. In both cases, the active sexuality of the women characters and their adoption of the subject, rather than object, position in relation to men constitutes a degree of female empowerment that severely challenges the dominant order of the chivalric-romantic ideology and leaves the male lover adrift and without identity. The consequence of the two Orlandos' painful recognition of the alterity and agency of the beloved (Angelica and Sasha respectively), is a falling into chaos, a world turned upside down and emptied of its meaning because the production of the male 'I' within the context of Ariosto's chivalric epic poem was predicated on a static and acquiescent female 'other' who, Ariosto and Woolf imply, does not exist. Woolf's transformation of her subtext into a farcical examination of the rigid patriarchal enforcement of traditional gender norms culminates in the final revelation that Orlando's gender transformation from man to woman ultimately costs her the estate she so loves, just as Vita tragically lost her beloved Knole House to the claim of a distant male relative. In upsetting traditional gender roles and unsettling clear distinctions between 'masculine' and 'feminine', Ariosto and Woolf each construct a critique of the gender-based social inequities that underlie the dominant discourses of their day. This is perhaps the most subversive statement that either could have made.

[23] 'Rimase al fin con gli occhi e con la mente / fissi nel sasso, al sasso indifferente' (Ariosto, *Orlando furioso*, ll. 23.111.7–8); ('Finally he fell to gazing fixedly at the stone — stone-like himself' [Waldman trans., p. 279]).

Chapter 7

Re-visible Spenser: the quest in Ralph Ellison's *Invisible Man*

Christine Herold

This chapter comprises a comparative analysis of what may seem to be strange print-fellows, Ralph Ellison's *Invisible Man* and Edmund Spenser's *The Faerie Queene*.[1] It is my contention that Ellison intended his novel as a modern Black version of the Renaissance English romance. Symbolic objects and allegorical episodes from Cantos 1–12 of Book One of *The Faerie Queene* are re-created in a twentieth-century American context. This modernized setting permits Ellison to examine the issues, barriers, torments and rewards for a coming-of-age quest that is at once socially and politically archetypal and contemporary, as was Spenser's work in its day. By playing off the 'establishment' goals and ideals of the Renaissance of English society against the historical and personal issues of a Black American struggle for individuation, Ellison reveals the paradoxical similarities and striking differences between the two cultural positions. Eric Sundquist broadly acknowledges Ellison's debt to 'paradigms of the quest narrative drawn from world literature — from the *Odyssey* and the *Aeneid* to *Don Quixote* and *Moby-Dick*'. Ellison himself acknowledges his debt to Shakespeare, among other Renaissance authors. Sundquist further states, '*Invisible Man* thus adds fragments, echoes, and whole passages from black public history in order to restructure the struggle for freedom and racial equality in the United States according to classic literary models'.[2] I would add to those sources noted by Sundquist one that has thus far escaped recognition: *The Faerie Queene*. Once this well-known European model has been recognized, one can better appreciate the extraordinary tensions consciously invoked by Ellison's combining White European and Black American literary and cultural traditions. I conclude that in these structural and thematic syntheses Ralph Ellison has created a literary work

---

An earlier version of this paper was presented at the Tenth International Conference on Medievalism, held in Worcester, Massachusetts, September 1995.

[1] All quotations of Ralph Ellison's *Invisible Man* are taken from the Vintage Books Edition (New York: Random, 1989). All quotations of Edmund Spenser's *The Faerie Queene* are taken from a facsimile of the 1596 edition, intro. Graham Hough, 2 vols (London: Scolar, 1976).

[2] Eric J. Sundquist, *Cultural Contexts for Ralph Ellison's 'Invisible Man'* (Boston, MA: Bedford-St Martin's, 1995), p. 5.

that embodies and promotes the author's integrationist philosophy of American life.

It was at Douglass High School that Ralph Ellison assimilated the knowledge and love of Renaissance poetry into the other elements of his American heritage. Thus, Elizabethan English literature and its traditional philosophical-poetic quest for individuation and enlightenment held its respected place in Ellison's intellectual development, alongside Afro-American English and the equally respected native musical traditions of jazz and the spiritual.[3] 'Going to the Territory' is Ellison's metaphor for his integrationist philosophy. It refers to the mutually catalytic effect of the often historically invisible mingling of White European and Black African cultural traditions and sense of individual identity. It is the quest for this elusive individual and true collective identity amidst the tensions of suppressed recognition of similarity and artificial constructs of historical difference that constitutes the mimetic and allegorical plot which places Ellison's *Invisible Man* in the tradition of Spenser's *The Faerie Queene*.

Ellison conceived of the experiences of his protagonist as 'a number of rites of passage, rites of initiation'.[4] His protagonist is at once an individual character and a representative type. Beside the realistic elements in his characters and plots, Ellison explicitly calls attention to their symbolic and mythic meanings as well. He describes this mythic level of meaning as it applies to a boxing match among blindfolded boys staged for the entertainment of a group of adult white men. The scene is described with all the militaristic grandeur and human futility of an epic confrontation between man and superhuman or divine opponent. It is reminiscent of the trick played on Gawain by Morgan the Goddess, the Redcrosse Knight's losing battle with Orgoglio or Gloucester's observation in Shakespeare's *Lear* that the gods torment us for their sport. In the 'battle royal', as he names it, Ellison's protagonist displays that determination and greatness of spirit with which epic heroes thrust themselves recklessly towards overpowering foes. On another level Ellison's 'battle royal' is an autobiographical event, reflecting allegorically the actual struggle of an American Black against an overwhelming White power structure. Ellison discusses his allegorical method:

> as one who was reading a lot about myth and the function of myth and ritual in literature, it was necessary that I see the 'battle royal' situation as something more than a group of white men having sadistic fun with a group of Negro boys. Indeed, I would have to see it for what it was beyond the question of the racial identities of the actors involved: a

---

[3] Ellison, 'Going to the Territory', *Going to the Territory* (New York: Random, 1987), pp. 125, 137.

[4] Ellison, 'On Initiation Rites and Power', *Going to the Territory*, p. 49.

> ritual through which important social values were projected and reinforced.[5]

Ellison identifies one of the purposes of his novel as revealing the 'sacred values' of American national identity through dramatization of ritual reversals of those values as they inform collective and individual behaviour. Ellison sees ignorance of the meaning and function of America's own inherited and amalgamated rituals as a great social and psychological fault.[6] In his stated allegorical purpose, Ellison acquires the weight of literary responsibility sought by Greek drama and Christian romantic epic. Ellison casts his protagonist initially as an innocent 'fool' (modelled on the sacred fools of ancient initiation rituals) whose idealism and 'passion' lead him on a fantastic quest for identity and truth.

Despite these similarities of purpose, however, we see the crux of the relationship between Ellison's novel and Spenser's poem in the sparks that fly when a Black American writer of the twentieth century confronts the value system expressed in a sixteenth-century English allegorical poem. Ellison takes the English Renaissance mode of individuation and the Spenserian allegorical language, and makes their incongruities for the plight and appearance of a Black American protagonist the starting-point for a quest that goes beyond the safety of illusory individuation within the stylized collective of orthodox behaviour. Such a reworking of the Spenserian quest challenges the easy answers of Spenser's black-and-white value system with a more complex, more frighteningly heroic overturning of the dragons of allegorical stereotyping. Ellison's is a self-questioning quest that overthrows the certainties of the old spiritual system of white Christian supremacy and replaces them with the potential openness of true integration, with its potential for true individuation. Identity and individual responsibility are guiding themes for Ellison. His lesser characters, and especially his antagonists, are programmed in their behaviour according to a rigid, theoretical system. By contrast, his hero is expected to respond individually, morally, consciously and intentionally to each new situation and to every unfamiliar personal or social challenge. He fails repeatedly, but he — and we — are more aware of the necessity for conscious moral action, especially with each additional failure due to repeated lapses into theoretically stylized modes of behaviour. According to Ellison, 'our failure to deal with the mystery of our diversity' prevents us from realizing our potential for freedom and self-awareness.[7] This is the moral message of *Invisible Man*; it is a message, however, that Ellison feels most Americans would rather avoid.[8]

---

[5] Ellison, 'On Initiation', pp. 49–50.

[6] Ibid., pp. 50–51.

[7] Ibid., p. 52.

[8] Ellison, 'Society, Morality, and the Novel', *Going to the Territory*, p. 261.

Such diversity has no place in the racially and theologically exclusive orthodoxy of *The Faerie Queene*. The protagonist in *Invisible Man* represents what is alien to the traditional Everyman, but without completely discarding the earlier model. For Ellison a primary function of the American novel is to 'identify that which is basic in man beyond all differences of class, race, wealth, or formal education'; in effect, to fashion a new Everyman, an all-inclusive moral being to replace the old exclusionary European Everyman.[9] 'It must be remembered', Ellison writes, 'that we are a continuation of a European civilization, not a thing in ourselves, although our variations upon the theme, our amplification of the themes, are unique'.[10] The Invisible Man embodies an ethnic mixture (descendant of master and slave) and pastiche of cultural traditions that distinguishes him as Other than the Anglo-Saxon Christian hero. He is not, therefore, invisible because of what is not there; rather, he is everything that is there in white America which white America refuses to acknowledge. By placing his non-canonical hero in a canonical environment, Ellison exposes the narrowness of the canonical ideal on the social as well as on the individual allegorical levels.

The following words initiate Invisible Man's quest for identity:

> He was an odd guy, my grandfather, and I am told I take after him. It was he who caused the trouble. On his death-bed he called my father to him and said, 'Son, after I'm gone I want you to keep up the good fight. I never told you, but our life is a war and I have been a traitor all my born days, a spy in the enemy's country ever since I give up my gun back in the Reconstruction. Live with your head in the lion's mouth. I want you to overcome 'em with yeses, undermine 'em with grins, agree 'em to death and destruction, let 'em swoller you till they vomit or bust wide open. ... Learn it to the younguns', he whispered fiercely; then he died. (p. 16)

Grandfather's instructions represent themselves as a great and mysterious element of the truth, the self-knowledge, that becomes the object of the boy's quest. The old man describes the mission he bequeaths to his offspring in militaristic terms: 'our life is a war'. Ellison's young protagonist resembles Spenser's description of the young untried warrior Redcrosse in the opening canto of *The Faerie Queene*: 'armes till that time did he neuer wield' (ll. 1.1.5). Ellison's hero, like Spenser's, bears the marks of his people's brutal history. The youthful knight, 'Ycladd in mightie armes and siluer shielde, / Wherein old dints of deepe wounds did remaine, / The cruell markes of many'a bloudy fielde' (ll. 1.1.2–4), prefigures Ellison's boy, his eye swollen, head pounding, mouth dripping bloody saliva,

---

[9] Ibid., pp. 273–4.

[10] Ellison, 'The Novel as a Function of American Democracy', *Going to the Territory*, p. 312.

gripping his 'badge of office', the 'gleaming calfskin brief case' (p. 32). The Knight of the Red Cross faces, as his first foe, 'a Dragon horrible and stearne' (ll. 1.1.27), Foule Errour. The enemy in Ellison's quest, the ' 'em' of Grandfather's exhortation, is a 'lion' ready to swallow alive the followers of Grandfather's prescription. There is a difference, nonetheless, in the manner in which each hero sets forth on his quest. The Renaissance knight Redcrosse is eager to fulfil Gloriana's request, to engage his foe; he is confident; 'euer as he rode, his hart did [y]earne / To proue his puissance in battell braue / Vpon his foe, and his new force to learne' (ll. 1.1.24–6). The twentieth-century Invisible Man finds himself fulfilling Grandfather's request against his will, and without comprehending its meaning or purpose at all:

> It was as though I was carrying out his advice in spite of myself. And to make it worse, everyone loved me for it. I was praised by the most lily-white men of the town. I was considered an example of desirable conduct — just as my grandfather had been. And what puzzled me was that the old man had defined it as *treachery*. When I was praised for my conduct I felt a guilt that in some way I was doing something that was really against the wishes of the white folks ... even though they were fooled and thought they wanted me to act as I did. (p. 17)

The hero complains, 'The old man's words were like a curse'. What he suspects is that virtuous behaviour is relative, and political. Redcrosse has no such qualms about his behaviour. The standards to which he adheres or aspires were made for him; they are white man's standards, grown out of white man's aspirations and beliefs. The confusion in Ellison's character's aspiring to these same standards derives from the fact that he is black. He feels that he is 'acting' white; and the whites, while they praise his 'white' behaviour, are made uneasy at the sight of black acting white. They suspect an alien behaviour lurks beneath the acquired façade. In associating his novel with the Renaissance English romance tradition, Ellison is, in fact, knowingly 'writing' white. He is certainly aware that in European Christian tradition white is associated with good and black with evil. Thus Ellison engages with the romantic epic on levels that reflect his blackness as a writer, and the blackness of his protagonist.

Ellison pointedly manipulates the traditional colour symbolism as it occurs in Spenser's poem. Not surprisingly, everything good in *The Faerie Queene* is white: the 'Asse more white then snow', the even 'whiter' Una, her 'milke white lambe'; virtue and innocence are white (ll. 1.1.29, 30, 36). Black signifies mourning ('And ouer all a blacke stole she did throw, / As one that inly mournd: so was she sad' [ll. 1.1.32–3]), error, or evil (Archimago, 'in long blacke weedes yclad' [ll. 1.1.254]; 'lustfull *Lechery* ... blacke, and filthy did appeare' [ll. 1.4.208, 212]; 'griesly *Night*, with visage deadly sad ... in a foule blacke pitchie mantle clad', 'coleblacke steedes yborne of hellish brood' [ll. 1.5.181–3, 188]). Perhaps the blackest of Spenser's images is that of vile Errour and her inky brood. Grandfather's description of his people's position in the white man's world bears a striking, yet complicated resemblance to Spenser's description of the monster. Errour herself lives in darkness, disdaining the light: 'For light she hated as the deadly bale, / Ay wont in desert darknesse to remaine, / Where plaine none might her see, nor she see any plaine' (ll. 1.1.142–4). It is her brood of Impes as 'blacke as inke' (ll. 1.1.196), however, that enact the vomit-inducing behaviour encouraged by Grandfather. True to his integrationist philosophy Ellison re-creates Spenser's black-versus-white image in such a way that all the factors are related — the monster, the lion (Redcrosse is compared to a 'Lyon' [ll. 1.1.146]), and the 'fruitfull cursed spawne of serpents small' (ll. 1.1.195). In Grandfather's conceit, the heroic lion and the deceit-swallowing monster are merged. Yet the fate he has decreed for the enemy of his people (vomiting or busting wide open), in his Spenserian model describes both the fate of Errour herself ('Therewith she spewed out of her filthy maw / A floud of poyson horrible and blacke' [ll. 1.1.172–3]; 'A streame of cole black bloud forth gushed fro[m] her corse' [ll. 1.1.216]) and that of her offspring:

> That detestable sight him [Redcrosse] much amazde,
> To see th'vnkindly Impes of heauen accurst,
> Deuoure their dam; on whom while so he gazd,
> Hauing all satisfide their bloudy thurst,
> Their bellies swolne he saw with fulnesse burst. (ll. 1.1.226–30)

In Ellison's concentration of Spenserian imagery, all are punished: those who require flattery and imitation — but are also deceived by them — as well as the deceiver-flatterers (Grandfather's 'younguns'). Indeed, the failure of Grandfather's vision of subversive 'treachery' to achieve anything positive is demonstrated again and again throughout the novel. Mirroring his grandfather's subversive behaviour in his graduation speech, for example, leads Ellison's hero directly to the pain and humiliation of the 'battle royal' (pp. 17–18).

Grandfather's duplicitous method resembles one of the great obstacles to Redcrosse's success. In Spenser's text, Redcrosse must test himself against his cultural ideals and rid himself of duplicity in order to be worthy of an heroic reward. The knight must learn to distinguish the one truth from duplicity, Una from Duessa. But duplicity is the mode of behaviour praised by the grandfather and imposed upon Ellison's hero by his circumstances as an outsider in his own culture. For a black hero in a white cultural context, the attainment of heroic stature is a complicated undertaking. Ellison's protagonist is possessed by the contradictions inherent in attempting to fit his behaviour to a univalent model of heroism.

The traditional representations of the quest themes of sexual identity, development and responsibility that Spenser imitates are, like the colour symbolism, reiterated yet complicated by Ellison. Veiled ladies, for example, play a role in both works. The veil has traditionally symbolized purity. Una hides her lovely whiteness 'vnder a vele, that wimpled was full low' (ll. 1.1.31). But the veil has also been associated with the mystery and potential danger of the feminine. Ellison draws upon both the positive and negative associations of the veil. His young hero is confronted with 'a magnificent blonde — stark naked', who, nevertheless, is veiled by 'the smoke of a hundred cigars'; 'She seemed like a fair bird-girl girdled in veils calling to me from the angry surface of some gray and threatening sea' (p. 19). His conflicting responses to the dancer duplicate those of the Redcrosse Knight to Una when Archimago causes him to believe she has betrayed him:

> In this great passion of vnwonted lust,
> ...
> He started vp,
> ...
> Lo there before his face his Lady is,
> Vnder black stole hyding her bayted hooke,
> And as halfe blushing offred him to kis,
> ...
> All cleane dismayd to see so vncouth sight,
> And halfe enraged at her shamelesse guise,
> He thought haue slaine her in his fierce despight. (ll. 1.1.433–4)

Ellison's hero betrays the same awe, fascination, and distrust for the female:

> I wanted at one and the same time to run from the room, to sink through the floor, or go to her and cover her from my eyes and the eyes of the others with my body; to feel the soft thighs, to caress her and destroy her, to love her and murder her ... (p. 19)

Spenser's archetypal motif of the red-robed duplicitous temptress,

> A goodly Lady clad in scarlot red,
> Purfled with gold and pearle of rich assay,
> And like a *Persian* mitre on her hed
> She wore, with crownes and owches garnished,
> The which her lauish louers to her gaue ... (ll. 1.2.110–14)

or Fidessa-Duessa (ll. 1.7.1–9), is several times repeated by Ellison. A version of the Lady in Red appears in a reminiscence of Jim Trueblood's:

> 'Kinda like when you watch a gal in a red dress and a wide straw hat goin' past you down a lane with the trees on both sides, and she's plump and juicy and kinda switchin' her tail 'cause she knows you watchin' and you *know* she know, and you just stands there and watches 'til you can't see nothin' but the top of her red hat and then that goes and you know she done dropped behind a hill — I seen me a gal like that once.' (p. 56)

Trueblood's description includes the traditional associations between the female, the colour red, sexual desire and guile. It is a fondly erotic and attractive image, though tainted by the animal-like simplicity of its sharecropper narrator.

The temptress in red appears again in the novel:

> She was a small, delicately plump woman with raven hair in which a thin streak of white had begun almost imperceptively to show, and when she reappeared in the rich red of a hostess gown she was so striking that I had to avert my somewhat startled eyes. (p. 411)

In the red and pink setting of her apartment, this 'symbol' of 'life and feminine fertility' (p. 409) seduces our inexperienced hero, who resists no more effectively than Redcrosse resists Duessa:

> ... Her humblesse low
> In so ritch weedes and seeming glorious show,
> Did much emmoue his stout heroïcke heart,
>
> [...]
>
> He in great passion all this while did dwell,
> More busying his quicke eyes, her face to view,
> Then his dull eares, to hear what she did tell ... (ll. 1.2.184–6, 230–32)

> The red robe swept aside like a veil, and I went breathless at the petite and generously curved nude. ... It was like a dream interval and in an instant it swung back and I saw only her mysteriously smiling eyes above the rich red robe. (p. 416)

The Lady in Red appears yet again in the novel, but in a more sinister form. Her name is Sybil ('She ran, the colors of her dress flaring flamelike in the bright places of the dark' [p. 531]; 'She was blushing, her cheeks, even her freckled bosom, were bright red' [p. 518]). In her drunken, sexually deprived *naïveté* Sybil delivers a shattering blow to the hero's newly acquired sense of identity by asking him to fulfil her rape fantasy as if he were a 'big black bruiser'. He responds, 'I no longer deluded myself that I either knew the society or where I fitted into it' (p. 520).

Dream visions are another aspect of the Christian epic and romance traditions imitated by Spenser and recreated by Ellison. Archimago's magic works confusion upon the Redcrosse Knight in false dreams, brought from the dark depths of Morpheus's house through the ivory door (ll. 1.1.343–1.2.54). In Ellison's text, Spenser's powers of Morpheus are re-visioned as the powers of Marijuana. 'Under the spell of the reefer', Ellison's character experiences a half-waking dream of descent into a cave in which he sees 'a beautiful girl the color of ivory' and hears a preacher preach on 'blackness' as the origin of everything. In the same hallucinatory state, he is helped further into confusion by an old singer of spirituals who poses as a source of wisdom. Confusion over truth versus appearances is characteristic of the state of mind of both questing heroes.

A nightmarish projection appears in Jim Trueblood,[11] whose incestuous dream-turned-reality of his daughter re-creates Redcrosse's tormented erotic dreams of Una:

> Then I turned my back and tried to move away, though there wasn't much room and I could still feel her touchin' me, movin close to me. Then I musta dropped into the dream. ... I'm whispering to Matty Lou, tryin' to keep her quiet and I'm figurin' how to git myself out of the fix I'm in without sinnin'. I almost chokes her. (pp. 57–9)

Whereas Spenser's knight is saved from murder or sexual ignominy, first by his own reason (ll. 1.1.442–7), then by Archimago (ll. 1.2.41–5), Ellison's narrator's shadow-character considers himself 'lost'. Much to his surprise, however, Trueblood is rewarded by the 'white folks' for behaviour that is the antithesis of the moral code they themselves espouse. Ellison thus exposes a hidden corruption in the white folk that associates them with this 'blackest' of black folk. They reward the sharecropper for committing a sin that tempts and fascinates them, which they may now enjoy vicariously while continuing to uphold their superficial position of moral superiority and without shrinking the perceived distance between the morally and socially undeveloped 'Negro' and themselves. Ellison intensifies the white–black association through the parallel between Trueblood's overt actions with Matty Lou and Mr Norton's romantic obsession with his dead daughter:

> A girl, my daughter. She was a being more rare, more beautiful, purer, more perfect and more delicate than the wildest dream of a poet. I could never believe her to be my own flesh and blood. Her beauty was a well-spring of purest water-of-life, and to look upon her was to drink and

[11] Ellison's narrator, like the rest of the college blacks, is embarrassed by the 'primitive' black lifestyle preserved by Jim Trueblood and the other sharecroppers (pp. 46–7).

> drink and drink again. ... A nature not of this world, a personality like that of some biblical maiden, gracious and queenly. I found it difficult to believe her my own. (p. 42)

Using the Redcrosse Knight's lust-induced betrayal of Una as palimpsest, Ellison rewrites Spenser's erotic scene, uniting the erotic obsession of the white benefactor for his daughter and the 'fouled' innocence of Trueblood's daughter in order to dramatize his theme of similarity in difference:

> He [Mr Norton] stood shakily, still staring intently at Trueblood. Then I saw him removing a red Moroccan-leather wallet from his coat pocket. The platinum-framed miniature [of his daughter] came with it, but he did not look at it this time.
>
> 'Here', he said, extending a banknote. 'Please take this and buy the children some toys for me'.
>
> Trueblood's mouth fell agape, his eyes widened and filled with moisture as he took the bill between trembling fingers. It was a hundred-dollar bill. (p. 69)

It is not insignificant, then, that the sharecropper's 'younguns' are 'playin' "London Bridge's Fallin' Down"', hinting that the impressive structure of White Western ethics may be riddled with hidden faults.

The episodic structure of chivalric romance is another characteristic that Ellison takes up. Many of the trials and episodic adventures of the questing knight of Spenser's poem are replicated, in modern guise, in *Invisible Man*. The Redcrosse Knight is nearly killed in Orgoglio's dungeon; the Invisible Man is almost killed in the basement of the Liberty Paint factory. The giant, 'puft up with empty wind', and 'growen great through arrogant delight' is parodied in the pompous Lucius Brockway, master of the basement: 'his withered face an animated black walnut with shrewd, reddish eyes' (p. 208). Spenser's foul pit is echoed in Ellison's factory basement:

> At last he came vnto an yron doore,
>
> ....
>
> Where entred in, his foot could find no flore,
> But all a deepe descent, as dark as hell,
> That breathed euer forth a filthie banefull smell. (ll. 1.8.327, 349–51)

> It was a deep basement. Three levels underground I pushed upon a heavy metal door marked 'Danger' and descended into a noisy, dimly lit room. ... And there were the odors ... he was *making* something down here, something that had to do with paint, and probably something too filthy and dangerous for white men to be willing to do even for money. (pp. 207, 212)

I would even venture to say that the Invisible Man's experiences during and following the basement episode constitute a parody of the double baptism of the Redcrosse Knight. Redcrosse is baptized by Water in The Well of Life:

> It fortuned (as faire it then befell)
> Behind his backe vnweeting, where he stood,
> Of auncient time there was a springing well,
> From which fast trickled forth a siluer flood,
> Full of great vertues, and for med'cine good.
> ....
> Into the same the knight backe ouerthrowen, fell. (ll. 1.11.253–7, 270)

The Invisible Man is baptized in Liberty White Paint:

> I seemed to run swiftly up an incline and shot forward with sudden acceleration into a wet blast of black emptiness that was somehow a bath of whiteness ... in that clear instant of consciousness I opened my eyes to a blinding flash. ... I was understanding something fully and trying again to answer but seemed to sink to the center of a lake of heavy water and pause, transfixed and numb with the sense that I had lost irrevocably an important victory. (p. 230)

Both heroes experience Baptism by Fire, Redcrosse in the fiery-hot armour

> He [the Dragon] lowdly brayd, that like was neuer heard,
> And from his wide deuouring ouen sent
> A flake of fire, that flashing in his beard,
> Him all amazd, and almost made affeard;
> The scorching flame sore swinged all his face,
> And through his armour all his bodie seard,
> That he could not endure so cruell cace,
> But thought his armes to leaue, and helmet to vnlace (ll. 1.11.227–34);

and Invisible Man by electric shock:

> They were holding me firm and it was fiery ... A whirring began that snapped and cracked with static, and suddenly I seemed to be crushed between the floor and the ceiling. Two forces tore savagely at my stomach and back. A flash of cold-edged heat enclosed me. I was pounded between crushing electrical pressures; pumped between live electrodes like an accordion between a player's hands. (p. 232)

Redcrosse emerges from his baptisms renewed, empowered and victorious. Invisible Man emerges 'bewildered', 'deflated', 'tired', 'lost' in a 'vast whiteness' (pp. 237–8). His white doctors, nurses and other attendants-torturers consider him to be 'cured', 'a new man'. But being immersed in all this whiteness is not, for Ellison's black hero, the same restorative experience it is for Spenser's culturally sanctioned white one. The operator of the electro-shock machine attempts to achieve what he calls 'absolute integrity' for his patient-victim, in the form of a brain which may experience 'no major conflict of motives'. This, the doctor suggests, will integrate the patient peacefully into society (p. 236). What the white attendants do not, or will not understand, is that life itself for a black person in white society consists of conflicts of motives. True integration would require an acknowledgement of, and respect for, both or all contributing traditions, not obliteration of all but a purified or idealized dominant white tradition. Unlike Redcrosse, who is at the same time liberated and reclaimed by the submersion of his individual will and passions into the idealized collective cultural ethic, Invisible Man is violently robbed of essential elements of his identity when forced into the same homogenetic cultural paradigm: 'Something [has] been disconnected' in him, and he no longer knows his own name. He feels as if he moves 'against a current sweeping swiftly against [him]' (p. 249). This entire process of emptying the individual black man of identity under the guise of providing integrity is called in the novel, 'enlightened humanitarianism' (pp. 237–42, 247, 249).

Other parallels of plot and motif connect these two works such as the doubling of the role of the false Holy Man (Archimago in disguise) and Ellison's factory director-doctor, this 'tall austere-looking man in a white coat' (reversing the blackness of the Hermit's long garment). Similarly, we find a correspondence between the ultimate destination towards which each of our heroes aspires. Each hero aspires towards a particular city as a topographical endpoint of his individual quest. For Spenser's knight it is Hierusalem, the Heavenly City and Christian shrine (ll. 1.10.505–13). For Ellison's black hero it is Harlem, the 'city within a city' (p. 234). This is where Mary lives, she who has the potential to save him from the burning streets. Mary, solitary, benevolent, compassionate intercessor between Invisible Man and his fate, is a Virgin-figure, like Spenser's Una. She offers her young patient a quest that counters Grandfather's method:

> 'It's you young folks what's going to make the changes', she said. 'Y'all's the ones. You got to lead and you got to fight and move us all on up a little higher'. (p. 255)

Mary requires behaviour that is uncorrupted, outspoken, grounded in Black American culture. She advises her patient to be in, but not of, the world, a traditional Christian teaching that provides an active yet kinder alternative to Grandfather's anger. Responding to this challenge, Ellison's hero begins the most consciously militant phase of his quest ('You're a soldier now, your health belongs to the organization' [p. 360]). The 'Brotherhood' appears at first to be a modern version of the Christian orders of knighthood. But ironically, this black knight chooses a white paradigm of heroism over that which reflects his own mixed identity, and one which is expressed in language that reflects Grandfather's imagery:

> 'Tell me, where did you find this young hero of the people?'
> 'I didn't', Brother Jack said. 'He simply arose out of a crowd. The people always throw up their leaders, you know ...'
> '*Throw* them up', she said. 'Nonsense, they chew them up and spit them out. Their leaders are made, not born. Then they're destroyed. You've always said that'. (p. 302)

As it turns out, the 'mission' of the white-initiated Brotherhood is as duplicitous a scheme as is Duessa's, as perfidious as Archimago's. The official position is stated thus:

> 'What are we doing? What is our mission? It's simple; we are working for a better world for all people. It's that simple. Too many have been dispossessed of their heritage, and we have banded together in brotherhood so as to do something about it. What do you think of that?' (p. 304)

What the Brotherhood wants in reality, however, is to programme the Black community to its own advantage, and according to its own social programme ('But don't you think he should be a little blacker?' [p. 303]). Here Ellison confronts openly the ideal of English-styled heroism with what it means to be a member of a suppressed minority with heroic aspirations. '"Do you really think you have the right man?"' the hero asks the white 'brothers'; '"You mustn't let that worry you"', they respond, '"You will rise to the task; it is only necessary that you work hard and follow instructions."' The hero–recruit realizes, '"Now was the time for me to decide or to say I thought they were crazy and go back to Mary's".' But the Brothers manage to separate him from his people and his past, handing him a 'new identity' written on a slip of paper (pp. 308–9). Significantly, in both texts identity is received from an external source; for Spenser's hero this signals revelation and restoration of his true nature, whereas for Ellison's this signals further deterioration of his personality.

In the House of Holiness, the Redcrosse Knight, representative of his Christian culture, is able to accept, untroubled, the identity given him by the 'agèd holy man', Heavenly Contemplation. His culture, his individual identity, and his temporal and spiritual goals coincide. He is without conflict:

> O holy Sire, (quoth he) how shall I quight
> The many fauours I with thee haue found,

> That hast my name and nation red aright,
> And taught the way that does to heauen bound? (ll. 1.10.595–8)

Invisible Man, on the other hand, while being similarly chosen for a messianic mission, experiences levels of conflicted identity unknown to the earlier hero: 'I would do the work but I would be no one except myself — whoever I was' (p. 311). Indeed, he recognizes the paradox in his choice of heroic quest. Invisible Man sees that he is caught between two inherited paradigms, which, for a Black hero caught up in a White tradition, are seemingly irreconcilable: the quest for individuation of the romance hero on the one hand, and the epic pull of God, country and race over individual desires on the other. He sees himself lured by the heroic demands of his Black culture, Grandfather's oracular message and even the professed ideals of White culture. He does not reason through the potential consequences of his choice:

> What a vast difference between Mary and those for whom I was leaving her. And why should it be this way, that the very job which might make it possible for me to do some of the things which she expected of me required that I leave her? What kind of room would Brother Jack select for me and why wasn't I left to select my own? It didn't seem right that in order to become a Harlem leader I should live elsewhere. Yet nothing seemed right and I would have to rely upon their judgment. They seemed expert in such matters. (pp. 315–16)

He was to be haunted in this endeavour by the 'grandfather part' of himself, 'the cynical, disbelieving part — the traitor self that always threatened internal discord' (p. 335). In his desire to identify himself with the aspirations of the dominant culture, Ellison's narrator must deny those parts of himself that are deemed unacceptable: 'I was becoming someone else. ... My name was different; I was under orders. Even if I met Mary on the street, I'd have to pass her by unrecognized' (pp. 335–6). Ellison, in this tragic parody of the heroic quest, starkly exposes the narrowness of the defining characteristics of the western heroic model.

Of course, Ellison reveals an equally narrow definition of the characteristics of the militant African-American heroic model represented by Ras the Exhorter. In Ras Ellison creates a Black version of the romance epic paradigm:

> 'Come with us, Mahn. We build a glorious movement of black people. *Black people!* ... Don't deny you'self! It took a billion gallons of black blood to make you. Recognize you'self inside and you wan the kings among men!' (pp. 371, 373)

These words of Ras the Exhorter are the African-American equivalent of those spoken to the Redcrosse Knight by the holy hermit when his true identity and heritage are revealed to him. Born of a king, but raised as a dirt farmer, Redcrosse will become Saint George, patron of his nation (1.10.461, 577–94). Like the descendants of African slaves, he was, according to Spenser, torn from his parents and raised among strangers. He, too, had to work the soil and live in poverty. Like the oppressed African Americans of *Invisible Man*, Redcrosse had to fight bloody battles to establish himself and earn the right to represent and lead his people:

> Then come thou man of earth, and see the way,
> [...]
> To yonder same *Hierusalem* do bend,
> Where is for thee ordaind a blessed end:
> For thou emongst those Saints, whom thou doest see,
> Shalt be a Saint, and thine owne nations frend
> And Patrone: thou Saint *George* shalt called bee,
> Saint *George* of mery England, the signe of victoree.
> [...]
> For well I wote, thou springst from ancient race
> Of *Saxon* kings, that haue with mightie hand
> And many bloudie battailes fought in place
> High reard their royall throne in *Britane* land,
> And vanquisht them, vnable to withstand:
> From thence a Faerie thee vnweeting reft. (ll. 1.10.461, 544–9, 577–82)

Ellison, however, portrays both exclusionary versions of the heroic model as ineffective and ignoble, as failing to encompass the variety of revered and meaningful traditions and ideals inherent in the mixed cultural and racial identity of the hero, failing to create in the protagonist a sustained, dynamic self-awareness. His democratic integrationist philosophy requires an heroic paradigm that conjoins both cultural identities.

In the Brotherhood, Ellison presents a parodic failure of Spenser's heroic paradigm. In *The Faerie Queene*, this model of white Christian heroism provides 'most glorious victory' for its hero. Redcrosse's rite of passage, his successful internalization of the ideals of his Christian culture, has resulted in the exposure of falsehood (the disrobing of Duessa), suppression of animal passions (defeat of the Dragon), rejection of confusion (imprisonment of Archimago), and unification of identity and purpose (marriage of Redcrosse and Una, and Redcrosse's continued mission against the 'other'). The hero will continue to wage holy war against those religious and ethnic elements rejected by the dominant Christian culture:

Ah dearest Lord, said then that doughty knight,
Of ease or rest I may not yet deuize;
For by the faith, which I to armes haue plight,
I bounden am streight after this emprize,
As that your daughter can ye well aduize,
Backe to returne to that great Faerie Queene,
And her to serue six yeares in warlike wize,
Gainst that proud P[a]ynim king, that workes her teene:
Therefore I ought craue pardon, till I there haue beene. (ll. 1.12.154–62)

A major part of the traditional Western romance hero's holy mission was the destruction of the 'Paynim', a term which in the Renaissance denoted Arab, Muslim, Moor and Black African alike.[12] Redcrosse defeats three such 'Paynims' in the poem. The colour black indicated, to the Renaissance Englishman, a potential, if not manifest, spiritual and political enemy. Ellison admires and imitates the literary traditions of the period, ethnically biased as they were, and uses them as a prop for his Black American perspective on the subjects of truth, heroism, and the individual quest for identity. Ellison is fully aware of the ironies of his personal and literary position and of the difficulties involved in his unique applications of White ethical models. He puts it thus in his introduction to *Invisible Man*:

> my task was one of revealing the human universals hidden within the plight of one who was both black and American, and not only as a means of conveying my personal vision of possibility, but as a way of dealing with the sheer rhetorical challenge involved in communicating across our barriers of race and religion, class, color and region — barriers which consist of the many strategies of division that were designed, and still function, to prevent what would otherwise have been a more or less natural recognition of the reality of black and white fraternity. (p. xxii)

In the Epilogue to his novel, Ellison uses key images from the ending of Canto 12 of Book One of *The Faerie Queene* to place his Black hero deep in the

[12] A large bibliography on this association of ethnic, religious and political terms exists. See, for example, Anthony Gerard Barthelemy, *Black Face, Maligned Race: The Representation of Blacks in English Drama from Shakespeare to Southern* (Baton Rouge, LA: Louisiana State University Press, 1987); Jack D'Amico, *The Moor in English Renaissance Drama* (Tampa, FL: University of South Florida Press, 1991); Kathleen Coyne Kelly, '"Blue" Indians, Ethiopians, and Saracens in Middle English narrative texts', *Parergon*, n.s. **11.1** (1993), pp. 35–52; and Kenneth Baxter Wolf, 'The "Moors" of West Africa and the beginnings of the Portuguese slave trade', *Journal of Medieval and Renaissance Studies* **24.3** (1994), pp. 449–69.

centre of the white western tradition. Invisible Man, like Spenser's Archimago, ends in a hole:

> I'm an invisible man and it placed me in a hole — or showed me the hole I was in, if you will — and I reluctantly accepted the fact. ... Nor do I know whether accepting the lesson has placed me in the rear or in the *avant-garde*. *That*, perhaps, is a lesson for history. (p. 572)

Like Satan cast into the pit of Hell, Archimago is placed in a deep dungeon, bound hand and foot with iron chains. But Invisible Man's is a hole filled with light. Such a hole is a sacred space. The sacred lamp, symbol of the union of Una and her Knight, the One True Faith and Holiness, is placed in such a chamber in contrast to the dark hole wherein the magician lies: 'And sacred lampe in secret chamber hide, / Where it should not be quenched day nor night, / For feare of euill fates, but burnen euer bright' (ll. 1.12.331–3). Here, where the truths of the western tradition converge, Ellison's narrator provides his unique archetypal perspective on those truths:

> When one is invisible he finds such problems as good and evil, honesty and dishonesty, of such shifting shapes that he confuses one with the other, depending upon who happens to be looking through him at the time. (p. 572)

Despite the fact that he has learned some things in his illuminated chamber, the reality of diversity in similarity, for instance: 'Our fate is to become one, and yet many', [pp. 576–7]), and feels that he has been 'chosen', like a prophet ('Why should I be the one to dream this nightmare? Why should I be dedicated and set aside — yes, if not to at least *tell* a few people about it?' [p. 579]), the hero of *Invisible Man*, unlike Spenser's hero, remains confused ('I try belatedly to study the lesson of my own life' [p. 572]; 'all life seen from the hole of invisibility is absurd' [p. 579]; 'The very act of trying to put it all down has confused me' [p. 579]), impassioned ('I denounce and I defend and I hate and I love' [p. 580]; 'I condemn and affirm, say no and say yes, say yes and say no' [p. 579]), and disunified ('I approach it [life] through division' [p. 580]; 'there's still a conflict within me' [p. 581]). He remains the Other, still forcibly rejected by the dominant western tradition in its creation of its own identity. He is the dark power represented by Spenser's Archimago, but he is also the enlightened hero. For, like Spenser's hero, Ellison's Invisible Man has a continuing mission, though his mission necessitates exposing the abominations of the western tradition hidden beneath the beauty of its surface. Having recognized that all exclusionist identities, such as that promoted and celebrated in *The Faerie Queene*, are artificial constructs, not genetic nor theological truths, he takes upon himself the heroic task of teaching us what he has learned:

> the mind that has conceived a plan of living must never lose sight of the chaos against which that pattern was conceived. That goes for societies as well as for individuals. Thus, having tried to give pattern to the chaos which lives within the pattern of your certainties, I must come out, I must emerge. (pp. 580–81)

The heroic task of the protagonist of *Invisible Man* reflects the integrationist philosophy of its author, who followed a quest not without its own dangers. The rejection of his novel by the Black separatist movement precisely because of its integration of Black American and White European cultural tropes is proof of this.[13]

[13] The situation is described by Stanley Crouch (David Remnick, 'Visible Man', *The New Yorker* [14 March 1994], pp. 34–8).

Chapter 8

The reformulation of Orlando in Giuseppe Bonaviri's *Novelle saracene*

Barbara De Marco

> 'The Puppet show is coming', we boys shouted. ... In fact, Orlando, Rinaldo, Charlemagne and — with black faces because they were Saracens — Ferraù, Sacripante, King Marsilio, crowded in among them, sighed upon seeing that great expanse of isolated countryside ... 'Go fill up your lungs with puppets', my godfather said to me, 'in a few days you'll have to go to Catania to study'.
>
> The last evening, before I left, don Mariddu presented the Dispute between Charlemagne and his nephew Rinaldo, who wanted his uncle to make use of new strategies of war against Marsilio, who was besieging Paris.
>
> Charlemagne, strutting around in his green robe, in his falsetto voice, spoke haughtily to his nephew: 'Since you don't want to fight according to my plans, you will go into exile outside the borders of the kingdom'.
>
> I, too, was going into exile to Catania, and for that reason, a shared sentiment grew up between Rinaldo and me. ... I wanted to cry. ('What are you doing? Are you crying?' Rinaldo said to me, riding through the woods.)
>
> 'O Rinaldo!' I answered, whispering the phrase. 'I am so sad, like you. Tomorrow I'm leaving for Catania'.[1]

A version of this essay was read at the American Association of Italian Studies annual meeting, Chicago, Illinois, April 1998.

[1] 'Arriva l'Opera dei Pupi', gridavamo noi ragazzi ... Infatti, Orlando, Rinaldo, Carlomagno e, neri in faccia perché saraceni, Ferraù, Sacripante, il re Marsilio, assiepati fra di loro, sospiravano vedendo quella gran libertà di campagne assolate. ... 'Va' a respirare una boccata di pupi', mi disse mio compare 'perche in questi giorni devi andar a Catania per i tuoi studi' ... L'ultima sera, prima che partissi, don Mariddu rappresentò la disputa fra Carlomagno e il nipote Rinaldo. Il quale voleva imporre allo zio una nuova tecnica guerresca contro Marsilio che assediava Parigi.

Carlomagno, girandosi su se stesso nel manto verde, con voce in falsetto, altezzosa, disse al nipote: 'Poiché tu non vuoi combattere seguendo i miei piani, andrai in esilio fuori dal Regno'.

Anch'io andavo in esilio a Catania, per cui fra Rinaldo e me si creò la stessa consonanza di sentimenti. ... Mi veniva voglia di piangere ('Che fai? vuoi piangere?' mi disse Rinaldo, cavalcando per i boschi).

In this brief excerpt from the autobiographical novel *Ghigò*, the Sicilian-born author Giuseppe Bonaviri reveals the intensity of his personal identification with stories of the Paladins, whose exploits were re-enacted every autumn when the *puparo* (puppet master) don Mariddu brought the *teatro dei pupi* (marionette theatre) to the Sicilian hill town of Mineo. The influence of the novels of chivalry on Bonaviri's early years is made more explicit in an earlier episode from the same novel, in which he describes the eighteenth-century edition of *Guerrin il Meschino*

> published in ottavo, on simple paper, that I still own. ... You can still see the two knights my godfather sketched in ink: each has a helmet, sword, leg guards, and an aquiline nose, exactly, in fact, like my Uncle Michael's.[2]

The family resemblance is reiterated in Bonaviri's essay on the epic of Orlando in Sicily:

> In my case, I projected the world of Paladins onto my father. I saw in him Rinaldo, or Oliver who goes out in search of the lost companions. I lived off the smile of my father, gentle and melancholy, or on his childlike, distracted air, or on his rare sudden fits of fury, similar to those of the maddened Orlando. ... Orlando, Rinaldo, my father, for us they had never been born. They had always existed, like the sun and the night.[3]

These autobiographical sketches also reveal that the stories from the Carolingian narrative cycle were transmitted to Bonaviri in forms both oral and

---

'O Rinaldo!' gli risposi sussurrando la frase. 'Sono molto triste come te. Domani parto per Catania' (Bonaviri, *Ghigò*, Scrittori italiani [Milan: Mondadori, 1990], pp. 150–53).

Unless otherwise indicated, all English translations are my own. I am in the process of publishing the first complete translation of the *Novelle saracene*.

[2] 'Stampato, in ottavo, su carta modesta, che tuttora conservo. ... Vi si vedono tuttora due Paladini abbozzati da mio compare con inchiostro: hanno elmo, spada, schinieri e naso aquilino, uguale, per l'appunto, a quello di mio zio Michele' (Bonaviri, *Ghigò*, pp. 110–11). Bonaviri's collection of poetry, *O corpo sospiroso*, intro. and notes Giacinto Spagnoletti (Milan: Biblioteca Universale Rizzoli, 1982) also makes particular use of chivalric imagery.

[3] 'Nel mio caso, una proiezione del mondo dei Paladini era mio padre. Le vedevo Rinaldo, o Oliviero che va alla ricerca dei compagni perduti. Mi nutrivo del sorriso di mio padre, mesto e buono, o della sua aria spaesata e infantile o dei suoi rari improvvisi furori simili a quelli d'Orlando impazzito ... Orlando, Rinaldo, mio padre per noi non erano mai nati. Erano sempre esistiti come il sole e la notte' (Bonaviri, 'Comparazione tra *Pinocchio* e l'epos d'*Orlando* in Sicilia', in his *L'Arenario*, La Scala [Milan: Rizzoli, 1984], pp. 12–14). As a child, the author was nicknamed 'figlio d'Orlando' (son of Orlando) because of his love of the stories about these knights (Bonaviri, *O corpo*, p. 81n).

written; this dual line of transmission is of fundamental importance in any attempt to read the chivalric themes in the work of Bonaviri.[4] In a classic study, Giuseppe Pitrè described the year-long cycle of stories that made up the repertoire of 'La storia dei Paladini' as performed in the *opra*, or regional puppet theatres, documenting the following medieval and Renaissance texts as sources: *Cronaca di Turpino*, Andrea da Barberino's *I Reali di Francia*, Luigi Pulci's *Il Morgante maggiore*, Matteo Maria Boiardo's *Orlando innamorato*, Ludovico Ariosto's *Orlando furioso* and Lodovico Dolce's *Le prime imprese del conte Orlando*. A second cycle took up matters after the death of the original Paladins, and included stories from Maestro Andrea's *Guerrino*, the anonymous *Figlio del Meschino*, *Gualfo ed Alfeo re di Negroponte*, *Trebatio*, *Ardente Spada* and *Alessandro Magno II*, among others.[5]

Alongside the puppet theatres were performances by the professional *contastorie* (street-singers), whose preferred material was also the Carolingian narrative cycle, represented by a series of texts in which *Reali* and *Guerrino* figured most prominently. Pitrè insisted on the essentially oral nature of this tradition, contrasting the Sicilian practice of reciting by memory to the Neapolitan, in which the *contastorie* read and then commented on the legends.[6] The blending of oral and written traditions in the nineteenth century was further complicated by Giusto Lodico, a schoolteacher from Palermo, who published bimonthly episodes of the *Storia dei Paladini di Francia*; their appearance between 1858 and 1860 caused a veritable 'epicomania'.[7] Lodico's *Storia* was an unabashed blending of retellings from texts composed in the fifteenth and sixteenth centuries, sprinkled with oral legends as recounted by the contemporary *contastorie*. The written sources for Lodico's episodic reworkings, as far as Pitrè could determine, included Pulci's *Morgante*, Boiardo's *Orlando innamorato* as re-worked by Berni, Ariosto's *Orlando furioso*, Dolce's *Prime imprese*, Teofilo Folengo's *L'Orlandino* and Francesco Bello's *Mambriano*. These major Renaissance epics were augmented with details from Vincenzo Brusantino's *L'Angelica innamorata*, Bernardo Tasso's *Amadigi* and Francesco Tromba's *Madama Rovenza*. The complete Lodico cycle closed with the *Rotta di Roncisvalle* (*The Rout at Roncesvalles*).[8]

Against this backdrop it becomes possible to situate Bonaviri in the centuries'-long tradition of Sicilian *contastorie*. Themes from the Carolingian

---

[4] The same dual influence is present in Gesualdo Bufalino's *Il Guerrin Meschino*, the subject of Gloria Allaire's chapter later in this volume.

[5] Giuseppe Pitrè, 'Le tradizioni cavalleresche popolari in Sicilia', *Romania* **13** (1884), p. 322.

[6] Ibid., p. 348.

[7] Carmel Alberti, *Il teatro dei pupi e lo spettacolo popolare siciliano*, Problemi di storia dello spettacolo 4 (Milan: Mursia, 1977), pp. 80–81.

[8] Pitrè, 'Le tradizioni', pp. 348–52.

epic cycle are played out in Bonaviri's *Novelle saracene*, a collection of 26 tales of unmistakable Sicilian stamp, as Bonaviri himself comments:

> I, too, have brought to these tales memories and humours, but their Sicilian matrix is found in the Mediterranean sunlight that permeates them. ... Most of these little tales form part of an ethnographic patrimony that is Indo-European, not to say universal, but they have obviously undergone notable alterations, cadences, and modes of speech that are typically Sicilian.[9]

In Italo Calvino's *Le città invisibili*, to the Great Khan's request that Marco Polo tell him something about Venice, the Venetian replies, 'What else did you think I was telling you about? ... Every time I describe a city I am telling you something about Venice'.[10] In an interview with Franco Zangrilli, Bonaviri made a similar response to the comment that Mineo, scene of Bonaviri's youth, is the locus of almost all of his literary work. Like Marco Polo's Venice, Mineo acts as Bonaviri's constant vantage point.[11] The close identification between the locus of his novels and his home village may be transparently clear, as in his early novels *Il sarto della stradalunga*, *La contrada degli ulivi* and *Il fiume di pietra*, or it may be thinly veiled as a novel of India, as in *È il rosseggiar di peschi e di albicocchi*. It may appear in the guise of another city, real or imaginary, as in *La divina foresta* or *Il dormiveglia*. It may also show up in the middle-Eastern garb of an imagined medieval Sicily, recalling centuries of Greek and Arab presence on the island as, for example, in *Notti sull'altura*, in *Dolcissimo* and, to a large

---

[9] 'Anch'io in questi racconti ho apportato memorie e umori, ma la loro matrice siciliana si trova in una solarità mediterranea che vi è diffusa. ... La gran parte di queste novelline fanno parte d'un patrimonio etnografico euro-asiatico, per non dire universale, ma indubbiamente hanno subito varianti notevoli, cadenze, recitativi tipicamente siciliani' (Bonaviri, *Novelle saracene*, La Scala [Milan: Rizzoli, 1980], pp. 147–8). See also Franco Zangrilli's interview with the author, 'Giusppe Bonaviri', in *La forza della parola. Incontri con Cassola, Prisco, Pomilio, Bonaviri, Saviane, Doni, Pontiggia, Altomonte*, Il portico Biblioteca di lettere e arti 96 (Ravenna: Longo, 1992), pp. 93–4.

[10] 'E di che altro credevi che ti parlassi? ... Ogni volta che descrivo una città dico qualcosa di Venezia' (Italo Calvino, *Le città invisibili*, Nuovi Coralli 182 [Turin: Einaudi, 1972], p. 94).

[11] 'Mineo resta ... il punto da cui si osserva il mondo. Ma potrebbe essere Verona d'Usa or Quilin in Cina, non conta ... mi imbosco in Mineo perché è nido a me noto, ma dentro mi porto tutta la mia personalità, carente e complessa che sia, non so. Sicché, Mineo, come Verona d'Usa o un paese della Alaska sono solo le specola d'osservazione' (Zangrilli, 'Cibo e fantasia a braccetto: a colloquio con Giuseppe Bonaviri', in Antonio Iadanza and Marcello Carlino (eds), *L'opera di Giuseppe Bonaviri*, Opere varie [Rome: Nuova Italia Scientifica, 1987], p. 125).

extent, in the *Novelle saracene*.[12] Umberto Mariani discusses the simultaneous levels of time and space that Bonaviri summons up in these repeated journeys into memory and imagination.[13]

In the *Novelle*, the memory of a childhood nourished on the figures and humours of the Paladins allows Bonaviri to set his heroes on an imaginary stage alongside figures from Greek myth, Biblical history, liturgical drama and Arabic folklore. Together they act out legendary adventures interspersed with remembered events of village life:

> there is not an event or wonder or marvel that does not have as its basis Mineo, the real and at the same time mythic homeland of the author, whose people and places and pastimes make up ... the *presepio-universo* of every possible adventure, earthly and unearthly.[14]

The *presepio*, or Christmas *crêche*, is an appropriate image for describing the *Novelle* only if it conjures up the dynamic and heavily populated tableaux of Italian Renaissance paintings, for example, Gentile da Fabriano's *Adoration of the Magi* or, more appropriately, the crowds of figures that populate the traditional Sicilian and Neapolitan Nativity scenes. In these, the posture of each figurine offers a meticulously detailed and even grotesquely accurate representation of village life, set against the mysterious and intangible events of the birth of the Christ.

Traditional religious iconography most certainly plays its part in the *Novelle*, but it never does so in a completely traditional way. Similarly, Orlando and his companions take their accustomed places on the stage of the *Novelle*, but find themselves in new and unusual roles:

> Jesus was sleeping when they seized him. Giufà was sleeping next to him. They chained Giufà up first, for they were afraid of his incredible strength. 'What's happening?' said Giufà, his eyes burning red.

---

[12] Bonaviri, *Il sarto della stradalunga*, Oscar Narrativa (Turin: Einaudi, 1954); *idem*, *La contrada degli ulivi*, Nuovi Coralli 122 (Venice: Sodalizio del libro, 1958); *idem*, *Il fiume di pietra*, Nuovi Coralli 230 (Turin: Einaudi, 1964); *idem*, *È un rosseggiar di peschi e di albicocchi*, La Scala (Milan: Rizzoli, 1986); *idem*, *La divina foresta*, Narratori moderni (Milan: Rizzoli, 1969); *idem*, *Il dormiveglia*, Scrittori italiani e stranieri (Milan: Mondadori, 1988); *idem*, *Notti sull'altura*, Narratori moderni (Milan: Rizzoli, 1971); *idem*, *Dolcissimo*, La Scala (Milan: Rizzoli, 1978).

[13] *Dolcissimo*, trans. Umberto Mariani (New York: Italica, 1990), esp. pp. x–xii.

[14] 'Non c'è vicenda o meraviglia o prodigio che non abbia come sfondo la reale e al tempo stesso mitica patria dell'autore. Mineo, i cui luoghi e personaggi e mestieri compongono ... il presepio-universo di ogni possibile avventura umana e celeste' (Giovanni Raboni, rev. of *Novelle*, quoted in Bonaviri, *O corpo*, p. 23).

But what could he do? By then he was covered in chains. Then they chained Jesus up, hand and foot, poor beautiful child.

Orlando was walking all alone, he was thinking of the enchanted Ardennes. They threw a cloud of tar in his face. They covered him with a silken sheet. They bound him hand and foot with silver chains...

'Have the Saracen Jesus taken to the castle!' ordered His Majesty King Frederick.

He was shut in there for three days and three nights. The horned owl didn't sing. The swallow flew away. Frederick had a thought. On the esplanade of the castle were three olive trees — one to the west where the sun dies, and one to the east where the star rises, and a third facing the northern wind.

'O soldiers, o captains', said the King, 'these olive trees have open branches like horns. Hang our three proud enemies on the cross there'.

A captain said, 'Majesty, but what will His Holiness think of this?'

The Pope made known his thought by a messenger, swift as lightning.

'King Frederick, my friend and shield of Christianity, scourge Jesus, destroyer of the world. He has made the rich poor, and the poor rich. Perhaps putting him on the cross is the just punishment'.

And so it was done. ...

The soldiers put Jesus on the cross facing the east where the shining sun rises, Orlando facing west where the day burns in its ending, and Giufà facing north ... The striking of the hammers was heard. They drove in the nails. The knight Orlando, dressed in iron, could not breathe. He heard his son playing, and he thought: 'O my son Orlandino, beloved fire, beauty and strength pass through into Nothingness'.

Giufà was writhing, the nails were too big for his hands. Oh, what pangs, our poor child Giufà! ... Jesus's turn came. The soldiers turned to him. His mother said:

Nail him with a little nail of silk
for my son is of divine flesh.
Should he fall slowly, slowly, into the black well
the day will draw him forth no more!

All the people were in tears, as the sun set in the infinite silence. Jesus, his forehead crowned with thorns, trembled all over. ... The king in the castle gave the order in a loud voice: 'Let loose the falcons. Let them fly, for they must suck the life from the heads of the three condemned men'.

There were one hundred and one falcons, of a wondrous beauty in both plumage and daring. ... The kites, circling in the sky, understood that they were to swoop down to the terrace of the castle. The soldiers had taken off Orlando's helmet, poor knight-errant. His old, white hair shone in the sun. A falcon with red plumage struck him in the forehead with his beak. Those birds, rapacious kites, swooped down, one after the other. Flying straight down, they struck the knight ... Orlando's pierced brain quivered. Blood and feelings flowed forth. Jesus felt in his eyes that the golden veil of his life was leaving. He screamed. He cried out. ... Jesus died like a bird with his mouth open. His thoughts sank into the black sea. Giufà alone remained, falling into the Nothingness announced by the soldiers' blast. In death, Orlando felt himself grow large, swelling over promontories and cliffs.[15]

---

[15] 'Gesù dormiva quando lo acchiapparono. Giufà dormiva con lui. Per prima incatenarono quest'ultimo, avevano paura della sua forza fortissima. 'Che succede?' disse Giufà con l'occhio rosso ardente.

Ma cosa poteva fare? Ormai era pieno di catene. Dopo incatenarono per mani e piedi Gesù, povero figlio bello.

Orlando camminava tutto solo, pensava alle fatate Ardenne. Gli buttarono polvere di pece in viso, con un lenzuolo di seta lo coprirono, lo legarono mani e piedi con catene d'argento. ...

'Il saraceno Gesù sia portato al castello!' ordinò sua maestà Re Federico.

Vi fu rinchiuso per tre giorni e per tre notti, non cantò l'assiolo, la rondine fuggì. Sapete che pensata ebbe Federico? Sullo spalto del castello c'erano tre ulivi, uno a occidente dove muore il sole, uno all'oriente dove s'alza l'astro, il terzo guardava il vento aquilone.

'O soldati, o capitani', disse il Re 'questi ulivi hanno dei rami aperti come corni, mettete in croce lì i nostri nemici fieri.

E un capitano disse: 'Maestà, ma sua Santità cosa ne pensa?'.

Il Papa fece sapere questo con un messo veloce come lampo.

'Re Federico mio amico, scudo della Cristianità, flagellate Gesù distruttore del mondo. Ha fatto i ricchi poveri, e i poveri ricchi. Forse metterlo in croce è il giusto castigo'.

E così fu. ... I soldati mettevano in croce Gesù ad oriente dove splendido spunta il sole; Orlando ad occidente dove si infiamma sul finire la giornata; Giufà ad aquilone. ... Si sentivano i martelli battere, ficcavano i chiodi. Orlando, cavaliere di ferro vestito, non fiatava, sentiva il figlio suonare, e pensava: 'O figlio mio Orlandino, diletto fuoco, la bellezza e la forza trapassano nel Nulla'.

Giufà smaniava, erano troppo grossi i chiodi per le sue mani. ... Venne la volta di Gesù, a lui si voltarono i soldati. La madre:

Inchiodatelo con chiuvuzza di seta
ché carni divine ha il figlio mio,
cali nel pozzo nero piano piano,
non lo lusingherà più il giorno!

Tutta la gente era in pianto mentre il sole scendeva nel silenzio infinito. Gesù con la fronte incoronata di spine tremava per tutta la persona ... Il Re nel castello a gran voce diede l'ordine: 'Slacciate i falconi, fateli volare perché la testa ai tre condannati debbono succhiare'.

I falchi erano cento e uno, in mirabile bellezza di piume e ardire. ... Quei nibbi dopo aver girato per il cielo capirono di dover tornare in basso sullo spalto del castello. Ad Orlando, povero paladino errante, avevano tolto l'elmo, i suoi capelli di bianco vecchio brillavano al sole. Lo colpì col becco sulla fronte un falcone dalle piume rosse. Quegli uccelli rapaci nibbi scendevano uno dietro l'altro, dritti dritti, colpivano il paladino. ... Forato il cervello vibrò ad Orlando, ne uscì sangue e sentimento. Gesù sentì che dagli occhi se ne andava l'aureo velo della vita. ... Gesù morì come un uccello dall'aperto becco, nel mare nero andarono i suoi pensieri. Giufà restò solo piombando nel Nulla suonato dalla tromba dei soldati. Orlando si sentì ingrandito dalla morte per promontori e balze' (Bonaviri, 'La morte di Gesù', *Novelle*, pp. 44–50; *idem*, 'The Death of Jesus', trans. De Marco, *Sicilia Parra* **9.1** [1997], pp. 7–9.

There is much to wonder at here, notwithstanding a certain familiarity of details, among them, elements from the Gospel accounts of the Passion of Jesus — he is seized by soldiers, crowned with thorns, his mother stands mourning at the foot of the cross, and so forth. Similarly, King Frederick with his falcons, the wandering knight Orlando and the Sicilian folk hero Giufà are each recognizable within a given narrative context.[16] However, not even the most apocryphal of legends has prepared us for the conjunction of a Saracen Jesus, his cousin Giufà, and an ageing knight Orlando put to death on the cross. The deliberate insertion of several independently recognizable characters into a representation of the central drama of the Christian faith is startling and strange. In this curious — even bizarre — juxtaposition, the three figures become emblematic of the entire collection of tales, for the *Novelle* have as their central feature the reformulation of the formulaic. In other episodes not considered here, Jesus loses his miraculous powers, the apostles incite to riot and banditry, and Giufà manages to rout King Frederick and rule over the island kingdom. Bonaviri provided his own gloss to the crucifixion scene:

> We find the ingenuous Giufà beside Orlando, symbol of an errant strength, together with Jesus, rendered in an original figure of a wandering Saracen. It is as though our peasant, held fast between village and nearby countryside by a destiny centuries-old, had wanted to create a Holy Trinity from heterodox characters ... the usual position of the Christian — and of Christological thought — is turned upside down to be remade into a pagan or perhaps pre-Christian drama, when two cultures, two hegemonies, two opposite mythographies, inevitably clashed. Everything undergoes a reversal (*rovesciamento*), in this case, even time and space and the way of understanding the Divine.[17]

Whether we agree that this 'Holy Trinity' is the creation of the village peasant or is, rather, the invention of the writer himself, the crucifixion scene places Orlando in a central, if unaccustomed, role. Bonaviri follows a well-established formula: the *Novelle* develop new stories out of old material. Just as Rajna de-

---

[16] The third of these contexts derives from a 'large cycle about the fool ... too important in popular narrative to be omitted. It comes from the Arabic world, and is appropriately set ... in Sicily. ... The Arabic origin is seen in the very name of the protagonist — Giufà' (Calvino, *Italian Folktales*, trans. George Martin, Pantheon Fairy Tale and Folklore Library [New York: Harcourt, 1980], p. 755).

[17] 'Troviamo il candido Giufà accanto ad Orlando, che era simbolo di peregrinante forza, e insieme a Gesù reso nella sua originaria figura di saraceno giramondo: come se il nostro villano, fermo per secolare destino tra borgo e terre vicine, si fosse voluto creare una Divina Trinità da eterodossi personaggi. ... Insomma, si rovescia la usuale posizione cristiana — e del pensiero cristologico — per rifarsi ad un dramma pagano, o forse pre-cristiano, quando s'ebbero a scontare due culture, due egemonie, due opposte mitografie' (Bonaviri, *Novelle*, p. 148).

scribed Ariosto's *Furioso* as a continuation, not of Boiardo's *Innamorato*, but of the material of chivalric romances,[18] so Bonaviri's *Novelle* are a continuation, not just of the Carolingian narrative cycle, but of the material of that cycle — along with material from the Bible, the *Qur'an*, classical mythology, *laude*, folk-tales and the author's own memories of life in a Sicilian village. I have discussed elsewhere the many literary strands that are woven into the *Novelle*.[19] The present chapter takes up just one of those threads, the retellings of the Carolingian cycle. The legends of the Paladins are only one feature in the work of a complex writer, one who, as Giorgio De Rienzo stressed, does not easily fit into any preconceived school or group of writers: 'He writes, nonetheless, as few writers know how to write: with the sense of a moral responsibility that does not wish to trick the reader'.[20]

The incongruity of an ageing Orlando, persecuted and crucified alongside the Saracen Jesus, is perhaps the most striking image of this *mondo alla rovescia*. Not every episode involving Orlando is as bizarre, though each is unusual. In the following episode, in which they discover Jesus teaching himself to fly, the two sets of cousins, Jesus and Giufà, Orlando and Rinaldo, are still young boys; from the description, in fact, it is clear that the two Paladins are actually puppets:

> One time Orlando and Rinaldo, still young, with graceful faces and gentle speech, happened to be passing through. They were wandering through the world because of the hatred of King Frederick, who had killed Charlemagne and his divine virtue. ... They stopped at Uncle Michael Gabriel's house to have him nail together better their leg guards and the small cords of their shields. ... And that's how these two cousins saw Jesus who, in low flight, his eyebrows knit, was flapping his wings.
>
> 'Oh, this is great', they said. 'Are you perhaps the son of Astolfo who flies on the horse Pegasus? Or the son of a cloud that opens up in a storm?'
>
> Then they discovered who he was. They laughed and made friends. These knights were boys too. Rinaldo set his bejewelled cloak on the ground, he wanted to try to fly. Jesus said to him, 'Do this, do that!' He couldn't do it. The cousins laughed, and bidding farewell to the peasants who were there, to Master Michael, and to Jesus and Giufà, they set out again through the world of adventure. Their iron footsteps, joined to the

[18] 'Il *Furioso* non continua l'*Innamorato*, sibbene *la materia dell'Innamorato*. Dalle cose narrate dal suo antecessore, Lodovico tien conto o no, a seconda che gli torna' (Pio Rajna, *Le fonti dell'*Orlando Furioso. *Richerche e studi*, 2nd rev. edn [Florence: Sansoni, 1900], pp. 40–41).

[19] 'Giuseppe Bonaviri's *Novelle saracene*', *Sicilia Parra* **9.1** (1997), pp. 6–7.

[20] 'Scrive, tuttavia, come pochi scrittori sanno scrivere: con la coscienza di una responsabilità morale che non vuole ingannare il lettore' (De Rienzo, '*Dolcissimo*', in Iadanza and Carlino, p. 90).

> clanging of their swords, could be heard as the moon, reclining in its shell, rising from the abyss, showed its face over the streets of the village.[21]

The innocence of this initial encounter is quickly lost. King Frederick, enemy of Paladins and Saracens alike, catches sight of Jesus in flight, mistaking him at first for one of his falcons. Jesus, forced into hiding from the Norman soldiers, catches malaria. Orlando and Rinaldo, learning of the matter, return to town at Michael's bidding:

> 'O Orlando, O Rinaldo', the old people cried out in recognition. 'Save us from the evil malaria'.
>
> But what could they do? Could they, with their swords Durendal and Fusbert, combat that evil that sprang up and afflicted the world? Do you know what they thought up? From the walls, with their beautiful shields, edged with cords of gold, they directed the dazzle of the setting sun upon those freezing old people, and upon the little child Jesus. The doors became white. The crown on Jesus's head was illumined. Virtue shone amidst the green fronds. And so everyone was happy, very happy. The people began to say:
>
> 'What, has the sun risen again?'
>
> But Orlando and Rinaldo had things to do. Ferraù and Sacripante had to run through the shimmering gardens, with pendulous oranges and tangerines. So they set off again.
>
> 'Jesus, we'll meet again', said Orlando. 'Fight off that sickness'.[22]

---

[21] Una volta si trovarono a passare Orlando e Rinaldo ancora giovanetti, col leggiadro volto e la leziosa parlata: andavano girando il mondo per odio di re Federico che aveva ucciso Carlomagno e la sua virtù divina. ... Si fermarono da zio Michele Gabriele per farsi inchiodare meglio gli schinieri e la cordicella dello scudo. ... Così quei due cugini videro Gesù che in volo basso — fermo il ciglio — batteva le ali.

'Oh, questa è bella', dissero. 'Sei forse figlio d'Astolfo che vola sul cavallo Pégaso? o figlio della nube che disserra nella tempesta?'

Dopo seppero chi era; risero, e fecero amicizia. Erano ragazzi anche i paladini. Rinaldo pose a terra il manto ingemmato, volle provare il volo. Gesù gli diceva: 'Fa' così, fa' colì!' Non ci riuscì. I cugini risero e, salutati i villani presenti, il mastro Michele, Gesù e Giufà, ripartirono per l'avventuroso mondo. Si sentiva il passo ferrato unito al tinnito della spada, mentre la luna adagiata nella conchiglia risalendo l'abisso s'affacciava sulle strade del paese' (Bonaviri, 'Gesù e Giufà', *Novelle saracene*, pp. 13–14).

[22] 'O Orlando, o Rinaldo' fecero grido i vecchi riconoscendoli. 'Aiutateci dalla malaria maligna!'

E come potevano fare? Potevano combattere con Durlindana e Fusberta quel male che saltava e affliggeva il mondo? Sapete cosa pensarono? Dalle Mura con gli scudi bellissimi, trapunti con cordelle d'oro, mandavano i barbagli del sole tramontante a quei vecchi affreddati e a Gesù bambinello. Si imbiancavano le porte, si allumava la corona che in testa aveva Gesù, virtù splendeva tra le fronde verdi. Così furono tutti contenti contentissimi. La gente a dire: 'Ma

The image of the knights healing the ailing *paese* with the rays of the sun is echoed in Bonaviri's essay comparing Pinocchio and Orlando, in which he further elaborated on the identification of his father with the knight Orlando:

> It would happen that, when the sun sank down behind the mountainous chain of Caltagirone, our father himself became a sun. ... If he went walking with us through the lime rocks of Camuti ... he reflected many suns. And the Paladins of France walking through the heights could become refracted solar rays, and exist as flames.[23]

A central figure in the *Chanson de Roland* is the Emperor Charlemagne who, as Rajna commented, towers over the action of the drama, even when he is an off-stage presence.[24] As part of the general process of *rovesciamento* in the *Novelle*, Frederick II, Norman king of Sicily, has usurped the role of Charlemagne. Indeed, in a splendidly anachronistic coupling of the historical and the legendary, the Frederick of the *Novelle* has killed 'Charlemagne and his divine virtue'. As a result, Orlando and Rinaldo, unsure of their own safety, must wander the earth. The animosity between the two knights and Charlemagne was already an established element of earlier versions of the Roland epic; the *Novelle* present a similar drama in a different setting and under a different king. Palermo and the Norman court replace Paris and the fields of war. Frederick II is portrayed as a venal and self-indulgent figure with a weakness for women and song ('King Frederick, returning to his castle where he used to amuse himself with his notary and with the ladies playing mandolas').[25] Suggestions of his uneasy alliance with the Pope reposition the tale within an actual historical context: it is true that tensions arose between Frederick and the Pope when Frederick proved unwilling to bestir himself to fight in the Crusades. In Bonaviri's retelling, there is just enough of the familiar to make plausible the shift of scenery, allowing the Holy War against the Saracen infidels to be waged on Sicilian soil:

---

rispunta di nuovo il sole?'

Ma quelli avevano il loro da fare, dovevano rincorrere tra gli scintillanti giardini, penzolanti d'arance e mandarini, Ferraù e Sacripante. E ripartirono.

'Gesù, ci rivedremo', fece Orlando. 'Combatti la malattia'. (Bonaviri, 'Gesù e Giufà', p. 17).

[23] 'A noi capitava che nostro padre, quando il sole precipitava dietro la catena montuosa di Caltagirone, diventasse lui stesso un sole. ... Se camminava con noi per i calcari di Camuti ... lui rifletteva tanti soli. E i Paladini di Francia camminando per alture potevano diventare rifratti raggi solari, ed esistere come vampe' (Bonaviri, 'Comparazione tra *Pinocchio*', p. 13).

[24] Rajna, *Le fonti*, p. 4.

[25] 'Re Federico, ritornato nel castello dove si divertiva col notaro e con le donzelle sonanti mandole ...' (Bonaviri, 'Gesù e Giufà', p. 14).

> The Pope decided to call upon King Frederick, who was enjoying himself by the sea, in a land that was not Sicily. He was corrupting his soul with ancient words.
>
> 'Majesty, King Frederick, His Holiness wishes to speak to you'.
>
> And he went off, with his mandola and his trusty steed.
>
> 'I don't wish to return to Sicily ever again', said the King.
>
> 'You must return there with your army. Jesus is turning every-one into Saracens, in adoration of the God Macone'.
>
> The Pope was the Pope, so Frederick reluctantly agreed.[26]

Other familiar motifs are open to reinterpretation and rewriting by Bonaviri. Orlando, now friend of the Saracens and foe of the Christian emperor, is cast in other unaccustomed roles as well, among them, that of Astolfo, who, in the *Furioso*, voyages to the moon to recover Orlando's wits. In the *Novelle*, it is Orlando himself who travels to the moon; his trip is motivated by a desire to console the Saracen Jesus who, overcome with sorrow at an outrage he himself has committed, has descended to the moon: 'Jesus was overcome with sadness, he walked alone. He seemed aged with the age of the world ... he descended to the moon that went walking below him as white as a young bride in May'.[27] Bonaviri's use of the moon as a narrative means to discover and explore relations among the individual, nature and the cosmos is, in the words of one critic, a recurrent and 'almost obsessive' theme.[28] Associating the moon with the loss of reason, the distortion of senses, and the desperation of the hero clearly follows the path of Astolfo's fantastic voyage. But here the *Novelle* take a divergent path. Whereas Ariosto's Orlando, his wits restored by Astolfo, at once resumes his duties to God and country, no longer distracted by the beautiful Angelica, Bonaviri's Jesus, notwithstanding his sojourn on the moon and the salutary presence of Orlando, returns yet again to madness. In a later episode, an aged Jesus, still

---

[26] 'Il Papa pensò di chiamare re Federico che se la godeva lungo il mare in una terra che non era Sicilia, corrompeva l'animo con parole antiche.

'Maestà Re Federico, sua Santità vi vuole parlare'.

E partì con mandola e il fido cavallo.

'In Sicilia non voglio più tornare' disse il Re.

'Dovete tornarci con il vostro esercito. Gesù fa diventare tutti saraceni in adorazione di Dio Macone'.

Il Papa era il Papa, e quello a malincuore accettò (Bonaviri, 'San Pietro suona il violino ... Gesù distrugge il mondo', pp. 38–9).

[27] 'Gesù si era intristito, camminava solo, sembrava vecchio della vecchiezza del mondo ... scese sulla luna che sotto lui camminava bianchissima come donzella sposa in maggio' (Bonaviri, 'La luna di Gesù', p. 32). It should be noted that, in Bonaviri's cosmography, the moon rides below the earth.

[28] Giuseppe Antonio Camerino, '*Il dormiveglia*. Note sulla narrativa di Bonaviri', in Sarah Zappula Muscara (ed.), *Mnemosine. Giuseppe Bonaviri* (Catania: Maimone, 1991), pp. 114–15.

suffering from his earlier bout of melancholy, decides, against the advice of his companions, to destroy the entire world. His destruction of the *locus amoenus* is on a scale unimagined by Ariosto's hero. Among the survivors are Giufà, Jesus's companions, the saints Peter, John, Joachim and Francis and, of course, Orlando.[29]

The madness that causes Jesus to destroy the world in the *Novelle* is provoked by human perversity, not by thwarted sexual desire as in the *Furioso*. Indeed, throughout the *Novelle* there is little mention of romantic love or desire. There is not even a hint of the two cousins' jealous fighting over Angelica that figured so large in the *Innamorato*, provoking the subsequent elaboration on the 'Combattimento di Orlando e Rinaldo'.[30] Angelica herself is given little more than passing mention in the *Novelle*. When her name does comes up in a later *novella*, the real focus is actually Orlando's courtesy and generosity to the poor:

> Into those parts came Orlando, the great knight. He was tired, all night long he had been pursuing Angelica.
>
> 'O our Orlando, o our dear Orlando', shouted the men. 'Take some gold pieces'.
>
> He filled his helmet. Then he said, modestly, 'Enough, brothers. Where the need is greater, lesser need gives way'.[31]

The only other mention of Angelica in the *Novelle* suggests that, while she has not been dropped from the repertoire, she has passed out of Orlando's memory altogether:

> Giufà ... saw Orlando, white of hair, still disdained by Angelica, that treacherous woman. He was carrying Durendal at his side and was wearing his cuirass, but he had no desires, for time passes like a perennial river that wipes out the rose, the lily, and memory.[32]

---

[29] Bonaviri, 'San Pietro suona il violino ... ', pp. 41–3.

[30] Already in the *Furioso* Ariosto had drastically altered the role of Angelica; whereas she was at the centre of Boiardo's *Innamorato*, in the *Furioso* she leaves the scene well before its end (Rajna, *Le fonti*, p. 43).

[31] Di là passò Orlando il grande cavaliere; era stanco, tutta la notte aveva inseguito Angelica. 'O nostro Orlando, o nostro Orlanduzzo', gridarono gli uomini. 'Prendi dei marenghi d'oro'. Lui si riempì l'elmo, poi disse in castità: 'Basta, fratelli; dove maggior bisogno c'è, il minore cessa' (Bonaviri, 'I monaci del tristo convento', *Novelle*, p. 86).

[32] 'Giufà ... vide Orlando, bianco nei capelli, ancora in sdegno per Angelica femmina traditrice. Portava la durlindana al fianco, la corazza, ma non aveva ardori ché il tempo passa come fiume perenne che cancella la rosa, il giglio, la memoria' (Bonaviri, 'San Pietro suona il violino ... ', p. 42).

Other fantastic episodes, threaded through Boiardo's *Innamorato* and Ariosto's *Furioso*, make use of enchanted castles, mysterious woods, magic rings, bewitchments, vendettas, fountains of love and hate — in short, all the trappings and entanglements of 'courtly love'. These find no place in the *Novelle*. Indeed, if there is any love interest to be found, it is that of the love of a mother for her child. In an essay on the *Novelle*, Franco Zangrilli discusses the prominence given to the figure of the mother, who 'becomes practically omnipresent, being transformed constantly into an image now fabulous, now mythic, now universal'.[33] Indeed Zangrilli's typology of transfigurations forms a litany of its own: 'madre irrequieta, madre narratrice, madre addolorata, madre regina, madre chiesa, madre protettrice, consigliera, guida, madre adottiva, madre animale ... materna Sicilia, madre di cultura, madre terra'.[34] The pervasiveness of the mother image is fully consonant with Bonaviri's own characterization of the *Novelle*, which he calls the 'meeting-place' between himself and his mother.[35] Bonaviri repeatedly searches out these autobiographical meeting places. Events related to his family history provide the central event of several novels, as Calvino describes in his introduction to the English translation of *Notti sull'altura*:

> An event, probably autobiographical — the protagonist takes a trip to his birthplace on the occasion of his father's death — is here transfigured into a fantastic pilgrimage. The death of the father is incarnated in a mysterious feathered creature, the 'thanatobird', and children, friends, wizards and mystagogues devote themselves to searching for this unreachable bird. ... In their search for the bird of death, they decipher the signs of minerals and the metamorphoses of plants as if these things constituted a tight network of mysterious relationships.[36]

In *Notte sull'altura*, it is Death that leaves behind its mysterious traces. Similarly, in the *Novelle*, Death walks openly, as part of the conscious daily reality of the villagers:

> The villagers, in the midst of the barren fields, the women with spindles in their hands, thought of their dead ones. They felt them in their hands and in their eyes. ... At night, the dead came up out of their communal grave. The darkness was an unsettling cloud.

---

[33] 'Diviene quasi onnipresente trasformandose costantemente in immagine ora favolosa, ora mitica, ora universale' (Zangrilli, *Il fior di ficodindia. Saggio su Bonaviri*, Quaderni dell'Istituto di storia dello spettacolo siciliano 3 [Acireale: Cantinella, 1997], p. 13).

[34] Ibid., pp. 14–18. See my review of Zangrilli, *Il fior*, forthcoming in *Italian Quarterly*.

[35] Bonaviri, *Novelle*, p. 147.

[36] Bonaviri, *Nights on the Heights*, intro. Italo Calvino, trans. Giovanni Bussino (New York: Lang, 1990), pp. xiii–iv.

> The dead walked, each one carrying on his shoulders a pitcher full of tears. On their breasts sat sorrow. ... Their families, in festive dress, waited for them behind the windows, or they set candles at the doorways. The departed dead retained the memory of their children, their mothers, the donkey, the grass, the courtly knight-errant. ... The living, as you know, watched them in hiding, their hearts were sorrowful, but the mothers were happy, seeing their dead children wrapped in their white sheets. They were freed from the pains they had suffered, and from the fear of dark, shadowy death that played like a reed pipe in their hearts.[37]

In stark contrast to the melancholy figures who haunt this nocturnal village landscape, in the chivalric tradition, the death of the Christian warrior on the battlefield was made holy with the palm of martyrdom. Over the course of time and retelling, the conversion of the Saracen also began to feature regularly in the narrative. The *rovesciamento* of the earlier crucifixion scene makes use of the conventional episodes from the chivalric legends while opening the way to a new disruption in the tradition of sanctified death. 'Blessed Roland', the glory of Christian militarism, after centuries of narrative retellings in which he gained glory for battling the Saracens, now loses his life because of his friendship for the Saracen Jesus. There is no deathbed conversion scene nor any palm of martyrdom. Death in the *Novelle* brings with it no final redemption; the burden of the Cross is not lightened by the promise of a resurrected Jesus, let alone sainthood for Orlando, who in death thinks only of Nothingness. Yet while the dying Jesus's thoughts 'sank into the black sea' and Giufà fell 'into the Nothingness announced by the soldiers' blast', Orlando, by contrast, 'felt himself grow large, swelling over promontories and cliffs'. If the crucifixion scene represents the clash of 'two cultures, two hegemonies, two opposite mythographies', there is every reason to believe that Orlando will survive the encounter.

In his 1956 essay on the survival of Carolingian legends in Sicily, Ettore Li Gotti asserted that

---

[37] I villani, in mezzo ai nudi campi, le donne con fusi in mano, pensavano ai morti; se li sentivano sulle mani e sugli occhi ... Di notte uscivano dalla fossa comune, era stridente nembo il buio.

I morti camminavano ognuno portando su una spalla una brocca piena di lacrime. Sul petto a quelli sedeva il dolore. ... I parenti li aspettavano in abiti da festa dietro le finestre, o mettevano lumiere alle porte. I trapassati morti avevano memoria dei figli, delle madri, dell'asino, dell'erba, del cortese cavaliere errante. ... I vivi, si sa, li guardavano di nascosto, si sentivano lagrimoso il cuore, le madri però erano tutte contente vedendo i figli morti in bianche foglie chiusi. Quelli si liberavano dalle pene passate dalla paura di scura morte tenebrosa che suonava come zampogna nel loro cuore' (Bonaviri, 'San Pietro suona il violino ... ', pp. 36–7).

> Sicily is one of the few regions in Italy (and not only Italy) where the legend of Roland in particular, and the legend of Charlemagne's knights in general, still continues to live and therefore to be transformed.[38]

In order to live on, the Carolingian cycle must have its *contastorie*, and the *contastorie*, Pitrè tells us, is a job like any other. One embraces it because one has a particular vocation, a particular genius for it: not everyone knows how to tell a story. Whoever takes on the job must have not only a profound love for the tales of chivalry, but an easy and pleasing manner of telling them.[39] Pitrè's remarks referred specifically to the oral story-tellers of the nineteenth century, whom he had heard recite from memory the year-long cycles of stories of Charlemagne's knights. Bonaviri's reminiscences of his youth in Mineo, quoted at the outset of this chapter, demonstrate that the popular theatrical representation of the chivalric hero, handed down through generations of *pupari*, was still alive in the 1920s and 1930s. Bonaviri's many novels and works of poetry show that he has fashioned for himself the role of modern *contastorie*. The representation of Orlando in the *Novelle*, his exploits as an ageing and white-haired knight, still capable of generous deeds and valorous acts, still willing to make the ultimate sacrifice of an honourable death, positions the *Novelle saracene* in a long tradition, yet another continuation of the material of chivalric tales.

[38] 'La Sicilia è una delle poche regioni d'Italia (e non dell'Italia soltanto), dove continua a vivere e quindi a trasformarsi la legenda rolandiana in particolare, e in genere quella dei paladini di Carlomagno' (Ettore Li Gotti, *Sopravvivenza delle leggende carolingie in Sicilia*, Biblioteca del Centro di Studi filologici e linguistici siciliani 9 [Palermo: Centro di Studi filologici e linguistici siciliani, 1956], p. 7).

[39] 'Il contastorie è un mestiere come qualunque altro, e per lo più s'abbraccia per vocazione, per genio. ... Chi si dà a questo mestiere vuol avere, oltre che amore sviscerato per la cavalleria, ritentiva felicissima, facile e pronta parola, maniera particolare di porgere' (Pitrè, 'Le tradizioni', p. 346).

Chapter 9

From medieval realism to modern fantasy: *Guerrino Meschino* through the centuries

Gloria Allaire

Perhaps no other chivalric text has captured and held in thrall the Italian imagination like the epic romance *Guerrino Meschino*. A largely original creation along the lines of an Old French *chanson de geste*, but infused with certain elements from Breton romance, it was composed by the Florentine Andrea da Barberino sometime between 1406 and 1431.[1] Although the content of the first and last of *Guerrino*'s eight lengthy Books is rather conventional (containing a three-day joust, a champion who fights incognito, besieged cities saved by the lone Christian hero and maidens spurned by or enamoured of him), the inner Books represent a unique synthesis of material from well-known medieval legends such as Prester John, the *Alexander Romance*, the Sibyl's cave and Saint Patrick's Purgatory. These characters and adventures are set within a naturalistic topography that is inhabited by a host of exotic people and animals drawn from the Plinian strain of natural history.

Far from being a loose aggregation of fantastic literary tropes, the original narrative derives its organic wholeness from the author's pseudo-historical style that employs verisimilar descriptions of characters, places and events. Maestro Andrea rationalized and clarified the sometimes confused material of his sources to make it more believable to the tastes of pragmatic and sceptical fifteenth-century Florentines. He eliminated most magical and supernatural elements, improved the language and generally elevated the material to suit his more critical audience.[2] Furthermore, Maestro Andrea's clear focus on the individual protagonist and his actions unifies to the text. Unlike the vague, unstructured wanderings of the typical knight errant, this hero's numerous adventures stretch

---

A shorter version of this study was read at the American Association of Italian Studies annual meeting, Chicago, Illinois, April 1998.

[1] 1406 marked the appearance of Jacopo Angelo da Scarperia's translation of Ptolemy's *Cosmographia*, a work that informed the detailed geographical infrastructure of *Guerrino*'s narrative. Maestro Andrea died between 1431 and 1433 (Michele Catalano, 'La data di morte di Andrea da Barberino', *Archivum Romanicum* **23** [1939], pp. 84–7).

[2] Charles Peter Brand, *Ludovico Ariosto. A preface to the* Orlando Furioso, Writers of Italy (Edinburgh: Edinburgh University Press, 1974), pp. 48–9.

logically through time and space: dates and time periods are carefully cited to emulate an actual late medieval travel account, and the protagonist's ten-year itinerary can be traced on actual medieval maps.

Surviving manuscript evidence reveals that not only were these narratives read aloud *in piazza* by the author himself,[3] but they were owned and read by the élite of Florence — wealthy bankers, merchants, guild members and the oligarchical élite.[4] *Guerrino*, known to them by its medieval title *Il Meschino di Durazzo*, was read by members of the Benci, Doni, Porcellini, Guasconi, Gaddi, Salviati and Orlandini families, among others. The text also enjoyed a wide transmission outside of Tuscany where its readers included nobles, princes and kings: the Venetian nobleman Francesco Contarini[5] and the Ferrarese prince Borso d'Este[6] commissioned copies; Federico Gonzaga owned a copy,[7] as did the Aragonese kings in Naples.[8] Of all extant exemplars of Andrea's works, only *Guerrino* was illuminated, indicating the special regard with which medieval book owners viewed it. A labelled engraving and three separate library inventories show transmission to Umbria and Sicily in the last decades of the fifteenth century.[9] Still later, multiple printed copies were found in the royal libraries of France.[10] There were at least ten incunabulum editions of *Guerino* — the spelling preferred by northern Italian printers — and its publishing history continued actively until 1967.[11] The nineteenth- and twentieth-century editions of *Guerrino*

---

[3] See Gloria Allaire, *Andrea da Barberino and the Language of Chivalry* (Gainesville, FL: University Press of Florida, 1997), p. 6.

[4] Allaire, The Chivalric 'Histories' of Andrea da Barberino', dissertation, University of Wisconsin-Madison, 1993, pp. 106–73.

[5] Fanny Autelli, *Codici e incunaboli miniati della Biblioteca Civica di Bergamo* (Bergamo: Credito Bergamasco, 1989), pp. 324–5.

[6] Giulio Bertoni, 'Notizie sugli amanuensi degli Estensi nel quattrocento', *Archivum romanicum* **2** (1918), pp. 36, 37–8.

[7] Alessandro Luzio and Rodolfo Renier, 'La coltura e le relazioni letterarie di Isabella d'Este Gonzaga', *Giornale Storico della Letteratura Italiana* **33** (1899), p. 10.

[8] Present-day Paris, Bibliothèque Nationale, MSS ital. 491 and 98. See also Tammaro De Marinis, *La Biblioteca napoletana dei re d'Aragona*, 4 vols (Milan: Hoepli, 1952), vol. 1, pp. 175–6.

[9] Arthur M. Hind, *Catalogue of Early Italian Engravings ...* , 3 vols (London: Trustees, 1910), vol. 3, p. 302; Henri Bresc, *Livre et société en Sicilie (1299–1499)*, Bollettino, Suppl. 3 (Palermo: Centro di Studi filologici e linguistici siciliani, 1971), pp. 325, 332, 336.

[10] Ministére de l'Instruction Publique, *Anciens Inventaires et catalogues de la Bibliothèque Nationale*, ed. H. Omont, 5 vols (Paris: Leroux, 1908), vol. 1, p. 401; vol. 2, pp. 352, 495; vol. 3, p. 12; vol. 4, p. 54, appendix.

[11] To avoid confusion, I will use the Tuscan form *Guerrino* to refer to the original medieval version and *Guerrin* for that of Bufalino. My own survey of printed editions of *Guerrino* reveals the following totals for each century: sixteenth century (18 editions), seventeenth (at least 7),

may well be called 'popular': printed for mass consumption, the quality of the text — both language and content — declined through numerous editorial retouchings and rewritings. *Guerrino*'s long and complex textual history thus represents a fascinating case for a study of narrative recastings.

One must begin with the 1473 *editio princeps* of *Guerino il Meschino* published in Padua by Bartholomaeus de Valdezocch[i]o and Martinus de Septem Arboribus. The language of this edition is heavily coloured by north-eastern Italian regionalisms in contrast to the majority of extant manuscript exemplars that are in clear, pure Florentine. One also notes that the title of all printed editions privileges the hero's baptized name 'Guerrino' over 'Meschino' ('poor wretch'), a nickname that indicates his apparent lack of high birth as well as his many misfortunes.[12] This phenomenon of renaming first began in manuscripts of the 1460s or 1470s: as the story circulated and became well known, copyists already familiar with the plot would inadvertently slip in the hero's baptized name where earlier exemplars had read only 'il Meschino'. In the story, the infant hero is captured by pirates and sold as a slave after his father's kingdom was sacked by invaders. Although the reader knows his true name, for much of the book the protagonist is ignorant of his noble birth and travels under the name 'Meschino'.

The original Tuscan text underwent further linguistic reworking when it was translated into Castilian and into French early in the sixteenth century.[13] The *Cronica del caualero Guarino Mezquino* by Alonso Hernández Alemán (1527, 1548) remains quite faithful to the original. For the French translation, however, textual disparities between an extant manuscript copy (Cambridge, Fitzwilliam Museum, MSS 25–6, written *c.* 1500) and print editions (1530, 1531, 1532, 1620, 1628) suggests that there were two different translators. The author of the Cambridge manuscript, Jean de Rochemeure, was rather free in his use of amplification, and oscillated between slavishly 'correct' translation and interpolating passages in his own voice according to his own narrative intent.[14] Thus one might call his text the first early modern reinterpretation of *Guerrino*.

Another sixteenth-century retelling was Tullia d'Aragona's extended reworking in octaves entitled *Il Meschino altramente detto Il Guerino* (Venice: Sessa,

eighteenth (7), nineteenth (29), twentieth (39).

[12] For a discussion of the etymology of this hero's name, see the chapter intitled 'Il Guerrin Meschino. Viaggiatore dell'Immaginario', in Franco Cardini, *L'invenzione dell'Occidente. Come la Cristianità europea divenne occidentale* (Chieti: Solfanelli, 1995), pp. 224–5n.

[13] Allaire, *Andrea da Barberino*, p. 12.

[14] Anna Maria Babbi, 'Le traduzioni del *Guerrin Meschino* in Francia', in *Il romanzo nella Francia del Rinascimento dall'eredità medievale all'*Astrea. *Atti del Convegno Internazionale di Studi, Gargnano, 7–9 ottobre 1993*, Gruppo di Studio sul Cinquecento francese 6 (Fasano: Schena, 1996), pp. 150–52.

1560).[15] Living in Counter-Reformation Italy and at a time when women writers and intellectuals were still struggling for public acceptance, Tullia had her own agenda for the changes she enacted on her probable Tuscan model. Although she maintained the principal characters and overall plot structure, many episodes have been abbreviated or elided while others were expanded. Since she composed it in part to demonstrate her *onestà* or respectability as a higher-class courtesan, not to be confused with a common prostitute, one finds a sterner moralizing and a harsher view of women that is not faithful to Maestro Andrea's original. Other changes were made for aesthetic reasons or to display her poetic ability at writing in the epic register.

Because early print editions of *Guerrino* represented a linguistic departure from the original Tuscan, an important task of nineteenth- and early twentieth-century publishers like Bietti and Salani was to 're-Tuscanize' the language for modern readers, a process that took the text ever farther from its medieval original. One may well ask what elements of the text allowed its cultural reclamation five centuries after its composition. The morally pristine hero took on an added modern Catholic dimension, and his ten-year quest to find his true heritage and deliver his realm from foreign occupation must have resonated strongly for pre-Risorgimento patriots. The proto-modern, desiring subject Guerrino was like a blank page or, better, a palimpsest, upon which the Italian people of a particular time or place could project its own hopes and desires, upon which it could write its own happy resolution to a long quest for political identity. The medieval protagonist Guerrino had originally represented royal lineage and feudal loyalties as reinterpreted anachronistically through the eyes of *nouveau riche* Florentines who consciously emulated the old aristocracy; he later came to stand for the Catholic right and the monarchy of post-Risorgimento Italy; finally, in the case of Sicilian puppet theatre and Bufalino's 1993 reworking, he opened a door to an exotic world of fantasy, a door that would brusquely slam shut when the need for such escapism had passed.

The text's second phase of modern reworking occurred in the early twentieth century when it was condensed, retold and marketed as appropriate reading material for Italian youths, a trend that had a precedent in the Renaissance when chivalric epic romances like *I Reali di Francia* and *Buovo d'Antona* were used to teach reading by Venetian schoolmasters.[16] With the modern increase in literacy, the text came to be viewed as suitable for adolescent readers. This is

---

[15] Published posthumously. For a discussion of its dating and significance, see Allaire, 'Tullia d'Aragona's *Il Meschino altramente detto il Guerino* as Key to a Reappraisal of Her Work', *Quaderni d'italianistica* **16.1** (1995), pp. 33–50.

[16] Paul F. Grendler, *Schooling in Renaissance Italy. Literacy and Learning, 1300–1600*, The Johns Hopkins University Studies in Historical and Political Science 107th Series, 1 (Baltimore, MD: The Johns Hopkins University Press, 1989), pp. 292–3.

demonstrated by Luisa Steiner Stabarin's Fascist era abridgement, *Dalle avventure di Guerino detto il Meschino* (Turin: Paravia, 1934). Her abridgement was described by a post-war journalist as a collection of harmless adventure stories that — ironically — the reviewer now reads with a strong Democratic Christian emphasis on faith, family and upright behaviour for which the hero provides a good role model:

> Long and perilous is his wandering through the world. ... He fights for all the abandoned, endangered waifs and strikes down the cruel oppressors, he lives among anxiety and dreams ... smiles at love and at grief, and succeeds finally *with the help of God and not that of magic, to find his parents and crown the end of his days with the joys of family and Faith.* ... [Stabarin's] reworking ... will certainly be effective reading matter for young souls who love these bizarre and fanciful stories, filled with the sounds of arms and knights ... (emphasis added).[17]

It is strange to find that, in its modern form, a text originally written for the no-nonsense, pragmatic merchants and diplomats who built Renaissance Florence was now being consigned to adolescent fantasies. The same thing happened with the mistaken analogy of its puppet theatre representations to children's entertainment. It is not easy to establish when such associations began,[18] but they were probably due to the critical prejudices of university-trained intellectuals who brought their own preconceptions to semiotically complex art forms in which they did not fully participate.[19] This problem recalls the reception of orally performed chivalric material in earlier centuries: even as such accounts were admired and eagerly consumed by the popular audience, Latin humanists like Francis Petrarch, Poggio Bracciolini and Mario Equicola mocked their enthusiasm.[20]

---

[17] 'Lungo e pericoloso è il suo errare per il mondo. ... [S]i batte per tutti i derelitti insidiati e abbatte i crudeli e prepotenti, vive di ansie e di speranze, ... sorride all'amore e al dolore, e riesce finalmente, con l'aiuto di Dio e non con quello della magia, a trovare i suoi genitori e a coronare la fine della sua esistenza con le gioie della famiglia e delle Fede. ... La sua rielaborazione ... riuscirà certamente efficace lettura per le anime giovanili, che amano queste storie, bizzarramente fantasiose, risonanti d'armi e cavalieri ...' (Giovanni Bitelli, 'Guerino detto il Meschino', *Corriere del Giorno* [Taranto] 15 December 1951, p. 3). All translations are mine.

[18] Antonio Pasqualino, *Le vie del cavaliere dall'epica medievale alla cultura popolare*, Studi Bompiani (Milan: Bompiani, 1992), pp. 267–8.

[19] For the semiotic complexity of reading a 'testo spettacolare' that was improvised in puppet shows, see ibid., pp. 231–3.

[20] Francesco Petrarca, Rime e Trionfi, Mario Apollonio and Lina Ferro (eds), (Brescia: La Scuola, 1972), p. 66; Mario Equicola, *Chronica di Mantua*, quoted in Carlo Dionisotti, 'Fortuna e sfortuna del Boiardo nel Cinquecento', in *Il Boiardo e la critica contemporanea, Atti del convegno di studi su Matteo Maria Boiardo, Scandiano-Reggio Emilia 25–27 aprile 1969*, ed.

In the nineteenth century, *Guerrino* was the most prestigious of stories performed in the Neapolitan and Sicilian puppet theatres.[21] No mere childish entertainment, these public shows drew an audience of adult males for whom the resuscitated tenants of chivalry, the echoes of bold arms resounding and the phantasms of indomitable heroes breathed life into their own *machismo* struggling impotently under the oppressive rule of the newly unified Italian government.[22] Thus, modern retellings of *Guerrino* — like their medieval counterparts — were transmitted along two different, but parallel, channels for reception: one written and one oral.[23]

Another modern version of *Guerrino* appeared in the world of bourgeois theatre. A melodramatic stage version by Domenico Tumiati was performed in Buenos Aires at the time of the First World War.[24] In a review of this production, Giustino Ferri alluded to the transformation *Guerrino* had undergone, comparing it to the various incarnations of the Doctor Faustus or Don Juan legends.[25] According to Ferri, such works are dynamic, possessing the potential of an 'indefinite metempsychosis' in time and space. Their contents and the sentiments that they express can be varied either in their retelling or in their reception, being variously interpreted by author or audience according to the tastes of different centuries and cultures. In the case of his play, Tumiati reduced the original — filled with individual heroism, epic travels and military victories — to a sentimental love story based on a single episode taken from the beginning of Book Two of the medieval source.[26] In the medieval original, Guerrino and his companion, a French knight named Messer Brandisio, help a Saracen princess Aminadam to free her besieged city of Media. Guerrino, just beginning his quest to discover his parentage, is never enamoured of this woman and leaves the city quickly, content that his companion Brandisio has married her and will rule the

---

Giuseppe Anceschi, Biblioteca dell'*Archivum Romanicum* Ser. 1: Storia-Letteratura-Paleografia 107 (Florence: Olschki, 1970), p. 234; Poggio Bracciolini, *Facezie*, ed. Marcello Ciccuto, Biblioteca Universale Rizzoli. I classici della BUR (Milan: Rizzoli, 1983), pp. 201–3.

[21] Pio Rajna, 'I "Rinaldi" o cantastorie di Napoli', *Nuova Antologia*, 2nd ser. **12** (1878), p. 572. See also Giuseppe Pitrè, 'Le tradizioni cavalleresche popolari in Sicilia', *Romania* **13** (1884), pp. 322, 345n, 348–9, 386, *passim*.

[22] For this hypothesis, see Marcella Croce, 'Manifestations of the Chivalric Traditions in Sicily', dissertation, University of Wisconsin-Madison, 1988.

[23] The same dual transmission influenced Giuseppe Bonaviri's chivalric inspired writings. See the chapter by Barbara De Marco earlier in this volume.

[24] Domenico Tumiati, Guerrin Meschino: *Dramma cavalleresco*, 2nd edn (1912; Milan: Treves, 1928).

[25] Giustino Ferri, rev. of *Guerrin Meschino*, play by Domenico Tumiati, *Nuova Antologia*, 5th ser. **164** (1913), pp. 454–5.

[26] For plot description, see Rodolfo Renier, 'Guerin Meschino', *Fanfulla della Domenica* (Rome), 9 June 1912, p. 2.

city. Tumiati was drawn to the potential love triangle in this episode around which he invented an anti-heroic story of sentimental love and masochistic suffering. His emphasis on lust and passion is completely at odds with the ethos of Andrea da Barberino's epic romances. Although lesser characters are sometimes involved in minor dalliances with willing Saracen maidens, Maestro Andrea's male protagonists consistently behave in a morally upright manner when confronted with sexual temptations: the original Guerrino proves his firm resolve to remain faithful to his betrothed when he repeatedly shuns the advances of seductive women who are attracted by his noble visage and physical prowess.[27] This is most evident in Book Five when he passes a virtuous year in the Venusberg-like cave of the Sibyl of Norcia.

A similar modern, post-Freudian insertion of psychological explorations of sexual desire appears in the opening pages of the most recent incarnation of *Guerrino* by the prize-winning author Gesualdo Bufalino. This is a short work of fiction, part prose and part poetry, entitled *Il Guerrin Meschino. Frammento di un'opra dei pupi* (Milan: Bompiani, 1993). Taking his inspiration from the two principal strands of modern *Guerrino* retellings — the popular prose edition and the puppet theatre — Bufalino pretends to re-enact performances of *Guerrin* by an ageing *puparo* (puppet master). According to the book's dust-jacket, the young Bufalino had worked in the shop of one of these folk artists, and also was familiar with the story through one of the popular Salani editions. The brevity of his chapters and the language of certain passages suggests that he may also have been influenced by the more abbreviated Bietti editions which also circulated in Sicily.[28] Bufalino narrates Guerrin's adventures in prose written as though one were reading yet another modern editor's retouched version of the medieval story, but he frames and glosses the chivalric adventures with introspective poems. Although in many ways this latest creative treatment violates the spirit of Maestro Andrea's original — a version that Bufalino could hardly have known since there is at present no critical edition[29] — the reinterpretation finds its justification in the dynamic metempsychotic process discussed above. Bufalino participates in an act of composition that is in many ways more medieval in its nature than modern: he takes up a pre-existing text, at once abbreviating, expanding, conserving and innovating within the narrative parameters bequeathed

[27] Similarly, in a scene that recalls the biblical Potiphar's wife, Andrea's Ugo d'Avernia flees the advances of his lord's wife (*Storia di Ugone d'Avernia volgarizzata nel sec. XIV*, F[rancesco] Zambrini and A[lberto] Bacchi della Lega (eds), Sceltà di curiosità letterarie inedite o rare dal secolo XIII al XIX, dispense 188–9 [1882; Bologna: Commissione per i testi di lingua, 1968], vol. 1, pp. 6–8).

[28] The actual Sicilian *pupari* had at their disposal numerous editions published by Bietti and Salani, as well as one by Nerbini purported to be written by Aldo Forlandi (Pasqualino, p. 290).

[29] I have begun work on such an edition.

to him by a long dead author of the past, making the ancient source text speak with a new voice to a new audience. The freedom with which Bufalino retells the story combined with the respect that he shows it — a kind of homage by a faithful reader/spectator — situate this latest *Guerrin* at the end of an already complex textual tradition.

Although many modernisms had crept into the story through the process of repeated editing, certain minutiae of dialogue or description that extend back to the manuscript tradition itself have remarkably been preserved and find their way into Bufalino's text. For example, the words from the Latin liturgy 'Salvum me fac' survived in the Salani and Bietti editions that Bufalino may have known even though the Purgatorial episode in which they were originally found was excised from print editions as a result of the Counter-Reformation.[30] Similarly, modern published versions have somehow managed to conserve details of a Dantesque damned soul, retaining both his name, Macco, and his physical description — lying across a path like a sack of wool (*un sacco di lana*) — from the manuscript tradition.[31] Bufalino begins with a fairly faithful, although severely truncated retelling of Book One and the first part of Book Two of Andrea's *Guerrino*. The general plot outline is preserved as are names of characters: the hero's father Milone, prince of Taranto, attacks the kingdom ruled by two Albanian brothers Madar and Napar. The war is largely a ruse to win for himself their beautiful sister Fenisia. In the counterattack, the nurse Sefera saves the infant Guerrino, who is then captured by pirates and sold to Epidonio. The foster father, a merchant in the original, is here called a seneschal. In both versions Guerrino grows to manhood at the court in Constantinople, suffers the unrequited love of the emperor's daughter Elisena, and wins a joust that he fights incognito.

In matters of style and description, the modern version departs radically from the original. One must remember, however, that Bufalino has inherited a wealth of later accretions from his immediate oral and printed sources so we must not accuse him of deliberately misrepresenting the medieval text. Some glaring anachronisms have crept in; for example, the female spectators at the joust carry fans and throw roses similar to the bullfight scene in *Carmen* (p. 21). Guerrino enters the lists wearing a device of black with silver teardrops (p. 24). Bufalino's equine characters accomplish impossible feats never proposed in the original: jumping into and out of the lists with the fully armed knight in the saddle, carrying three men to safety by jumping across a river three times, and successfully fighting off a gryphon attack (pp. 24–5, 43, 62–3). (Horses were the favourite food of gryphons in medieval bestiaries; a mount in Andrea's original

---

[30] *Guerrino detto il Meschino* (Florence: Salani, 1926), p. 280; *Guerino Meschino* (Milan: Bietti, 1900), p. 175.

[31] Salani edn (1926), p. 283 names Macco, but changes the wording of the description; Bietti edn (1900), pp. 175–6 is closer to Andrea's original.

is swiftly killed.) Weapons such as the *giavellotto* (javelin) are anachronistically mentioned (p. 31). There is a moment of racial tension à la *Othello* as the emperor fearfully imagines that a 'Moor' (a term rarely employed in Andrea) may win his daughter in the joust and bed her (p. 23). When Guerrino splits a Saracen opponent in two (p. 32), a ray of sunlight shines through the wound similar to King Arthur's piercing of Mordred; such a description of wounding is without precedent in the Carolingian cycle texts of Andrea da Barberino or indeed in any late medieval Italian known to me. Bufalino summarizes Book Two somewhat less faithfully, retaining the beginning of the hero's travels, his fight with the giant Maccabeos, and the rescue of French knight Brandisio and an Armenian Christian. But the retelling ignores Maestro Andrea's careful geographical plot and very quickly deteriorates into a reordered listing of names and places derived from the medieval text, but lacking its orderly structure. Bufalino briefly mentions the adventures that will follow: Guerrino's encounters with the homosexual king Pacifero, Prester John, an innkeeper's lusty daughter, the princess of Media Aminadam and the two rival Saracen kings who duel to win her. As if there were not enough toponyms in the story (well over 800 in the manuscript tradition), Bufalino invents some fantastic countries of his own: the Kingdoms of the White Stones, the Land of Discomfort and the desert of Lòp. He also inserts a character named 'Babele' who speaks in a mixture of languages,[32] reminiscent of the heteroglossic Salvatore in Umberto Eco's *Il nome della rosa* (*The Name of the Rose*).

Bufalino clearly has his own agenda for his retelling: beyond the obvious notions of reworking a famous text or of paying literary homage to a cultural phenomenon, he also expresses certain apparently autobiographical complaints. Through various symbolic and metaphoric additions not in the original, he expresses a melancholic regret for the loss of innocence and youth, the danger and pleasure of illusions, the failing physical capacities of a man past his prime and the inevitability of ageing and death. The old age/death theme is introduced in his opening poem/proem and is a leitmotif throughout the prose account of Guerrin's adventures. The opening poem alludes to the *puparo*'s once carefree life of riding horses to various fairs throughout Sicily, of games of chance, of a vigorous body with acute senses and of attracting women with his manly physique. The author uses parts of the body (hands, teeth, eyes, ears) as synecdoches to contrast the strong body of his youth to its now failing capacities. This regret is not expressed only in sensual terms, but in professional ones: as a puppeteer his livelihood depends on quick hands, clear voice and good memory. The arthritic hands of an old man cannot manage the puppets

> Io non so chi mi ha tolto quelle mani.

[32] Bufalino, *Il Guerrin Meschino*, pp. 72, 74–5, 82, 126.

Annaspano ora, imbrogliano i fili,
i pupi cascano da tutte le parti (p. 8).

(I don't know who stole those hands from me.
They grope along now, they tangle the wires;
the puppets fall down all over.)

nor can the voice of an old man properly articulate his heroic stories:

Ora la voce, ch'era tromba, flauto e tamburo,
suona unica per tutti i pupi,
cristiani e mammalucchi, vassalli e re di corona.
Il gemito dell'amante, il gemito del moribondo,
un'uguale tosse li recita ... (pp. 8–9)

(Now the voice that was once trumpet, flute and drum,
sounds the same for all the puppets,
Christians and Saracens, vassals and crowned kings.
The moan of the lover, the moan of the dying,
an identical cough delivers them all ...)

Although these claims for such expressive vocal powers may seem mere poetic hyperbole, eyewitness evidence attests to their realism. For instance, an early twentieth-century British traveller to Sicily furnishes a moving tribute to the power of the puppeteer's voice. His discussion of puppet performances is written in a light-hearted, though condescending tone, mocking the credulity of the simple folk who watch them. Yet even this sophisticated and sceptical modern man falls under the spell of the Sicilian puppeteer, and he is forced to conclude admiringly:

> Art abounds in miracles, and not the least is this, that a man can take a few watery commonplaces and by the magic of his voice transmute them into the golden wine of romance. The audience drank in the glowing drops that poured from his lips. ... What did they know of loosely jointed wooden dolls or of toy stages? They were no longer in the theatre. They had wandered the woods with Marfisa, they had sought Bradamante in the leafy glades, they had found her dying in the grotto ... and the world would never be the same to them again. A voice that can do this is rare and, like the power of a giant, rarely found in the possession of one who knows how to use it worthily.[33]

[33] Henry Festing Jones, *Diversions in Sicily* (London: Fifield, 1920), p. 128. For a typology of vocal sounds used by the traditional puppeteers, see Pasqualino, pp. 237–8.

In the opening poem, Bufalino drives home his lament about old age, twice repeating the line 'Non si dovrebbe diventar vecchi' ('One should not have to become old' [pp. 8, 9]). This thematic extends to his retelling of Andrea's *Guerrino* and accounts for several elements that simply are not found in the medieval tradition. For much of Bufalino's *Guerrin*, the hero travels alone through unpopulated wilderness with only his horse, a modern addition here called 'Macchiabruna' ('Dark Spot'), as a partner. This is in stark contrast to the bustling medieval landscape through which Andrea da Barberino's hero passes. In the medieval version, the hero is at times forced to cross deserts and uninhabited regions, but he always travels with companions, guides or interpreters, if not at the head of an army. Bufalino's general tone of melancholy is faithful to certain passages of the original, but the medieval Guerrino is hardly the brooding Romantic or depressive that we find in this retelling.

In one fantastic episode of Bufalino's *Guerrin*, a fairy messenger in the guise of a butterfly (!) leads the hero to the Castle Without Time, also called the Palace of the Immortals (pp. 87–94). Within this enchanted castle dwell ancient Elders who survived Noah's Flood. Time has stopped for them, and they have the gift of immortality, but after so many centuries of *ennui* the gift has become burdensome. Because Guerrin has 'youth, courage and innocence' (p. 89), he is able to locate and enter the castle, and break the spell. Remarkably, although the scene of the demise of the Immortals was invented by Bufalino to emphasize his own old age thematic in an existentialist key, a similar scene existed in Maestro Andrea's original, Book Six, in which Guerrino makes a pilgrimage to Saint Patrick's Purgatory located on an Irish island. *En route*, he passes the 'isola carnefice' ('Executioner's Island'). This is a place where the inhabitants cannot die as long as they remain on the island; leaving it would cause their immediate deaths. After their long lives become too burdensome, they must receive special dispensation from the Pope to step off the island, an action tantamount to committing suicide. This minor episode was among the 28 chapters of Saint Patrick's Purgatory that were excised from print editions of *Guerrino* after the Council of Trent and are absent in all the modern printed editions I have examined. There is thus no way Bufalino could have known this episode unless he had studied an early print edition or manuscript of Andrea's *Guerrino*. It is also possible that remnants of the scene may have survived in popular lore, and that Bufalino may have learned it from the oral tradition of the puppet theatre.

The lament for old age recurs in its most potent, concentrated form in the fourth and final section of Bufalino's little book. After years of bearing his master, the horse Macchiabruna can no longer support his weight, and Guerrin proceeds on foot out of compassion for his mount. The scene of the faithful horse's death 'without uttering a complaint' (p. 107) is not without a certain pathos, but the details that the knightly hero 'piously' buried him in a cave and prayed that heaven accept his departed soul are far removed from medieval literary topoi and would have shocked medieval Catholics who believed that animals had no souls.

The death of Guerrin's horse resonates beyond the puppet stage to the puppeteer/author himself because the next fragment is a poem entitled 'Chiuso per lutto' ('Closed for mourning').[34] In this short poem, the *puparo* says he is closing and will refund admissions because he doesn't feel like performing this evening. He then states that a wake would serve Guerrin well. The poem's meaning pivots on the words 'mourning' and 'Sicily'. It suddenly becomes a complex lament for Sicily, combining symbols of Christ's passion with the image of the angel's trumpet call at the Last Judgement and juxtaposing Guerrin's heroic gestures to the *petit bourgeois* modern life represented by two objects that rupture the fabric of fantasy, piercing it with the banality of the quotidian: the telephone and the cigarette. There will be no heroic salvation of Sicily nor any Final Judgement; medieval heroism and medieval Catholicism are conjoined as once potent, now lifeless beliefs, drained of energy like the hands of the tired ageing puppeteer. The only hope that this complex of beliefs may live again is found in a child waiting at the foot of the stage.

The frustration with lost physical capacities and the themes of death and grieving bring a desolate tone to the book's final section. As in the introductory poem, the personal becomes a critique of the professional. The ability of the puppeteer to enthral his audiences with fables of the most fantastic invention is at once celebrated and deplored. As in the moment when a child suddenly accepts the fact that there is no Santa Claus, the willing suspension of disbelief demanded of the *puparo*'s viewers has abruptly ceased to function. For the medieval readers of *Guerrino*, seeing was believing: during his travels, the protagonist encounters all manner of exotica, but these were described in concrete, naturalistic terms. On the other hand, Bufalino's Guerrin treads a landscape of fantasy populated by improbable creatures such as the Phoenix. Whereas the medieval hero's response was most often to dominate or even slay opponents, monsters and wild animals along his route, his modern descendant most often emerges from such encounters confused, bemused and wondering if he had been dreaming. Early in his journey, Bufalino's hero meets a monkey that metamorphoses into various birds, a squirrel and, finally, a hairy rustic before revealing himself to be the old magician Eudocio (p. 39). (No such scene appears in the original.) When the hero tries to grab this shapeshifter, he escapes 'in a column of sulphur and smoke. ... A diabolical deceit, therefore' ('in una colonna di zolfo e fumo. ... Un diabolico inganno, dunque'). Similarly, the uniquely

[34] Pages 110–11. This closing may also be seen as the author's protest over the May 1992 murder of anti-Mafia investigator Giovanni Falcone (Charles Knopp, rev. of *Il Guerrin Meschino: Frammento di un'opra dei pupi*, by G. Bufalino, in *World Literature Today* **69** (1995), p. 115.

coloured butterfly guide floating on the air before Guerrin is a relatively charming image, however incongruous its appearance may be in a story of a world-renowned warrior. The insect seems real enough: it speaks to him in a woman's voice, he catches it, it lands on his shoulder and it helps him release the Immortals from their enchantment. However, the episode ends with Guerrin opening his eyes, 'sticky from sleep' ('vischiosi di sonno' [p. 93]). Natural creatures take on fabulous qualities, and then become real or illusionary in succession. For the disillusioned puppeteer/author, seeing is a trick of the mind that can be skilfully employed to perpetrate deceptions upon the too willing spectator/reader. The old *puparo* now realizes that times have changed and that people have no need for such complicit deceptions. Modern contraptions such as the telephone and the motorbike wrench the spectator away from the comforting grasp of fantasy that is found within the theatrical space and thrust him into the too harsh world of the concrete.

Bufalino strips away the last vestiges of childlike believing in two reflexive gestures. In the last prose segment, Guerrin is confronted by the Old Man of the Mountain who tries to convert him to become one of his Assassins — a scene nowhere found in the manuscript tradition of *Guerrino* although it is certainly not without medieval analogues. Guerrin confesses that he has many times shed blood, and is therefore already a murderer, but he cries out in frustration:

> 'Non vedi i fili che mi sono attaccati alle ascelle? Non senti che parlo con la gola d'un altro? Che sono una marionetta?' (p. 120)
>
> ('Don't you see the strings that are attached to my armpits? Don't you hear that I speak with the throat of another? That I am a marionette?')

He has no will of his own and therefore cannot be held responsible for his actions. The second stripping away of pretence and belief is even more brutal and occurs in the closing poem. The show has ended and with it, the theatre season. The puppet master is preparing to leave town when townsfolk beg him to stay. He rejects their invitation with finality:

> 'Quando una cosa finisce, finisce.
>
> ...
>
> Vi ricordate Buovo d'Antona,[35]
> che morì mentre pregava
> ginocchioni nella chiesa del Salvatore,
> accoltellato a tradimento?
> Un giorno l'uno, un giorno l'altro,

[35] The principal regal character from Book Four of Andrea da Barberino, *I Reali di Francia*, Giuseppe Vandelli and Giovanni Gambarin (eds), Scrittori d'Italia 193 (Bari: Laterza, 1947).

tutti finiamo così.' (p. 124)

('When a thing ends, it ends.
...
Remember Buovo d'Antona
who died while he was praying,
on his knees in the Church of the Saviour,
treacherously stabbed?
One day one, one day another,
we'll all end up like that.')

To convince them that even the great hero Guerrin is finished, he grabs the marionette that represents him and cruelly snaps its neck with his two fingers, shouting: 'Non l'avevate capito? / Sono io, Guerrino il Meschino' ('Haven't you understood? I, I am Guerrino Meschino?' [p. 125]) It is with these moving lines that Bufalino's narration concludes.

The tone of sadness and nostalgia for a past that can never be replaced and a loss of innocence that can never be regained reflect two moments found in the original medieval version. In these episodes, which reveal a surprising psychological depth for a fifteenth-century literary creation, the hero, well along on his quest to discover his parentage and his true identity, raises a plaintive lament for the sufferings he has endured on his travels and gives way to momentary self-pity over the apparent hopelessness of ever finding his parents. He utters his first soliloquy at the Ganges, the eastern edge of the world. This is echoed when he arrives at Finisterre, the westernmost point of the European continent. In Bufalino's poems, the author's fictional alter ego looks at inventions like the telephone and the motorbike with the same sense of bemused wonder with which the medieval Guerrino once viewed gryphons, manticors and monstrous races in the East. Through the eyes of his re-created Guerrin, Bufalino experiences a similar sense of detachment from his own world, yet expresses regret and nostalgia because he no longer belongs to it. While Guerrin/*puparo*/author were immersed in pursuing their own fantastic adventures, the real world changed and left them behind, exiled from real space and time. Like the Immortals in their palace, time has also stopped for them and they are condemned to live forever in eternal *ennui*, as entertainment for a cruel god who made them. When viewed through the lens of this episode, the *puparo*'s final gesture takes on new meaning. Instead of the heartless cruelty of a creator toward his creature, it can now be read as a merciful release from an endless existence in a sphere where being no longer has any meaning.

Chapter 10

Coming full circle: romance as *romanzo* in Elsa Morante's *L'isola di Arturo*

Myriam Swennen Ruthenberg

Di te, Finzione, mi cingo,
fatua veste.
Ti lavoro con l'auree piume
che vesti prima d'esser fuoco
la mia grande stagione defunta
per mutarmi in fenice lucente!

(O Illusion, I draw about me
your concealing garment
and adorn it with the golden plumage
that was mine in the great lost season
before I grew all fire
and rose a radiant phoenix.)
'Alla favola' ('To the Story')[1]

Elsa Morante. *L'isola di Arturo*. Romanzo. This is what we read on the cover and title-page of Einaudi's edition of Morante's second novel, published in 1957. The deliberate inclusion of the word 'romanzo' precludes dismissing the word as a mere editorial explication. Although the same could be said for Morante's other novels *Menzogna e sortilegio*, *La storia* and *Aracoeli* which also include the word 'romanzo' as part of their titles, the denomination 'romanzo' prominently placed by the author in contiguity to the name of a principal hero of medieval

---

A shorter version of this chapter 'Romancing the Novel: Elsa Morante's *L'isola di Arturo*' appeared in *Romance Languages Annual* 9 (1997), pp. 336–41. Special thanks are due to Anthony Julian Tamburri and Deborah Starewich for allowing inclusion of this revision in the present volume.

[1] Morante, *Menzogna e sortilegio* (Turin: Einaudi, 1948), unpaginated at front; *House of Liars*, trans. Adrienne Foulke (New York: Harcourt, 1951).

romance, Arthur, is particularly relevant.[2] Hence, the title significantly resonates with the echoes of courtly literature (especially the Arthurian cycle), of the Old French romances (in particular the *Roman de la Rose*) and of Renaissance chivalric epics (Ariosto's *Orlando furioso* to name just one). In addition, allusions to Dante's Paolo and Francesca point indirectly to the reading, if not the misreading, of the story of Lancelot and Guinevere. They redirect our gaze in the direction of Celtic legends and their Old French romance derivative, *Lancelot du Lac*, while exposing the reader to questions of fictionality versus truth.[3]

However, the importance of these early romances in Morante's work as they relate to the modern novel as a genre has not been generally acknowledged. Giovanna Rosa rightly point out Morante's clear debts to particular genres:

> Da *Menzogna e sortilegio* ad *Aracoeli* tutti i libri dichiarano subito la loro appartenenza di genere. Così è nelle indicazioni di copertina, nei risvolti di quarta, nelle note bibliografiche, nei commenti, sempre di mano dell'autrice, che accompagnano le ristampe.[4]
>
> (From *House of Liars* to *Aracoeli*, all of Morante's books immediately proclaim their belonging to a genre. This is evident from her at all times personal directions for the cover, the frontispiece, bibliographical data, introductions, and commentaries in all reprints.)

Whereas Rosa examines Morante's literary self-consciousness as a 'romanziere', this critic fails to connect the notion of 'romanzo' to its narrative ancestors. Giacomo Debenedetti, one of Morante's earliest critics and admirers, noticed that the writer's characters are reproductions of archaic archetypes. Morante's indebtedness to the legend of King Arthur did not escape him. Debenedetti points out that the protagonist is often called 'Artù', a medieval form which strengthens the novel's connection to the Matter of Britain. Yet the critic fails to explain the relevance of these archetypes within the context of genre.[5] Sharon Wood displays an awareness of the ambiguous nature of Morante's novels in a statement she makes about Morante's work as a whole. Wood notes that '"romanzo" is not a straight-

---

[2] Morante, *La storia: Romanzo* (Turin: Einaudi, 1974); *idem*, *Aracoeli: Romanzo* (Turin: Einaudi, 1982). Although the subtitle 'romanzo' tends to be omitted in translations, William Weaver perceptively retained it in his, as *History: a Novel* (New York: Knopf, 1977) and *idem*, *Aracoeli: a Novel* (New York: Random, 1984).

[3] Luisa Guj, 'Illusion and Literature in Elsa Morante's *L'isola di Arturo*', *Italica* **65** (1988), pp. 147–8.

[4] Giovanna Rosa, *Cattedrali di carta: Elsa Morante romanziere* (Milan: Saggiatore, 1995), p. 10.

[5] Giacomo Debenedetti, 'L'isola della Morante', in Franco Contorbia (ed.), *Saggi (1922–1966)*, (Milan: Mondadori, 1982), pp. 384–5.

forward, transparent word in Morante's texts'; that it can mean 'a matter of feeling and passion ... novel ... a reference to the tradition of the old chivalric tales and legends in the manner of Ariosto'; and that 'in Morante all these meanings of "romanzo" operate simultaneously'.[6] None the less, Wood's parallel reading of *L'isola di Arturo* and *Menzogna e sortilegio* focuses instead on tracing 'the links between the construction of identity and the act of writing'.[7] Only Luisa Guj's reading of *L'isola di Arturo* signals the meta-narrative qualities of Morante's second novel. In her article 'Illusion and Literature in Elsa Morante's *L'isola di Arturo*', Guj demonstrates how Morante uses literary references 'to plot Arturo's illusionary perception of reality' and 'to point to the dangers of clinging to a type of myth-making literature totally unrelated to life and history'.[8]

In view of these allusions and statements, the references to *fin' amors* ('courtly love') that lie scattered among Morante's narratives in general, and *L'isola di Arturo* in particular, make us inquisitive about the true significance of this work.[9] The nature of the novel's literary recallings reinforces one's suspicion that *L'isola di Arturo* was a conscious artistic *tour de force* aimed at questioning the very notion of 'romanzo' by bringing the 'universal truths' found in these texts and so cherished by Morante into the present. These truths are filtered through personal experience in such a way as to become the experience of all humanity.[10] In doing so, the writer could exploit the ambiguous meaning of the Italian word 'romanzo'. Whereas anglophone readers refer to and translate the modern word somewhat simplistically as 'novel', the Italian noun contains the entire semantic load of the English concepts of 'novel' and 'romance' in so far as they relate to notions of reality and fiction — if we believe that what we today call 'novel' portrays real events, an ambiguity of which Morante is well aware. In this chapter, I will begin with this dichotomy and trace its development inside the textual boundaries of *L'isola di Arturo*. Furthermore, I will analyse this tension in relation to Morante's theoretical writings on the novel. I will conclude by

---

[6] Sharon Wood, 'The Bewitched Mirror: Imagination and Narration in Elsa Morante', *Modern Language Review* **86.2** (1991), p. 313.

[7] Ibid., p. 310.

[8] Guj, p. 145.

[9] 'Courtly love' was, of course, a nineteenth-century cultural construction, but the notion pervades twentieth-century popular imagination concerning the Middle Ages. Neither Morante nor her critics could have escaped its influence. On the ambiguity embedded in the term, see Paolo Cherchi, *Andreas and the Ambiguity of Courtly Love* (Toronto: University of Toronto Press, 1994), pp. 3–6.

[10] See, for example, Morante's essays 'Il poeta di tutta la vita' and 'Sul romanzo', in *Pro o contro la bomba atomica e altri scritti* (Milan: Adelphi, 1987), pp. 31–40 and 41–74. All translations from these essays are my own.

offering a reading of *L'isola di Arturo* as a novel that asks to be read as a romance.

The dichotomy between reality and fiction is as old as writing itself, as old, indeed, as the first *romanzi* which have this tension built into their very code. The oscillating movement between these two opposing forces in Morante's *romanzo* manifests itself from the first pages. In the initial chapter, the male first-person narrator introduces his writings from the perspective of a present-day reality, but also as the memories of his childhood's fantastic perceptions. Indeed, the second subtitle of the novel is 'Memorie di un fanciullo' ('A Boy's Memories'). The initial chapter title 'Re e stella del cielo' ('King and Star of the Sky') forces the narrative that follows into an ambiguous frame: not only does the narrator Arturo share his name with the brightest star visible in the Northern skies, but also with one of the earliest heroes of medieval romance, King Arthur. Both star and legend, while equally distant, are attractive to those who contemplate them. The legendary king's existence, once assumed to be an historical reality by the narrator, has now turned out to be uncertain:

> venni poi a sapere che questo celebre Arturo re di Bretagna non era storia certa, soltanto leggenda. (p. 11)
>
> (As I later discovered, this famous king of Britain wasn't real history at all, but just a legend. [p. 3])[11]

The reality–fiction dichotomy is thus problematized from the start. The reality of perception, as it is conditioned by reading, is in the eye of the beholder. In one dramatic instance in Morante's novel, Arturo learns that once fiction becomes reality, it reveals its deceptive nature. The epiphany occurs when he passionately kisses his stepmother, Nunziata (his homosexual father's first wife had died during childbirth). The childlike, dark Neapolitan newly-wed becomes Arturo's fleeting object of desire, the target of adulterous love befitting a hero of medieval romance. An important literary precedent for his own actions and for his awareness of the illusionary nature of fiction is the episode of Paolo and Francesca in Canto 5 of Dante's *Inferno*. Morante makes this literary debt explicit:

> Non ignoravo, si capise, che i baci non sono tutti gli stessi. Avevo letto, fra l'altro, anche il Canto di Paolo e Francesca, per esempio. Senza contare le dozzine di canzoni che sapevo, e che parlavano di carezze e

---

[11] Morante, *L'isola di Arturo* (Turin: Einaudi, 1957); *Arturo's Island*, trans. Isabel Quigly (New York: Knopf, 1959). All translations from *L'isola* are Quigly's.

> baci d'amore. ... Ma ero stato troppo avvezzo, finora, a venir considerato un ragazzino, per mettermi al posto di Paolo, il dannato del Girone Infernale. ... L'amore vantato nelle canzoni, nei libri e nelle riviste illustrate, per me era rimasto una cosa remota e leggendaria, fuori della vita vera. (*L'isola*, p. 263)

> (I knew, of course, that kisses weren't all alike. I had read the canto of Paolo and Francesca, for instance, not to mention that I knew dozens of love songs all talking about caresses and kisses. ... But I had got so used to being thought a child that I couldn't suddenly put myself in the place of Paolo, who was damned in hell. ... The love that they talked about in songs, and books, and magazines had seemed to me something remote and legendary, something outside real life. [p. 255])

The fatal kiss suspends Arturo temporarily in the illusionary world of secular medieval romance, a fictitious world in which the child narrator lives and loves in a very literary way. It is the only way in which he is able to love, having had no real-life experience of either motherly love or of its erotic counterpart. Nunziatella, whom Arturo considers 'la regina delle donne' ('queen of women') is both mother and object of devotion, very much like the Virgin Mary whose effigy she carries with her and whose title ('queen of women') she shares. Arturo's love for his young stepmother is a forbidden one and as such appropriate for one who performs his relationships in compliance with 'courtly love' tenets. To underscore the courtly nature of his behaviour is Arturo's sudden interest in Assuntina, Nunziata's friend and a kind of *donna-schermo* or 'screen lady', a prose version of the figure who in medieval lyric traditionally serves to provoke the jealousy of the longed-for lady. But despite Assuntina's availability and seductive manners, she does not constitute an object of desire precisely because she does not behave according to the 'rules' conventionally associated with 'courtly love'. As a hero on a quest for what actually constitutes the denial of love, Arturo is no different from the ancestors of Elisa in Morante's first novel, *Menzogna e sortilegio*, whose torments are caused by the pursuit of impossible relationships. It was in this novel that Morante first examined the dangerous attraction of reading and misinterpreting texts as exemplars for life. The novel's main character, Elisa (also her own family's historiographer), expressly states that the fantastic literature in her library was the wrong guide, a *menzogna* or lie:

> farsi adoratori e monaci della menzogna! far di questa la propria sapienza! rifiutare ogni prova, e non solo quelle dolorose, ma fin le occasioni di felicità, non riconoscendo nessuna felicità possibile fuori

> del non-vero! Ecco che cosa è stata l'esistenza per me! (*Menzogna*, p. 19)[12]
>
> (to make oneself a worshiper, a disciple of illusion! Deliberately to make falsehood the substance of one's thought and one's wisdom — to reject all experience, not only painful experience but even one's chances for happiness because one denies that happiness is possible beyond the confines of unreality. That is what my life has been. [Foulke trans., p. 11])

Similarly, within the diegesis of *L'isola*, it is books in which Arturo mirrors himself and from books he learns that women are associated with love.[13] Yet experience will teach him that this is a false certainty, as the discovery of his father's homosexuality reveals; from books such as *Le vite degli eccellenti condottieri* (*The Lives of the Excellent Condottieri*), the young Arturo has isolated some of the principles to live by. The most important of these is not to be afraid of death:

> Il primo pensiero, il massimo di tutti è questo: *Non bisogna importarsi della morte*! (*L'isola*, p. 117)
>
> (The first thought, the greatest of all is this: *Not to worry about death*! [p. 108])

His failed suicide attempt teaches him the fallacy of this maxim. Death is very much on Arturo's mind at the birth of Carmine Arturo, when the young protagonist envisions a re-enactment of his own mother's death during childbirth. It was a commonplace of classical and medieval narratives that the mythical hero be born in dramatic circumstances.[14] These are often abandoned at birth, kidnapped, or left to the care of a humble woman or even an animal. One thinks of Moses, Romulus, Orlando, Siegfried or Percival. In Arturo's case, when his stepmother is about to give birth to his namesake, the young hero relives the drama of abandonment. And yet, his was not a mythical *enfances*, but 'true history':

> Questo qui non è un libro di racconti inventati, è proprio storia vera, è scienza! (*L'isola*, p. 117)

---

[12] Wood uses this passage to illustrate the meta-literary qualities of Morante's first novel (p. 314).

[13] Tonia Caterina Riviello, 'The Motif of Entrapment in Elsa Morante's *L'isola di Arturo* and Dacia Maraini's *L'età del malessere*', *Rivista di studi italiani* **8** (1990), p. 77.

[14] Debenedetti, pp. 386–7.

> (This isn't a book of invented stories; it's proper history, science! [p. 108])

Arturo's literary experience echoes that of the medieval reader of chivalric epics whose authors claimed to be writing true vernacular accounts, but were what the modern reader would call fiction. Arturo accepts these claims as truth: he lives his books, he turns writings into life, thus making himself guilty of the same sin for which Dante condemns Paolo and Francesca. The Dantean lovers are guilty not only of excessive love (*dismisura*), but also of excessive reading. We note that variants on the verb *leggere* ('to read') occur four times in the 12 verses (*Inferno* 5, 127–38) that contain the episode: Francesca's story starts with the words 'noi leggiavamo' ('we were reading') and ends with 'non vi leggemmo avante' ('there we read no further'). As the emphasis on the act of reading in the tragic episode indicates, the doomed couple's excess was conditioned by their perception of the story of Lancelot and Guinevere. In Kristeva's terms, the lovers are guilty of attributing to the text they read 'excessive meaning',[15] that is, Paolo and Francesca adopted it as an exemplar for their own erotic relationship. The memory of this brief submission to excess constitutes their eternal suffering: their punishment is to ponder the impossible moment in which they allowed fiction to replace reality. Now, as they are blown and beaten by the winds of passion, they remember the *galeotto*, the book that led them there.

If the name Galeotto as employed by Dante refers to excessive loving and reading, one must recall that it is the Italian form of *Galehault*, the friend of Lancelot who entices him to kiss the married queen. Furthermore, the modern Italian word carries an additional semantic load: convict. It recurs with this meaning in *L'isola* to describe a convict friend of Arturo's father.[16] The loaded term provides evidence for the existence of a link between a transgressive romantic love and the romance as love literature experienced as 'prison'. The wrong book or the misread book can actually condemn the individual. The polysemous interpretation of *galeotto* is not surprising, given that in Morante's world, love and the literature that articulates it manifest themselves alongside the notions of prison and confinement and constitute the very core of her writings.[17]

---

[15] Julia Kristeva, *Tales of Love* (New York: Columbia University Press, 1987), p. 288.

[16] Guj, pp. 148–9.

[17] See Rocco Capozzi, '"Sheherazade" and Other "Alibis": Elsa Morante's Victims of Love', *Rivista di studi italiani* 5–6 (1988), pp. 51–71 (revised as 'Elsa Morante: The Trauma of Possessive Love and Disillusionment', in Santo Aricò (ed.), *Contemporary Women Writers in Italy: A Modern Renaissance* [Amherst, MA: University of Massachusetts Press, 1990], pp. 10–25). See also Riviello, p. 78.

To underscore the semantic links between love and prison, and reading about love as 'imprisoning', the oblique reference to Lancelot and Guinevere recurs further on in the novel, where a subtle word play foreshadows a more explicit reference to Galehault, the accomplice and witness of Lancelot and Guinevere's ill fate. The passage in which Arturo describes the young prisoner whom his father is courting illustrates this well:

> Mostrava ancor meno dell'età minima necessaria che certo doveva avere, per essere un *galeotto.* (p. 273, emphasis added)
>
> (He looked even younger than a *convict* was allowed to be. [p. 265])

The semantic coexistence of love and prison comes as no surprise. After all, it constitutes the backdrop for the novel: we remember that the island of Procida, seemingly an amatory space, an apparent *locus amoenus* for idealized courtly pursuits, is overshadowed by a penitentiary. For outsiders, the name of the island is synonymous with its prison:

> 'Per molta gente, che vive lontano, il nome della mia isola significa il nome d'un carcere'. (p. 15)
>
> ('People who live far away often think of Procida as just the name of a prison'. [p. 6])

Morante's delicate allusion to Galeotto and the resulting connection, via Dante, to Arthurian legend is very appropriate. In context of the father's amorous relationship with Wilhelm Gerace, *galeotto* is also associated with forbidden love. In addition, Arturo's choice of words to indicate the friend's status inevitably recalls *Inferno* 5. As a semantic hybrid, love and prison have made their way into the child narrator's world and into his language.

The semantic load of the word *galeotto* comes to fruition when it is repeated in more fitting literary surroundings later in the novel under the significant heading 'Perle e rose convenzionali' ('Conventional pearls and roses'):

> A tradimento, dalla mia infanzia, ritornavano, anche, ad adornarlo, certi miei pregiudizi romanzeschi. Voglio dire che già il titolo di *galeotto* valeva quanto un blasone secondo i miei pregiudizi di ragazzino. E altrettanto, aggiungerò, secondo quelli di Wilhelm Gerace adulto! (*L'isola*, p. 301, emphasis added)
>
> (And to betray me, various romantic prejudices of mine returned from my childhood to adorn him. When I was a child, the title of *convict*

> meant more to me than a coat-of-arms; and, I might add, it still meant as much to Wilhelm Gerace, who was grown up! [p. 292])

This confirms our suspicion that the Galehault of Arthurian romance as restaged by Dante has the power of conditioning our reading of *L'isola*. Arturo himself admits having been prejudiced because of a previous literary experience. Unlike his father, he is, both in retrospect and as the adolescent Arturo who appropriates the narrative voice, aware of the deceptive nature of reading (and writing) as he remembers having experienced its magic spell as a child. The association is a felicitous one, when considering that Dante's unfortunate lovers owe their eternal captivity in the turbulent winds of passion to precisely such 'pregiudizi romantici' ('romantic prejudices') acquired in book form: 'Galeotto fu 'l libro e chi lo scrisse' ('Galeotto was the book and he who wrote it' [*Inferno* 5, 137]). Morante's choice of the word *galeotto* is deliberately open-ended thereby allowing for the simultaneous association of love — and writing about love — with the image of prison and the Galehault of Arthurian legend as retold by Dante.[18] Guj points out that the notion of 'galeotto' inspired by Dante illustrates how 'the mental picture he [Arturo] has of his father does not quite match reality' (p. 148). Morante's *double entendre* confirms that Arturo's earlier perceptions were based on his literary preconceptions, a distorted, fictitious image of reality.

The last occurrence of the word *galeotto* confirms the dangers that lurk behind the reading of romances by underscoring Wilhelm Gerace's inability to detach himself from their spell:

> Difatti ... la fede di Wilhelm Gerace ambiva, per accendersi, la primitiva scintilla di una qualche seduzione convenzionale: il personaggio di Galeotto si addiceva bene ai suoi sospiri, che erano infantili eternamente, come quelli dell'universo! ... E così in eterno ogni perla del mare ricopia la prima perla, e ogni rosa ricopia la prima rosa. (p. 301)

> (Indeed ... Wilhelm Gerace's devotion needed the crude glitter of something conventionally seductive like that to kindle it, and the theatrical figure of that *convict* suited his melancholy very well because it was everlastingly childish. ... And thus every pearl in the sea eternally copies the first pearl, and every rose the first rose. [p. 293, translator's italics])

---

[18] The love–prison connection is repeated in Morante's last novel, *Aracoeli*. Capozzi notes that the name of the famous church recalls that of another Roman institution, the Regina Coeli prison (p. 62).

The resurgence of Galehault focuses our attention back on *Inferno* 5. At this point, however, the literary reference seems to be endowed with additional meaning: Arturo's father's feelings can be triggered by the primitive sparks of 'something conventionally seductive'. The episode of Paolo and Francesca has at this stage in the novel and in the eyes of Arturo become an emblem for conventional seduction through its equation with Galeotto. In other words, Morante has touched on a fundamental characteristic of the reader's perception of a written text: it is based on conventional interpretation. Is Morante, like Dante, challenging her readers to question their own preconceptions about the genre called 'romanzo'?

Let us for a moment assume that Morante's 'romanzo' is actually a 'meta-romanzo', and that the rose image in the above passage is, indeed, an allusion to another medieval romance, the *Romance of the Rose*. The emblem of the rose frames and dominates this chapter through its presence in the chapter's title and its recurrence in such close vicinity to the *seduzione convenzionale* scene. One cannot help but wonder if Morante employed the conventional medieval topos of the rose to remind her readers of the *Roman de la Rose* composed by Guillaume de Lorris about 1236 and continued at least a quarter-century later by Jean de Meung.[19] Without rehearsing details about this intriguing and intricate allegorical romance, it is nevertheless useful to note a few of its general characteristics that are rewritten by Morante. The first part by Guillaume de Lorris is developed along the axis of memory as a dream narrative told by an enamoured narrator-poet who expresses himself in the first person and is both author and actor of his story. The quest for the rose is a quest for the transcendence of literal meaning. It is a work that is inevitably mentioned as having engendered the prose romance and as having led the way to the modern novel.[20] Similarly, *L'isola* is a recollection of a dream-like world, of the *enfances* of a hero on an enchanted island. It is also a book about the slow awakening to the non-literal meaning of fiction, told by an omnipotent narrator who is author of, and actor in, his story. Furthermore, *L'isola* employs the romance-like atemporality and aspatiality of its literary predecessors in which time and space are subject to symbolic interpretation.[21] With this in mind, how should we interpret Arturo's belief that each pearl copies the first pearl, and each rose copies the first rose? Considering the

---

[19] In the French romance, the rose is associated with heterosexuality, but in *L'isola* it is linked to the bisexuality of Wilhelm Gerace, who is called both *ape* (bee) and *rosa* (rose) (Guj, p. 152).

[20] Kristeva, pp. 288–96; M.M. Bakhtin, *The Dialogic Imagination*, trans. Michael Holquist (Austin, TX: University of Texas Press, 1981), pp. 155–8.

[21] Bakhtin, p. 156.

meta-literary context into which it is inserted, the reading of this maxim as a conscious allusion to the repetitious nature of romance is all but out of the question. It is plausible to see in this brief passage a stance on the state of the novel as a genre that in Morante's day had come to represent a particular world and a particular reality rather than the universal truths, the world in its entirety, that Morante prefers. *L'isola* can be read as a romance from which emanates an awareness of a mission aimed at distancing writing from the twentieth-century, post-war, neo-realistic notions of novel dictated by ideological prerogatives. Written in 1957, this novel contains truths that transcend temporal and spatial boundaries and are common to all humans: love, jealousy, the quest for happiness and freedom, the prisonhouse of memory of good times in bad. Every rose copies another rose, and one romance copies another romance. With this in mind, Wilhelm Gerace's reflections on his last name — chosen at random because any last name can suffice — in the very beginning of the novel can be read retrospectively and be interpreted:

> un nome ne vale un altro. Lo dice pure una poesia, di quelle che le ragazze scrivono sull'album dei pensieri: *Che importa il nome? Chiama pur la rosa con altro nome: avrà men dolce odore*? (pp. 57–8)
>
> (one name is as good as another. It even says so in a poem, one of those that children write in autograph albums: *What's in a name: that which we call a rose by any other name would smell as sweet.* [p. 48])

Wilhelm Gerace has borrowed Juliet's words to Romeo to reflect on his identity which remains unaltered in spite of his randomly selected last name, thereby freeing him from notions of ancestry. In short, what on the surface seems an unobtrusive word — rose — becomes a metonym for the whole text and the genre.

That the image of the rose must be connected to the novel becomes apparent in Morante's famous essay, 'Sul romanzo' ('On the novel'), where the author states that words are born naturally from life's experience and that, since every day each experience is new, words too are fresh every day like a rose.[22] Furthermore, the tools that the writer employs — words and expression — are one. The value of words cannot be distorted or transferred since words, being the names of things, are those things themselves. Morante's essay concludes in Gertrud Stein fashion: 'Una rosa è una rosa è una rosa è una rosa'. Morante comes to that conclusion within the context of her observations on the state of the novel and its ontology. The writer has entrapped her reader in a meta-literary game played, through the

---

[22] Morante, 'Sul romanzo', p. 69.

rose image, along a time-, place- and genre-crossing itinerary stretching from the medieval *Roman de la rose* to Shakespeare to Stein and including her own reflections on writing novels.

When we return to the text of *L'isola*, we notice how this very law of inevitable, continuous mutation that nevertheless leaves the original content intact is indicative of a topos that pervades Morante's whole body of work: the myth of the phoenix, which exemplifies the repetitive nature of experience, including literary experience.[23] Similarly, reflections in mirrors, water, words and sounds abound in *L'isola*, evoking the myth of Narcissus. There are sounds that reverberate in apparently identical yet contrasting patterns, such as the ones that echo — literally — between the rocks on the island of Procida:

> 'Esiste, nell'isola, una piana fra rocce alte, in cui c'è un eco'. (p. 31)
>
> ('On the island there is a piece of level ground lying between high rocks, where you find an echo'. [p. 22])

Significantly, Arturo interprets the reverberations of this echo as a 'duello epico' (an epic duel):

> 'Siamo a Roncisvalle, e d'un tratto, sulla spianata, irromperà Orlando col suo corno'. (p. 31)
>
> ('We were at Roncesvalles and, suddenly, on the terrace Roland would appear with his horn!' [p. 22])

As sound reverberates in the rocks, so the contents of past readings reverberate in the mind of Arturo. In this case, the past readings were the duels from Ariosto's *Furioso*, itself a kind of far-off echo of its many medieval predecessors. Language, too, obeys this law of eternal mutation by which everything is born out of previous experience, yet maintains essentially the same internal characteristics. The same words can take on different meanings according to their user:

> 'Anche le stesse parole mie napoletane ch'egli usava spesso, dette da lui [Gerace] diventavano più spavalde e nuove, come nelle poesie'. (p. 32)
>
> ('Even my own Neapolitan words, which he [Gerace] often used, grew bolder and newer when he said them, like [in] poetry'. [p. 23])

---

[23] On the importance of this myth in Morante, see Capozzi, pp. 51–71.

Again, the comparison is to literary expression, this time, poetry. The most obvious lexical echoes are found in the name of the protagonist, Arturo. 'Arturo' is not only a king and a heavenly star, he is also repeated in his half-brother, Carmine Arturo, who physically and emotionally resembles a king. Carmine Arturo's face is crowned by small, stubborn, blond curls that form a 'coroncina d'oro': 'a little crown of gold' (p. 231). The child is endowed with kingly attributes: from the small rings formed by the wrinkles in the flesh around his wrists and ankles Nunziatella's women friends predict that, like the great kings of romances, he will be bold, yet gentle-hearted; the defender of women and the poor; he will remain untouched by age, will travel far and wide, and will be praised by all (p. 231). He is the echo of Arturo the narrator as he remembers his own childhood.

To confirm her characters' double identities, Morante doubles their names: Arturo is seldom called just 'Arturo'; in direct address, his name is called out twice: 'Arturo, Artù'. The same can be said for Nunziata, who is most often addressed as 'Nunziatella, Nunz' or other combinations of her name and nickname. Thus, Nunziata's double nature of mother and lover is underscored on the lexical level. Furthermore, the pale complexion and the curved shoulders of Nunziatella as a pregnant woman recall those of Arturo's mother in a portrait (p. 176). Later, as mother, she also resembles the many traditional images of the Virgin Mary that Nunziatella brought with her from her native Naples and whose description she shares. The semantic link between her name, a diminutive form of 'Annunziata', is filled with allusions to the Virgin Mary's Annunciation. Even the only animal in the novel, Arturo's dog Immacolatella, replicates a previous scenario: both his mother and dog died giving birth.

A similar symbolic meaning can be found in the abundance of circular objects that lie scattered in Morante's pages: rings, bracelets, gold chains, earrings.[24] There are the 'cerchietti' (small circles) of Nunziatella's earrings, one of which becomes Arturo's amulet; the round face of his father's watch is the 'cerchio' (circle) that when lost underwater, Arturo searches for as though it were the Grail itself; the 'braccialettini' (little bracelets), i.e. the small, perfect circles formed by the wrinkles in Carmine Arturo's babyflesh; the 'coroncina d'oro' of blond curls that crown Carmine's infant face; and, finally, the imaginary magic ring that grants invisibility and that Arturo imagines to be wearing one night as he follows his father. In short, Morante's novel yields an abundance of circular objects all of which are placed in contexts that recall legends, myths and romances. They constitute an omnipresent, collective literary memory from which there is no escape.

---

[24] For the relevance of jewelry in Morante, see Felix Siddell, 'Jottings and Jewels in Elsa Morante's *Alibi*', *Forum Italicum* **29** (1995), pp. 91–102.

The novel as genre obeys this repetitive, circular motion. In Italian the very word *romanzo* has many connotations and can refer as much to medieval verse romances or to chivalric epic romances as to the modern historical novel inaugurated by Sir Walter Scott and developed during the nineteenth century.[25] In rather explicit terms, Morante states her indebtedness to a previous literary tradition, one that permeates the pages of *L'isola*:

> (Perfino le leggende mitologiche e popolari sono già una specie di romanzo collettivo). Il romanzo in prosa, che ha prevalso (sebbene non esclusivamente) dal Seicento in poi, non è altro che il successore diretto del poema narrativo, ossia del romanzo in versi. ('Sul romanzo', in *Pro*, p. 46)
>
> ([Even mythical and popular legends are a kind of collective romance]. The prose romance, that has prevailed [albeit not exclusively] since the seventeenth century, is nothing but the direct descendent of the narrative poem, i.e. the prose romance.)

Morante's oft-quoted definition of the term 'romanzo' complicates matters further:

> 'Romanzo' sarebbe ogni opera poetica, nella quale l'autore — attraverso la narrazione inventata di vicende esemplari (da lui scelte come pretesto, o simbolo delle 'relazioni' umane nel mondo) — dà intera una propria immagine dell'universo reale (e cioè dell'uomo, nella sua realtà.) ('Sul romanzo', in *Pro*, p. 44)
>
> ('Romance' is every work of poetry in which the author — through the invented narration of exemplary material [which he choses as a pretext or symbol of human 'relations' world-wide] — presents the whole picture of his own way of seeing the real universe [and thus of man, in his reality].)

This definition emphasizes the 'imaginative and symbolic nature of this [the novel's] genre',[26] but also indicates the novelist's responsibility of creating a picture of reality in its universality poured through the filter of personal experience. The juxtaposition of universality versus individuality is repeated when Morante defines the task of the romance writer: 'Il romanziere, al pari di un filosofo-psicologo, presenta, nella sua opera, un *proprio*, e *completo*, sistema del

[25] For a brief history of the romance genre, see William Paden, 'Europe from Latin to Vernacular in Epic, Lyric, Romance', in David W. Thompson (ed.), *Performance of Literature in Historical Perspectives*, (Lanham, MD: University Press of America, 1983), pp. 90–97.

[26] Paola Blelloch, 'Elsa Morante's Use of Dream', *La Fusta* 8 (1990), p. 61.

mondo e delle relazioni umane'.[27] ('The novelist [i.e. romance writer] is like a philosopher-psychologist: through his work he presents his *own, complete* system of the world and of human relations'.) Given this definition, even the poems of *Alibi* are 'romanzi' in that they reflect, like an echo, the same universal truths contained in preceding novels by Morante. In the introduction to her collection of poems, the author states this clearly:

> L'autrice prega i lettori di perdonarle l'esiguo valore e peso di queste pagine. Essendo infatti lei, per sua consuetudine (oltre che per sua natura e per suo destino) scrittrice di storie in prosa, i suoi radi versi sono, in parte, nient'altro che un eco, o, se si voglia, un coro, dei suoi romanzi.[28]
>
> (The author asks her readers to forgive her for the scarce value and weight of these pages. In fact, out of habit [and because it is her nature and her fate to do so] she is a writer of stories in prose. As a result her occasional verse is, in part, merely an echo, or, if you prefer, a chorus, of her *romanzi*.)

In other words, Morante echoes her own narrative voice as *romanziere* in the format of poetry which is a reverberating, reflected sound of her own previous creations, the result of her own created literary experience, that of *romanzi*.

We now have a better understanding as to why *L'isola* would be 'crowned' with a few verses by Umberto Saba, the Triestine poet for whom Morante reserved her most glowing praise. The title of her essay on Saba, 'Il poeta di tutta la vita' ('The Poet of Life in its Entirety') accurately summarizes Morante's judgement of the poet. She considers him a *romanziere* because of the universal truths his verses emit, for their ability to reflect the human condition in its entirety. Although this is a characteristic of 'poemi, o romanzi in genere ... nelle quali si riconosce l'intenzione di rispecchiare l'uomo nella sua interezza'.[29] ('Poems or *romanzi* in general ... in which we can recognize an intention of mirroring man in his entirety'.) Saba's famous cycle of poems partakes of this fundamental quality of *romanzo*:

> Il *Canzoniere* di Saba è il poema, o *il romanzo*, dell'uomo che, uscito dall'Ottocento, attraverso l'esperienza angosciosa dell'epoca presente, cerca i segni di quello che Saba chiama il 'mondo nuovo'. ('Il poeta', in *Pro*, pp. 34–5, emphasis added)

---

[27] Morante, 'Sul romanzo', p. 44.

[28] Morante, *Alibi* (Milan: Longanesi, 1958), unpaginated.

[29] Morante, 'Il poeta', p. 35.

> (Saba's *Canzoniere* is the poem, or *romanzo* of man who, living the end of the nineteenth century in anguish, looks for signs of what Saba calls the 'new world'.)

Morante goes so far as to call his *Canzoniere* a 'romanzo dell'universo reale' ('a *romanzo* of the real universe' [p. 36]). Hence it is not surprising to find in *L'isola*, after the subtitle 'Memorie di un fanciullo' ('A Boy's Memories'), the first line of 'Il fanciullo appassionato', a poem by Saba: 'Io, se in lui mi ricordo, ben mi pare' ('If I see myself in him, I am content'). One realizes the appropriateness of this Saba quotation only after reading it in its entirety. Its third line, not cited by Morante, reads: 'Ha qualcosa di me, di me lontano/nel tempo'[30] ('He has something of me, of a me remote / in time'). In other words, the remembering 'I' — echoed in a first person, reflexive pronoun ('mi ricordo') and the indirect object ('mi pare') — is tied to an 'I' who feels part of a whole, a *pars pro toto*, a fragment of an ancient precursor. The line confirms that we are repetitions of a previous 'first'. The same can be said for Morante's novel which is based on the memory of literary precedents whose universe has been filtered through the experience of a first-person narrator:

> nel momento di fissare la propria verità attraverso una sua attenzione del mondo reale, il romanziere moderno, in luogo di invocare le Muse, è indotto a suscitare un 'io' recitante (protagonista e interprete) che gli valga da alibi. ('Sul romanzo', in *Pro*, pp. 53–4)

> (at that moment in which he establishes his own true self by paying attention to the real world, the modern *romanziere*, rather than invoking the muses, tends to call upon a first-person narrator [both protagonist and interpreter] who functions as his alibi.)

This 'prima persona responsabile' (responsible first person), as Morante calls him, depicts reality only as it relates to him. Consequently, reality is reinvented. As a result, a novel can claim to be true to life in so far as a particular author's experience of reality has filtered it in such a way that the personal becomes universal, as Saba did in his *Canzoniere*. Truth, then, has to do with great, universal thoughts. In the novel in question, Arturo as a first-person narrator confirms this when commenting on the *Le vite degli eccellenti condottieri*:

> I condottieri storici ... erano persone uguali alle altre in tutte le cose, fuorchè nei pensieri! Uno, per principiare ad essere come loro, e anche

[30] Quoted in Rosa, p. 107.

> meglio di loro, deve prima tenere nella mente certi veri, grandi pensieri ... (p. 117)
>
> (The historical condottieri ... were people just like everyone else in everything but their thoughts. And when someone wants to start being like them, and even better, he's got to have some true, great thoughts in his head ... [p. 108])

Even texts that record historical actions are only true in as much as they spring from great thoughts. Truth is not constrained by formal boundaries. What is conventionally categorized as *romanzo* does not necessarily deserve this denomination unless it contains universal truths. One of these is that all writings are subject to being misread. The earliest *romanzi* attest to this truth, Paolo and Francesca re-experience it, and Arturo re-enacts it yet again.

Our reading of 'novels' is no different from that of Paolo and Francesca. As readers, we inevitably do the same as writers and confuse reality and fiction. We are imprisoned in a turbulence where every experience is a repetition of a previous one. We carry the burden of the memory of this earlier experience. The same is true for the experience of writing *romanzi*. Thus, *L'isola di Arturo* is a refracted image of a literary tradition that goes back as far as the earliest romances. Or better, *L'isola di Arturo* is, in the eyes of Morante, an ever-changing, golden-feathered phoenix, born over and over again from the fire that consumes it and from which it rises again. The novel's fate is like the kingly protagonist of Celtic romance whose story has been written and rewritten *ad infinitum*. Is it surprising, then, that Morante should identify her young protagonist Arthur with the hero of this oft-repeated legend? Should one be astonished that the child Arthur shares his name with a star that is part of an ever-circling, but ever-changing firmament? Should it startle us that in *L'isola di Arturo* the cyclical nature of experience, written or lived, is reflected both symbolically and lexically in the abundance of circular objects and is recognizable in the circular motion of the narrative discourse? Finally, could we not wonder then, if Morante's *romanzo* as a synthesis of her 'own, complete system of the world and human relations' is caught in that same rotating movement? For Morante, that system is one in which fiction and reality are living in a *discorde concordia* ('harmonious discord') to borrow a Tassean oxymoron. Morante's fictional and personal worlds move in an ever-changing, circular motion where the fiction–reality tension is ominously present. Finally, what makes this dialectic more intriguing is that it problematizes the very notion of *romanzo* at a time when the 'crisis of the novel' is almost a cliché, when writing has to be 'true', when the ideal knight is still expected to take his seat at the Round Table.

Index